S0-CAV-007

Becoming Partners

Marriage and Its Alternatives

Becoming Partners

Marriage and its Alternatives

by Carl R. Rogers, Ph.D.

CENTER FOR STUDIES OF THE PERSON
LA JOLLA, CALIFORNIA

A DELTA BOOK

Published by
DELL PUBLISHING CO., INC.
1 Dag Hammarskjold Plaza
New York, N.Y. 10017

Copyright © 1972 by Carl R. Rogers

*All rights reserved. No part of this book may be re-
produced in any form or by any means without the
prior written permission of Delacorte Press, New York,
New York, excepting brief quotes used in connection
with reviews written specifically for inclusion in a
magazine or newspaper.*

Delta ® TM 755118, Dell Publishing Co., Inc.
Reprinted by arrangement with Delacorte Press

Excerpts from GETTING BACK TOGETHER *by Robert
Houriet, copyright © 1971 by Robert Houriet. Reprinted
by permission of Coward, McCann & Geoghegan and
Julian Bach Agency.*

Excerpt from ON BECOMING A PERSON *by Carl R.
Rogers. Reprinted by permission of Houghton Mifflin
Company and Constable and Co. Ltd.*

*Excerpt from "Interpersonal relationships: USA 2000"
by Carl R. Rogers, from* JOURNAL OF APPLIED BEHAV-
IORAL SCIENCE, 4, #3, 1968. *Reprinted by permission of
NTL Institute for Applied Behavioral Science.*

Printed in the United States of America
Sixth Printing

TO HELEN

a person in her own right—giving, loving, stalwart;
my companion in our separate but intertwined pathways of growth;
an enricher of my life;
the woman I love;
and—fortunately for me—
my wife

Contents

Becoming Partners

Marriage and Its Alternatives

Introduction ✒

Why Am I Writing This Book?

THIS IS A QUESTION I have not infrequently asked myself as I have worked on these chapters. Curiously enough, the unexpected answer pops into mind, "Because I enjoy young people." This has been true for many years, and is exceedingly true at the present time. Much of what I have learned about the modern world comes from listening to young people—young colleagues, friends, and grandchildren—and being willing to go deeply with them into the elements of life that excite, anger, and perplex them. I count it a privilege that most of my associations and friendships are with individuals who are from thirty to fifty years younger than I. Some of these young people whom I meet represent for me whatever hope there is for this "blue-white planet" as it courses through a universe of *very* dark space.

Through my contacts with young people I know well the uncertainties, the fears, the beautifully honest casualness, the joys, and frustrations that mark their attempts to build some type of partnership between a man and a woman which has some thread of permanence in it—not necessarily a lifetime permanence, but something much more meaningful than a transient relationship.

So there began to form in my mind the thought that I might have something to offer to them in some of their pioneering struggle to build new kinds of marriages and alternatives to marriage. Not a stupid book of advice, certainly, but perhaps something that is *new*.

Then there began to take form a vague concept as to what this newness might be. I know that you can find out anything you want to know about the *externals* of marriage and partnership. You can find out the differences in male-female sexual needs and timing. You can read books on how to improve the sex act. You can study the history of marriage. You can find out what percentage of young people of college age are living together without marriage. You can read lists, compiled from questionnaires, of the major sources of satisfaction and dissatisfaction in married couples—and on and on and on. We are inundated by data. But rarely do we discover a true picture of what a partnership is like, as perceived and lived and experienced from the *inside*. That might be the new element I could add.

I began to think of the richness of experience involved in some of the marriages and other relationships I know. Could I draw out that richness? Would couples or individuals actually reveal themselves? Of all the unions I know something about, which might provide the most learning? Would it conceivably be possible to provide a living picture of the struggles, moments of "grooving together," the agonizing hours and months of perplexity, jealousy, despair which go to make up a partnership—whether it "works" or dissolves?

So I began to interview some couples, tape-recording our contacts. I asked others to write of their intimate experiences together. I have been astonished at the response. I have never been flatly turned down. Instead, both individuals and couples have given freely an intimate picture of marriage (or its alternatives) as the relationship is perceived from within. Such understandings and insights constitute for me—and for this book—the data for learning. To see all the vicissitudes of such unions from the perspective of the person who is living the experience achieves what are, for me, several important ends. Such material does not push itself on the reader saying, "This is the way you must be"; it does not point with alarm saying, "Don't go down this path"; it does not come to clear conclusions; it is very simply a person or a couple saying to the reader, "Here is the way it is and was for *me* or *us*—and perhaps you can learn from this some things which will help you in making your own changing, risky choices."

To me such a highly personal "view from within" is not only the best source of learning; it also points the way, perhaps, toward a new and more human science of man. But to follow that lead would take us far afield from the purpose of this book.

From the interviews and personal written material available to me I have tried to choose a reasonably wide spectrum of people and situations which I thought might be of the greatest interest and use. I have carefully edited the material to disguise names, places, and other identifying material. But I have not tampered with the personal psychological content. However, since I have been definitely selective in what has gone into this book, I should like to set forth the criteria which have guided me.

First. Would the individuals (singly or together) express themselves freely, spontaneously, honestly about the partnerships in which they have lived? Whether talking or writing about marriage, living together, sex experiences outside of the partnership, would they tell it as it is (or was)? I felt that the "objective," externally factual picture of a relationship would serve no useful purpose, no matter how accurate, while a glimpse from deep within might speak to issues the reader is inwardly facing. You will have to form your own judgment as to whether I have successfully met this criterion.

Second. I endeavored to select persons whose length of experience was sufficient to provide some perspective on the union or on its disintegration. One will not find an account by a couple on their honeymoon or by a couple in the throes of divorce. I tried to choose persons who were close to all the ups and downs and painful or exciting byroads of a partnership, and who were able to see and remember clearly these occurrences, but whose perceptions were not too distorted by some ecstatic or traumatic present moment. One result of this is that many of the partnerships described have lasted for from three to fifteen years, and most of the persons range in age from twenty to thirty-six. The major exception to this statement comes in my attempt to describe my own marriage: we are both seventy.

Third. I wanted to include partnerships which spanned a wide range of either positive or negative experiences, or both. As the persons present themselves in this book, one can see that by society's standards they would run from "success" to "failure," with many instances our culture would find hard to classify. In my terms they cover some exceedingly satisfying elements, and some tragically unsatisfying, with many of mixed character.

Fourth. I wanted it written from first-hand experience with these people, so that whatever were my own deeper learnings from the contacts could be woven into their own learnings as distinctly separate threads. The only exception to this is the chapter on communal experiments, in which I had to rely heavily on others to furnish me with the first-hand personal data.

I have stated these criteria as being clear. Actually they developed gradually as the book grew into being, taking some sort of irregular natural pathway of its own which I tried to follow. Perhaps this seemingly clear statement of what was chosen should be balanced by some statements of what the book is *not*, of pathways it did not naturally take.

It is not a study of partnerships or marriage in all cultures. It is about the search of men and women for relationships in the United States in the 1970s. It makes no attempt to deal with the European or Oriental patterns in such things, though I believe we are all moving—for better or for worse—toward similar styles.

It does not cut evenly across all class or cultural lines and levels in this country. Because of the kinds of contacts I have, it includes no account of a wealthy marriage nor of a strictly poverty-level partnership. Some of these persons have been from lower economic levels and one black lived in a ghetto, but most of the individuals could not be called seriously deprived from an economic point of view. This is not, to me, too unfortunate, since I suspect most of the readers will fall into somewhat the same group.

It is not, as I have already made clear, a book of advice or a collection of statistics—though there are a few figures in the first chapter—or a profound analysis of sociological trends.

The book is, instead, a series of slices, pictures, perceptions—of relationships, breakdowns, restructurings—in a wide variety of partnerships. These inner views are presented in a nonevaluative fashion. Are the unions "good" or "bad" or do they belong in some other judgmental category? I do not know. They *exist*. It is my belief that you will find here highly intimate and meaningful accounts of the man-woman relationship as it is actually lived—with all its tragedies, dull plateaus, ecstatic moments or periods, and instance after instance of exciting growth.

My deepest gratitude goes to the necessarily anonymous couples and individuals whose recorded statements constitute such a large portion of this book. I appreciate their opening of their lives to me, and even more their permission for me to open their lives to you.

One further word about my own relationship to the work. I have been a therapist for forty years, have facilitated many encounter groups, and have had unusually rich opportunities for friendships with young couples. Yet when I came to write the book, I found I simply could not, to any extent, draw on these past experiences. I could only record and write what had freshness and immediacy for me. Otherwise I would have felt as though I were writing a book of "cases." So, though in my comments I undoubtedly draw on a reservoir of past as well as present experiences, the essential material which follows is new and, with few exceptions, has all been gathered in the past twelve months.

If in any way it aids you in this risky process which we call living, and in the special risks of partnership with another person, then the book will have fully served its purpose.

1 ℐ Shall We Get Married?

IN TRYING TO FEEL MY WAY into this question, a difficult one for almost every young person and many who are older, I should like to start where the book started. I was challenged, some time ago, to try to picture human relationships as they might exist in the year 2000. What I wrote down then about man-woman relationships will perhaps give us a backdrop against which we can place some much more current examples of marriages that have dissolved and marriages that have held together or been restored. So, as a beginning, here is what I thought (and think) are the most likely trends in marriage and its various alternatives.

What do the coming decades hold for us in the realm of intimacy between boy and girl, man and woman? Here, too, enormous forces are at work, and choices are being made which will not, I believe, be reversed by the year 2000.

In the first place the trend toward greater freedom in sexual relationships, in adolescents and adults, is likely to continue, whether this direction frightens us or not. Many elements have conspired together to bring about a change in such behavior, and the advent of "The Pill" is only one of these. It seems probable that sexual intimacy will be a part of "going steady" or of any continuing special interest in a member of the opposite sex. The attitude of prurience is fast dying out, and sexual activity is seen as a potentially joyful and enriching part of a relationship. The attitude of possessiveness—of owning another person

—which historically has dominated sexual unions—is likely to be greatly diminished. It is certain that there will be enormous variations in the quality of these sexual relationships—from those where sex is a purely physical contact which has almost the same solitary quality as masturbation, to those in which the sexual aspect is an expression of an increasing sharing of feelings, of experiences, of each other.

By the year 2000 it will be quite feasible to insure that there will be no children in a union. By one of the several means currently under study, each individual will be assured of lasting infertility in early adolescence. It will take positive action, permissible only after a thoughtful decision, to reestablish fertility. This will reverse the present situation where only by positive action can one *prevent* conception. Also by that time computerized matching of prospective partners will be far more sophisticated than it is today and will be of great help to an individual in finding a congenial companion of the opposite sex.

Some of the temporary unions thus formed may be legalized as a type of marriage—with no permanent commitment, with no children (by mutual agreement) and—if the union breaks up—no legal accusations, no necessity for showing legal cause, and no alimony.

It is becoming increasingly clear that a man-woman relationship will have *permanence* only to the degree to which it satisfies the emotional, psychological, intellectual, and physical needs of the partners. This means that the *permanent* marriage of the future will be even better than marriage in the present, because the ideals and goals for that marriage will be of a higher order. The partners will be demanding more of the relationship than they do today.

If a couple feel deeply committed to each other, and mutually wish to remain together to raise a family, then this will be a new and more binding type of marriage. Each will accept the obligations involved in having and raising children. There may be a mutual agreement as to whether or not the marriage includes sexual faithfulness to one's mate. Perhaps by the year 2000 we will have reached the point where through education and social pressure, a couple will decide to have children only when they have shown evidence of a mature commitment to each other, of a sort which is likely to have permanence.[1]

[1] A proposal suggesting the licensing of births, and "substantial" payments to women who have no children during the normal reproductive period, age 15–44, has been submitted to the Massachusetts Legislature. A sign of the times?

What I am describing is a whole continuum of man-woman relationships, from the most casual dating and casual sex relationship, to a rich and fulfilling partnership in which communication is open and real, where each is concerned with promoting the personal growth of the partner, and where there is a long-range commitment to each other which will form a sound basis for having and rearing children in an environment of love. Some parts of this continuum will exist within a legal framework, some will not.

One may say, with a large measure of truth, that much of this continuum already exists. But an awareness of and an open acceptance of this continuum by society will change its whole quality. Suppose it were openly accepted that some "marriages" are no more than ill-mated and transitory unions, and will be broken. If children are not permitted in such marriages, then one divorce in every two marriages (the current rate in California) is no longer seen as a tragedy. The dissolving of the union may be painful, but it is not a social catastrophe, and the experience may be a necessary step in the personal growth of the two individuals toward greater maturity.[2]

To some it may seem as though this statement is too casual in its assumption that conventional marriage, as we have known it in this country, is either on its way out or will be greatly modified. But let's look at a few facts. In California in 1970 there were 173,000 marriages and approximately 114,000 "dissolutions of marriage." In other words, for every 100 couples who married there were 66 who were permanently parting. This is admittedly a distorted picture because a new law became effective in 1970 permitting couples to "dissolve" their marriages without trying to blame the "guilty party," simply on the basis of an agreement. The dissolution becomes final in six months instead of a year, as previously. So let us look at 1969. In that year for every 100 couples marrying, 49 were getting divorced. Somewhat more would have been divorced, but they were waiting for the new law to come into effect.

[2]Rogers, C. R. "Interpersonal Relationships: USA 2000." For this and every reference in this book, as well as notes on others that are relevant, see "To Carry On," an annotated bibliography at the end of the book for those who wish to explore further any aspect of the subject.

In Los Angeles County (essentially the city of Los Angeles) in 1969 divorces equaled 61 percent of the number of marriages. In 1970, under the new law, the number of dissolutions of marriage in the county was 74 percent of the number of marriages. Three couples were getting their marriages dissolved while four couples were getting married! And in 1971 in Los Angeles County there were 61,560 marriage licenses issued and 48,221 suits filed for dissolution of marriage, 79 percent as many as were marrying. These are not final *actions*, because the final outcomes will not be known for some time, but they are steps indicating *intent*. Thus in 1971 for every five couples intending to marry, four were intending to dissolve their marriages! In the course of three years there was a *61 percent, 74 percent, 79 percent* ratio of divorce to marriage in one of the country's largest cities. I believe those couples, and these figures, are trying to tell us something!

Some may say, "Yes, but that's *California*." I have purposely chosen that state because in social and cultural behaviors what Californians do today the rest of the nation—as has been shown in numerous ways—does tomorrow. And I have chosen Los Angeles County because what an urban center does today appears to become the national norm tomorrow. So as a very modest statement we may say that more than half the marriages in California end in dissolution of the partnership. In urban areas the rate is clearly higher. And for the country as a whole one expert estimates a 50–55% rate of marriage failure—35% divorced or permanently separated and 15–20% living together very unhappily (Saxton, p. 250).

In my contacts with young people it has become clear to me, beyond the shadow of a doubt, that the contemporary young person tends to have a distrust of marriage as an institution. He has seen too many flaws in it. He has often seen it fail in his own home. Instead, a relationship between a man and a woman is significant, and worth trying to preserve, only when it is an enhancing, growing experience for each person. There are very few reasons why marriage makes for economic well-being, as used to be true in early Colonial days in this country when husband and wife constituted a very necessary working team. The young person of today is not impressed by the fact that, religiously, a marriage should last "until death do us part." Rather he tends to regard the vows of complete permanence in marriage as clearly hypocritical. It is obvious from observing the behavior of married couples that if they were truthful, the persons involved would vow to live together "in sickness and in health" so long as the marriage was an enriching and satisfying experience for each one.

There are many who "view with alarm" the present state of marriage. To them it is proof that our culture has lost its moral standards, that we are in a period of decadence, and that it is only a question of time until we are penalized by an angry God for creating this sink of immorality in which we flounder. While I would agree that there are many signs that our culture is indeed in crisis and that it may be coming apart at the seams, I tend to see it in a different perspective. These are ago-nizing times for many, including many married couples. It is perhaps that we are living under the malediction contained in the ancient Chinese saying "I *curse* you; may you live in an im-portant age."

To me it seems that we are living in an important and uncer-tain age, and the institution of marriage is most assuredly in an uncertain state. If 50 to 75 percent of Ford or General Motors cars completely fell apart within the early part of their lifetimes as automobiles, drastic steps would be taken. We have no such well-organized way of dealing with our social institutions, so people are groping, more or less blindly, to find alternatives to marriage (which is certainly *less* than 50 percent successful). Living to-gether without marriage, living in communes, extensive child-care centers, serial monogamy (with one divorce after another), the women's liberation movement to establish the woman as a person in her own right, new divorce laws which do away with the concept of guilt—these are all gropings toward some new form of man-woman relationship for the future. It would take a bolder man than I to predict what will emerge.

Instead, I want in this chapter to present a number of vig-nettes of real marriages, each of which takes a different form, each of which raises profound questions—of morals, of practicality, of personal desirability. It is my hope that even if no answers are provided, there will be much data for thought and for personal decision-making.

WHY JOAN MARRIED

Listen to Joan, a young woman, now divorced, as she shares with an encounter group some of the background components of her marriage. I find that her account has many significant meanings for me, and I will share some of those later. Here's Joan:

I guess I got married for all the wrong reasons. At the time it was the thing to do. "Here are all my friends getting married, what am I gonna do? I'm a senior in college, that's pretty old. I better start thinking about marriage. I don't know what else I can do. I can teach but that's not enough.

The person that I married was a very popular man and I was a very insecure person, *very* insecure; and I thought, well, golly, I'm going with this person and everybody likes *him,* so maybe if I marry him, everybody will like *me!* The man that I married, I didn't feel he really listened, but I did feel security. That, and not knowing what I'd do when I graduated—that's why I got married.

A bit later she goes into more detail as to the kind of thinking that preceded her marriage.

The reason why I got engaged was because a very good friend of mine had gotten engaged and she had a very pretty ring, and was making all these wedding plans. My friends were saying, "God, Joan, when are you and Max getting married? You've been going together for three years now. You better not let him get away. If you let *him* get away, you're stupid!" My mother said, "Oh, Joan, when are you going to find another person like Max? He's so outstanding and responsible and mature and secure." I felt, "This is the one I should marry because my close friends, my roommate, my mother all say it," and although I had these doubts going on inside me, I thought, "Well, you're so insecure and so stupid that you don't know your own feelings." I thought, "They know what's best for you and you don't so you had better follow their advice."

I had guts enough to tell Max why I was doing it and I said I was really kind of scared to get married and said, "I don't know if this is really right for me." And he said, "Don't worry. You'll learn to love me." I did learn to love him in a brotherly way, but it didn't go beyond that.

When the wedding gifts were unwrapped and all the newness wore off, and the newness of having a baby wore off, then I really started feeling, "Oh you stupid idiot, you should have listened to *yourself*": Because I had been saying those things to me, but I just wouldn't listen because I thought I was too screwed up to know what was best for me. So I was right after all.

There are several elements which, for me, stand out in Joan's experience. First of all, it shows how prone we all are to yield to social pressures. A female college senior should be planning to get married, and socially that's *that*.

The dangers of advice stand out so very clearly. Out of love and caring and concern her mother and her good friends all know what is best for her to do. How easy it is to direct the life of another and how very difficult it is to live your own!

The fear of squarely facing one's own problems. Joan knew she was insecure. She knew she was frightened of the future. She realized she couldn't get to her own feelings. But instead of facing those inner problems squarely and directly, she did what so many of us do; she built the illusion that she could find the solution outside herself—in another.

Finally, what impresses me is that Joan, as is true of so many others, experiences no trust in her own feelings, her own inner unique reactions. She is dimly aware of the doubts she has about the relationship, of the lack of a feeling of deep love, of her unreadiness really to commit herself to this man. But these are only feelings. *Only feelings!* It is not until after marriage, and after having a child, that she realizes what reliable guides her gut reactions were, if she had only *trusted* them enough to *listen* to them.

LOSING ONE'S SELF—AND ITS EFFECT ON A MARRIAGE

Next I would like to present a picture of a good marriage which disintegrated. I think we can see some of the elements at work in causing it to fail. So here is the story of Jay, a promising young instructor in journalism, and Jennifer, a sociology major interested in international problems as well as art. I have known them for many years and their parents are friends of mine. They were both about twenty when they met, and their initial acquaintance grew up around the mutual interest they discovered in world issues. They are in their early forties now. They both came from educated backgrounds, though Jay's father, a highly cultivated person, was largely self-educated. They were of different religious faiths, but neither of them took any great stock in orthodoxy, and their beliefs could more adequately be described as humanistic. They were married, and the marriage seemed a very happy one indeed. In the course of several years a boy and a girl arrived. Here was the first point at which the possibility of a rift emerged. Jay came from a familial and cultural background in which a child was adored. He felt that nothing was too good for his children and that every whim of each child was to be obeyed. Jennifer went along with him to some extent, but this was not *her* way and she differed openly with Jay on this. Jay seemed an admirable father. Unlike many men, he loved nothing better than to spend a day with his children, and he had the capacity of becoming at those times very much of a child himself.

As Jay moved up in his profession he was called upon to spend periods of time abroad—in European, Latin American, and Asian countries. On any extended trip the whole family went along. They met interesting people, explored new cultures, and Jay and Jennifer even worked together on some of the foreign projects. It seemed to be an idyllic marriage and a very close-knit family. Yet there were subtle flaws in the personality and behavior of each—deficiencies which seemed to feed on the other's deficiencies, until little by little, since they were not openly faced and mutually talked out, they made this idyllic marriage intolerable. Let me give a very condensed account of this subtle downward spiral.

Jennifer, before her marriage, had been an extremely independent, creative, innovative person, always starting things and carrying out projects which others were not bold enough to do. Yet in her marriage she adopted the role of being her husband's support, of doing what he wanted done in the way he wished it done. She felt this was the way a wife should behave. She even wrote to him before their marriage, she tells me, that she was not too sure of herself and that she wanted to live her life through his.

Jay is a charming person with a high degree of charisma; a brilliant intellectual, an exciting conversationalist. Not surprisingly, his were the friends invited to their home. He was the central focus of the evening, while Jennifer did a splendid job of providing the food, the drinks, the aesthetic setting for the evening. She would try, but usually ineffectually, to enter the conversation or to introduce a topic of her own. At some level her resentment at this situation built up, though it never really surfaced until they had been married twelve or fourteen years. Up to that time she was really unaware of any of her resentments. Perhaps this was due to her life in her own family, where negative feelings were almost never expressed.

At any rate, without being conscious of what was happening, she turned her resentment inward. How could she be so inadequate, so worthless, so unappreciative that she could not enjoy her husband as others did? She simply gave up her own self in order to try to be the wife whom Jay wanted and needed. Sören Kierkegaard's statement (1941 translation) comes to mind: "The greatest danger, that of losing one's own self, may pass off quietly as if it were nothing; every other loss, that of an arm, a leg, five dollars, etc., is sure to be noticed." Though this sentence was written more than a century ago, it was incredibly true of Jennifer and it took her years to discover the loss.

Another important facet of their relationship was Jay's dependence on her, evident in many ways, but especially in the making of important decisions. Though outwardly a highly competent professional person, he seemed to have great difficulty arriving at decisions and frequently managed to get Jennifer to make a statement as to what decision *she* thought he should make. Then he would make that choice. If it didn't work out well, she was certainly partly to blame and in subtle ways he let her know it.

His dependence and his inability to be a strong and decisive father built up more and more suppressed anger in Jennifer, until she found, to her horror, that she hated to hear his car coming in after work. Her reaction was "Here comes my third child," and a deeply despondent feeling settled on her like a cloud.

This unconscious turning inward of all her negative feelings about the relationship caused her to be more and more depressed until thoughts of suicide were increasingly frequent. One day she found herself taking the steps that would lead to her own death. She was sure that she was worthless, that neither Jay nor her parents would miss her, that no one cared for her, and she might as well end it. Then *something* in her rebelled. There was at least a dawning feeling that she had a *right* to *live*. She immediately sat down and wrote to a psychiatrist whom she knew and in whom she had confidence, asking for an early appointment, which was given. She entered therapy and continued for a long time.

This was definitely the turning of the corner for her, but not for the marriage. As she became more open in the relationship, some of her long-pent-up anger and resentment poured out on Jay, often to his bewilderment. He had given her everything she wanted. He had been a father who loved his home, his wife, and his children. Who was this angry new woman who called him dependent, who felt he was not enough of a man sexually for her, who resented the excitement he created in social conversations? Her parents felt some of the same puzzlement, for she heaped on them the accumulated resentments of long ago, which often had little to do with the present relationship.

Jay felt strongly that he was not to blame for the situation, that he had always acted as a proper husband should, and that obviously Jennifer was "sick." He had been generous, helpful, stimulating, and completely faithful. He was at a loss to understand the situation, and certainly felt that he was not the one who needed to change. Hence, though they made several attempts to work out some of their problems with a marriage counselor, these efforts were not successful, and in some respects they worsened the situation. Jay could always present himself in such an articulate and favorable way that even the counselor was to some extent won over, leaving Jennifer more angry than ever.

Jennifer began demanding that Jay be the husband whom she wanted and expected. Jay for his part simply wanted Jennifer to go back to being the helpmate whom he had known for almost fifteen years. He would continue to be the loving person he had been if she would return to being the loving wife she had been. The marriage became more and more acrimonious, the air between them full of hostility, until divorce remained the only sensible answer.

I would make only two comments about this marriage. Though Jay and Jennifer were not perfectly matched, there is every reason to believe that it could have been a satisfying marriage. It is easy enough with hindsight to see that if Jennifer had from the first insisted on being her true self, the marriage would have had much more strife *and* much more hope. Ideally, if when she first felt dominated in conversation she had expressed her resentment to him, as a feeling in herself, it is highly likely that some mutually satisfactory solution could have been found. The same is true of her unhappiness over being forced to be the one who guided the children, of her annoyance at his dependent weakness, of her disappointment in his lack of sexual aggressiveness. If she could have voiced these attitudes as they arose, before they had built up to a high pressure; if she could have voiced them as feelings existing in her, not as the accusations they later became, then the likelihood that they would be met by the expression of feelings from him, and the possibility of coming to a deeper mutual understanding and to a resolution of the difficulties, would have been far greater. It seems tragic that a marriage with great and exciting potential should have become a failure. Out of it, however, has come a strong and creative Jennifer who will never again, I believe, sacrifice herself to meet the needs and demands of another.

And Jay—had he been faced with these feelings when they

occurred—would of necessity have realized that he was not always the excellent father and husband he felt he was, that he was not always right, that he was not only contributing to the marriage love and caring (which he was) but was also arousing anger and resentment and feelings of inadequacy in his wife. He then could have become openly a more human, childish, fallible person. Instead, he feels confirmed in his view that he was an excellent husband and father, that there was no sense of strain in the marriage so far as he could see, until Jennifer for unknown reasons "went off the track." He sees the breakup of the marriage as unnecessary and wrong. For him, Jennifer's thinking about the relationship gradually became an ugly caricature of something that was truly beautiful, creative, and often joyful. He simply does not understand this at all, except that he is sure that it was not his doing. It is sad to see such a lack of insight in so brilliant a person.

THE RESCUE OF A MARRIAGE

I learned a great deal from counseling a young wife, Peg Moore. Although this took place a number of years ago, her concerns, and my learnings, are as "now" as the latest pop record. I had known Peg in one of my classes, a bouncy, spontaneous, good-humored young woman with the wholesome appearance of the All-American Girl. But a bit later she comes to me for counseling. Her complaint is that her husband, Bill, is very formal and reserved with her, that he doesn't talk to her or share his thinking with her, is inconsiderate, that they are sexually incompatible and rapidly growing apart. I found myself feeling, "How tragic it is that such a lively, exciting girl is married to a wooden image of a man." But as she continues to talk out her attitudes she becomes more open, a mask drops away, and the picture changes drastically. She expresses the deep guilt feeling which she has regarding her life before her marriage, when she had affairs with a number of men, mostly married men. She realizes that though with most people she is a gay and spontaneous person, with her husband she is stiff, controlled, lacking in spontaneity. She also sees herself as demanding that he be exactly what she wishes him to be.

At this point counseling is interrupted by my absence from the city. She continues to write to me, expressing her feelings and adding, "If I could only say these things to him [her husband] I could be myself at home. But what would that do to his trust in people? Would you find me repulsive if you were my husband and learned the truth? I wish I were a 'nice gal' instead of a 'Babe.' I've made such a mess of things."

This is followed by a letter from which a lengthy quotation seems justified. She tells how irritable she has been—how disagreeable she was when company dropped in one evening. After they left,

I felt like a louse for behaving so badly. . . . I was still feeling sullen, guilty, angry at myself and Bill—and just about as blue as they come.

So, I decided to do what I've been really wanting to do and putting off because I felt it was more than I could expect from any man—to tell Bill just what was making me act that terrible way. It was even harder than telling you—and that was hard enough. I couldn't tell it in such minute detail but I did manage to get out some of those sordid feelings about my parents and then even more about those "damn" men. The nicest thing I've ever heard him say was, "Well, maybe I can help you there"—when speaking of my parents. And he was very accepting of the things I had done. I told him how I felt so inadequate in so many situations—because I have never been allowed to do so many things— even to know how to play cards. We *talked, discussed,* and really got down deep into so many of both our feelings. I didn't tell him as completely about the men—their names, but I did give him an idea of about how many. Well, he was so understanding and things have cleared up so much that I TRUST HIM. I'm not afraid now to tell him those silly little illogical feelings that keep popping into my head. And if I'm not afraid then maybe soon those silly things will stop popping. The other evening when I wrote to you I was almost ready to pull out —I even thought of just leaving town. (Escaping the whole affair.) But I realized that I'd just keep running from it and not be happy until it was faced. We talked over children and though we've decided to wait until

Bill is closer to finishing school, I'm happy with this arrangement. Bill feels as I do about the things we want to do for our children—and most important the things we *don't* want to do to them. So if you don't get any more desperate sounding letters, you know things are going along as okay as can be expected.

Now, I'm wondering—have you known all along that that was the only thing I could do to bring Bill and me close? That was the one thing I kept telling myself wouldn't be fair to Bill. I thought it would ruin his faith in me and in everyone. I had a barrier so big between Bill and me that I felt he was almost a stranger. The only way I pushed myself to do it was to realize that if I didn't at least try his response to the things that were bothering me, it wouldn't be fair to him—to leave him without giving him a chance to prove that he could be trusted. He proved even more than that to me—he's been down in hell too with his feelings—about his parents, and a good many people in general. (Rogers, 1961, pp. 316–317.)

It is interesting to ask how much psychological energy is consumed by spouses who are trying to live behind a mask in their marriages. Peg had clearly felt that she was acceptable only if she maintained a façade of respectability. Unlike Jennifer, she was somewhat *aware* of her feelings, but believed that if she showed them, she would be utterly rejected.

For me the significance of the story does *not* lie in the fact that she told her husband of her past sexual experiences. I do not think that is the lesson to be learned from it. I have known happy marriages in which one spouse has concealed certain experiences from the other, but has been able to do so comfortably. In Peg's case this concealment had built up an enormous barrier, so that she could not be real in the relationship.

One rule of thumb which I have found helpful for myself is that in any continuing relationship, any persistent feeling had better be expressed. Suppressing it can only damage the relationship. The first sentence is not stated casually. Only if it is a significant continuing relationship, and only if it is a recurring or persistent feeling, is it necessary to bring the feeling into the open in the relationship. If this is not done, what is unexpressed gradually poisons the relationship, as it did in Peg's case. So when she asks, "have you known all along that that was the only thing I could do to bring Bill and me close?" my answer would depend on what she means. I certainly believe that it was the sharing of her real feelings which rescued the marriage, but whether it was necessary to tell Bill the details of her behavior is something only she could decide.

Incidentally, a birth announcement and a note several years later indicated that both the marriage and their child seemed healthy.

MY OWN MARRIAGE

I would like to tell you something of the marriage in which I have, as of this writing, been involved for over forty-seven years! To some of you it may seem unbelievably square, but I cannot agree. Helen and I often marvel, however, at how enriching our life together still is and we wonder how and why we have been so fortunate. I can't answer those questions, but I would like to give you something of the history of our marriage, as objectively as I can. Perhaps you can gain something from the account.

We lived within a block of each other in a Chicago suburb during most of our grammar school days. There were others who were often part of the group too, though she had more friends than I did. I moved away when I was thirteen, and I do not remember any special pangs at being away from her, nor did we communicate.

When I went to college, I was surprised to find that she had chosen the same university, though her interests were entirely different. She was my first date in college, largely because I was too shy to date a stranger. But as I dated other girls, I came to appreciate her many qualities which appealed to me—her gentleness, her straightforwardness, her thoughtfulness—not a brilliant academic glow, but the willingness to think openly about real issues, while I was more caught up in the desire to appear scholarly. I can remember being ashamed of her sometimes in social groups because she seemed lacking in general and academic information.

Our friendship deepened. We went on hikes and picnics on which I was able to introduce her to the world of nature, which I loved. She taught me to dance and even sometimes to enjoy social events. I became more and more serious in my feelings for her. She liked me, but was not at all sure she wanted to marry me. Then, due to several circumstances, I was out of college for a year but kept writing her more and more passionate letters. When I returned, she had left college to take a job as a commercial artist in Chicago, so we were still separated most of the time. But at last she said yes. The night she told me she was now sure that she loved me and would marry me, I had to spend the rest of the night riding on a dirty bumpy train to get back to my college classes, but I couldn't have cared less. I was in seventh heaven, walking on clouds. "She *loves* me! She loves *me!*" It was a peak experience I can never forget.

There were still twenty-two months of separation before we were married, and the correspondence was heavy. (Today it would have been phonecalls.) I was fortunate in developing a business during my last two years of college which brought in a surprising amount of money, enough to get married on before starting graduate school.

Our parents approved the match, but not the marriage. To marry before completing one's education! How would I support her? Unheard of! Nevertheless, we were married (at age twenty-two) and went off to graduate school together. As we look back on it, we realize it was one of the wisest decisions we ever made.

We were both sexually inexperienced, extremely naïve (though we thought ourselves very sophisticated); yet for months we lived in a joyous romantic haze, having moved a thousand miles from our families (a great idea!), finding the world's smallest apartment in New York, furnishing it to suit us, and loving each other mightily.

Because we had chosen to go to New York together, we could *grow* together. Helen took some of the courses I was taking. I learned from her art work. We discussed the books and shows we indulged in on next to no money. We both changed incredibly in our attitudes toward religion, politics, and all the issues of the day. She worked part-time jobs, I had a regular weekend job, but still we were together a great deal of the time, learning to share ideas, interests, feelings—in all but one area.

I became very dimly aware that though our sexual relationship was great for me, it was not that great for her. I realize, though, how little I understood the deeper meaning of her phrases: "Oh, not tonight"; "I'm too tired"; "Let's wait 'till some other time." There is no doubt the situation could have led to a crisis.

At this point sheer luck gave us a break, though like most good luck, it needed to be used. In my graduate school I learned that a psychiatrist, Dr. G. V. Hamilton, needed a few more young married men to complete a research study he was engaged in. Probably there was some pay involved, which would account for my snatching the opportunity so promptly. (Actually the study was a more personalized forerunner of the Kinsey researches, and very well done, though never widely known.) I went to Dr. Hamilton's office for two or three lengthy interviews. He questioned so calmly and easily about every aspect of my sexual development and life that I gradually found myself talking with almost equal ease. One thing I came to realize was that I just didn't *know* whether my wife had ever had an orgasm. She often seemed to enjoy our relationship, so I *assumed* I knew the answer. But the most important thing I learned was that the things in one's private life which cannot *possibly* be talked about *can* be talked about, easily and freely.

So then came the question, Could I translate this into my personal life? I began the frightening process of talking—*really* talking—with Helen about our sexual relationship. It was frightening because every question and every answer made one or the other of us so vulnerable—to attack, to criticism, to ridicule, to rejection. But we weathered it! Each learned to understand much more deeply the other's desires, taboos, satisfactions, and dissatisfactions in our sexual life. And while at first it led only to greater tenderness, and understanding, and improvement, gradually it led not only to orgasms for her, but to a full, continuing, satisfying, and enriching sexual relationship—in which we could talk out new difficulties as they arose.

That was terribly important to us and undoubtedly saved us from deep estrangements which might have split us asunder. But the even more important thing was that we seem to have realized that the thing which cannot *possibly* be revealed to the other *can* be revealed, the problem which you *must keep* to yourself can be shared. While many times we have temporarily lost this learning, it has always returned in periods of crisis.

I certainly will not try to recount all of our marriage experience. There have been periods of greater remoteness from each other, and periods of great closeness. There have been periods of real stress, squabbles, annoyance, and suffering—though we are not the kind who fight—and periods of enormous love and supportiveness. And we have always continued to share. Neither has become so involved in his own life and activity that he has had no time for sharing with the other.

There is one annoying behavior which we have both exhibited at times, though I much more often than Helen. When one spouse, in a social or public situation, ridicules or humiliates or puts down the other, almost always as a "joke," trouble is brewing. It must be a mark of my defensiveness that I can't think of a simple specific example of my own behavior, so I will use one from another couple recently in our home. We were speaking of drinking when he said, "facetiously," "Of course, my wife drinks too much." She flared up because she felt it was untrue and she resented being criticized in public. His reply was, "Oh, I was just joking." This is the kind of behavior in which I too have indulged, but Helen definitely calls me on it when we get home. I have come to see it for what it is—a cowardly copout. If I have some negative feeling about something she has done, I would much prefer to take the more courageous step of voicing it to her when we are alone, rather than "jokingly" needling her in a social situation. In similar fashion I learned, early in our marriage, that the sarcasm which was so much a part of my family life, where we were continually throwing verbal barbs at one another, was something which hurt her deeply and which she would not tolerate. I have learned much from her (and she from me).

One point on which we have never fully agreed is whether there is an element of possessiveness in a good marriage. I say no. She says yes. I formed a real attachment to another woman, an attachment which to my mind did not exclude Helen, but was *in addition* to my love for her. She did not see it the same way *at all* and was very upset. It was not so much jealousy as it was a deep anger at me, which she turned inward, feeling that she was "on the shelf" and inadequate. Here I am grateful that our grown-up daughter helped Helen to recognize her true feelings and to reestablish communication between us. When we were able to share our real feelings, a resolution became possible, and Helen and I both remain good friends of the woman who was such a threat to her. Incidentally, each of us, on a number of important occasions, has been deeply helped by our son or daughter, and this is a priceless experience.

I think each of us has stood by the other very well in periods of individual pain or torment. I would like to give two examples of the way she has stood by me, and one in which I know she feels that I stood by her.

The first I will mention is that during my forties there was a period of nearly a year when I felt absolutely no sexual desire —for anyone. No medical cause was found. Helen was confident that my normal urges would return and simply "stood with me" in my predicament. It is easy to think up possible psychological causes, but none of them "clicks" as far as I'm concerned. It remains a mystery to me. But her quiet continuing love meant a great deal to me and probably was the best therapy I could have had. At any rate, I gradually became sexually normal once more.

A more serious crisis built around an incredibly lengthy, poorly handled therapeutic relationship which I had with a severely schizophrenic girl. The story is a long one, but suffice it to say that partly because I was so determined to help her, I got to the point where I could not separate my "self" from hers. I literally lost my "self," lost the boundaries of myself. The efforts of colleagues to help me were of no avail and I became convinced (and I think with some reason) that I was going insane.

One morning after an hour or so at the office I simply panicked. I walked home and told Helen, "I've *got* to get out of here! Far away!" She of course knew something of what I had been going through, but her reply was balm to my soul. She said, "Okay, let's go right now." After a few phonecalls to staff members to ask them to take over my responsibilities, and some hasty packing, we were on the road inside of two hours and didn't return for more than six weeks. I had my ups and downs, and when I returned I went into therapy with one of my colleagues, gaining great help. But my point here is that throughout this whole period Helen was certain this state of mind would pass away, that I was not insane, and showed in every way how much she cared. Wow! That's the only way I can express my gratitude. That's what I mean when I say she has stood by me in critical periods. I have tried to do the same when she has been suffering one or another kind of torment.

Helen's mother suffered several strokes as she grew older. This had the unfortunate (but not rare) effect of markedly changing her personality. Where she had been a warm and kindly person with strong intellectual interests, she became a carping, suspicious, sometimes viciously hurtful person. This was terribly hard on her daughters, but particularly on Helen, who would feel terribly crushed and hurt by the psychological jabs which came from a mother with whom she had been very close. Her mother became impossible to live with and could not live alone. Then came hard decisions—to take her from her apartment; to place her in a nursing home (the best of which are forlorn places); to face the fact that she was no longer the person she had been. Helen felt terribly guilty about what she was doing to her mother, and her mother retained enough shrewdness to know how to intensify that guilt. Through six long and very trying years I believe I stood by Helen. She could not help but feel hurt, guilty, and upset by her twice-weekly visits to her mother. I could let her have those feelings, but also let her know that I thought the accusations false and the decisions sound, and that I believed she was doing the best anyone could in a most distressing and complex situation. I know that she was strengthened and helped by my "standing by." Our physician son also greatly helped her to understand the physical and psychological deterioration which had taken place, and that her mother's complaints were not to be taken at face value.

As I look back over the many years of our life together, there are certain elements which appear important to me, though naturally I cannot be objective.

We came from the same community, with similar backgrounds and values.

We complemented each other. Someone has suggested that of the many types of marriage, two exist at opposite ends of a continuum. One is the "geared" marriage in which each partner supplements the deficiencies of the other and they mesh comfortably, sometimes too placidly. The other is the conflictual marriage, in which the success of the marriage depends on the fact that the couple is continually endeavoring to work out constructively the many conflicts which would otherwise destroy the marriage. Ours is somewhere in the middle of this continuum, but slightly closer to the "geared" marriage. I tend to be a shy loner; Helen is more naturally and comfortably social. I tend to persevere at what I'm doing; she is the one to say, "Why don't we do this or that?" "Why don't we take a trip?" I grudgingly agree, but once under way I'm the more adventurous and childish and she is more steady. I've been a therapist, with an interest in research; she has been an artist and a lifelong worker in the planned-parenthood movement. Each of us has had the opportunity to learn much from the other's fields of interest. We have also been able to deal constructively with most of our conflicts and differences.

Consequently, each of us has always had a *separate* life and interest, as well as our life together. So we have never competed directly. When we have come close to it, it has been uncomfortable. When I took up painting for a time and did one or two passably good paintings, it made her uneasy. When I see her being far more helpful to a person than I could be, I confess my reaction is, "Oh my God! She's better than I am!" But these envies and this competitiveness have rarely been important.

In another area we are astonishingly noncompetitive, and this is in our taste. From the early years of our marriage we have found that if we are selecting a piece of furniture, a car, a gift, or even an item of clothing, we tend to choose the same thing. Sometimes I will say, "Okay, I've made up my mind; let me know when you've made your choice." When she does, it is, with astonishing frequency, the same selection I have made. I don't account for this. I just state it.

She was an excellent parent when the children were young. I would rate myself only fair as a father then—curiously enough, in those days I was more concerned with whether they were disturbing me than with whether what they were doing was in the direction of promoting their own growth. As our two children became older I could communicate with them fully as well as and sometimes better than she.

Perhaps that's enough to indicate some of the many ways we supplement each other. But these balances shift: where I always used to be the better read of us, in recent years, as more and more demands have been made on my time, she is better read and I rely on her to keep me informed of much that is going on.

We have been through periods of sickness and operations, but never at the same time, so each has been able to see the other through the difficult period. In general, though the troubles of older years occasionally assail us, we have retained fundamentally good health.

David Frost gave a definition of love on TV which went something like this: "Love is when each person is more concerned for the other than he is for himself." I think this description fits all the best moments of our marriage. I realize that this can also be a disastrous definition of love, when it means that one or the other gives up his self out of consideration for the other. This has not been true in our case.

I suppose the most profound statement I could make about our marriage—and I can't explain it adequately—is that each has always been willing and eager for the other to *grow*. We have *grown* as individuals and in the process we have grown together.

One final paragraph about our present state, as we have reached the Biblical "threescore and ten." We have so much of shared living and suffering and struggle and joy that we also fulfill Truman Capote's definition of love: "Love is when you don't have to finish the sentence." In the middle of some event or scene Helen may say to me, "Do you remember when we. . . ?" and I say, "Of course," and we both laugh together because we know we are both thinking of the same experience. And while our sex life is not quite the same as in our twenties or thirties, our physical closeness, our "snuggling," and our sex relationships are somewhat like a chord which is beautiful not only in itself, but also for its many, many overtones which enrich it far beyond the simple chord. In short, we are incredibly fortunate though at times we have had to work very hard to preserve that good fortune.

Lest you think that this makes everything rosy, I should add that our two children have had their full share of marital difficulties. So our growth together into a satisfying relationship for ourselves has constituted no guarantee for our children.

SOME CONCLUDING REMARKS

So what do we conclude from the experience of Joan, of Jay and Jennifer, of Peg and Bill, of Carl and Helen? I believe you will have to write your own conclusions.

I have tried to indicate that whatever marriage is now, it will almost certainly be different in the future.

I have tried to choose examples which show some of the elements that can interfere with the success of or break up a marriage; and similarly some of the elements that can restore or renew a marriage or cause it to "work."

I hope it has been clear that the dream of a marriage "made in heaven" is totally unrealistic, and that every continuing man-woman relationship must be worked at, built, rebuilt, and continually refreshed by mutual personal growth.

In the following chapters we will see many more facets of this man-woman phenomenon, which is so central to the lives of almost all people.

2 ✐ An "Unmarried-Married" Couple

I KNOW A YOUNG COUPLE who met when she was eighteen, he was nineteen. I was aware that they had lived together for several years. I was surprised when I heard that they had been married, in a quite conventional ceremony—white dress for the bride, tuxedo for the groom, and all that. I thought that if they were willing to talk freely of the different phases of their relationship, it might have meaning for many young people. They did talk with me very freely about their past and present relationship, about six months after their marriage, and I would like to present some extended (but condensed) excerpts from that tape recording. I will call them Dick and Gail.

THE EARLY RELATIONSHIP

They told me about getting acquainted, and then came an amusing instance of distorted memory:

DICK: Well, I remember just thinking I liked Gail a lot. I put out a little more effort for Gail than I did with other girls at the time. I guess that's the only overwhelming impression I can remember. I think for a long period of time there wasn't any sexual relationships. I think that was significant. I think probably it was . . .
GAIL: A week . . .
DICK: A week? No, it was longer than a week, Gail . . .

GAIL: A week and two days after we met.

DICK: Really?

GAIL: Yes. *I* didn't think it was so long. Don't you remember the first time, it was . . .

DICK: That was nice. It was on the beach, but I thought it was longer than a week.

They had a rather stormy courtship, which Gail describes as follows:

GAIL: Well, I saw Dick first. I liked him first. I saw him on the first day of school. I thought he was good-looking but I thought he was obnoxious. He wore these dark glasses inside. I found out later he had broken his real glasses and couldn't see without glasses, but he gave this impression of being very snooty. . . . I couldn't *stand* him. His roommate told me he really wasn't so obnoxious, and we started seeing each other. But I liked him almost immediately, after thinking he was just a brat. From the first I was pretty intense. Somewhere along the line I think he talked me into letting go of my feelings and just letting myself fall in love. I can remember making up my mind and saying, "Well, why not? What's it going to hurt?" And I think there were really a lot of hard times 'cause, you know, I was quite willing to keep at it heavily and steadily and Dick was different—he would start to back off. And my feelings were hurt.

ME: The difficult times really came before you started living together, when you were sort of up and down in your relationship?

DICK: Yeah, up and down. I was taking drugs heavily at one point, having gone to San Francisco on Christmas vacation from college, and I went through some *awful* experiences there and decided that that wasn't what I wanted to do. And all this time while I was in San Francisco, which probably wasn't more than two months—it seemed like ages—being away from Gail sort of reinforced my feelings about her. It was easier to make up my mind as to what I felt about her when I wasn't around her.

COMMENT. Why do we distort things selectively in our memory? Because of some need or other. Dick has a need now to feel that he was quite slow in entering this relationship in a significant way. At the time it probably seemed to him that they were very slow in having sexual relations because his needs were stronger than Gail's, though later we will see a change in this.

The inadequacy of first impressions is well illustrated. Given a few clues, Gail comes to the conclusion that Dick is impossible. Later she finds quite the opposite.

Nearly every relationship probably has a type of imbalance similar to that between Dick and Gail. Gail soon finds that she is ready to involve herself heavily in the relationship. Dick is not. He gets involved but then backs off and gets involved and backs off again (later in the interview one reason for his behavior comes out).

We see some of the factors which influence choice in a relationship. When Dick gets away from Gail, he gains a more meaningful perspective on her and on her behavior and becomes more positive in his attitudes. "Absence makes the heart grow fonder!" It is also probable that his very dissatisfying experience with drugs made him lean toward an interpersonal relationship rather than trying to find satisfaction simply in chemicals.

LIVING TOGETHER

They tell of moving to Boston, and moving into the same apartment.

ME: Did living together make any difference whatsoever, whether for worse or better?

GAIL: We couldn't get away from it so easily. Dick couldn't walk out and disappear and stay gone for a month because, well, he did that when we were dating, but if he did that when we were living together, he would have to find somebody else to feed him. And it forced me to have to talk about it a little bit more, which is still going on. It puts us up against the wall, so to speak, and the big change, I think, was putting theory into practice. You know, when you're dating you can say, "Well, I'll be this way or this would happen when we're living together," but when you're living together, it *happens* and you can't theorize any more.

DICK: We never mentioned love in our relationship. And that's for at least three years. We never committed ourselves to loving one another until well into the fourth year, although I don't know *why*. We'd ask each other if we liked each other and placed a great deal of significance on that, but just as significantly we avoided the word "love," and all I remember about the first time we did mention love was that it was kind of a trauma.

GAIL: I can remember everything. I think we were arguing about us. And Dick was trying to tell me, without telling me, that he was leaving me. You know, saying there's this problem and that it's stale and it's . . . and so on. And I'm all ready to change and work it out and then he just got frustrated and he said, "But I love you and I really care for you," and then he walked out. That I really couldn't understand. You told me you loved me and walked out and left me! I thought, "Well, that's crazy." I thought that was just the nuttiest thing I ever heard. I thought, "Well, does he feel guilty about hurting me and is that why he's saying it?" And if he was all that crazy about me, he wouldn't have been walking out to somebody else! And he didn't tell me, you know, he never told me he had another girlfriend, which bugged me a lot because I thought he could at least do that. And I had to go through this whole painful thing of finding out, when somebody said they saw Dick with this little blonde. And I thought, "Well, if that's true, he's probably at her house," and so I went over there and there they were and Dick was mortified. I was bitchy and I wouldn't go away. I just sat there making small talk —and I know now that I loved every minute of it. And so I really didn't believe it.

DICK: You mean you didn't believe it when I said I loved you. . . .

GAIL: Yeah. But I guess I sort of had it in the back of my mind that we would get back together.

DICK: I was very dissatisfied with this other girl after a very short period of time, and it was interesting, because she outwardly seemed to have everything. I could, you know, I could list off consciously what I wanted and she had it, but it wasn't enough. I think one thing that I was very impressed about was that in comparing the two girls, this girl seemed not to have an independent life of her own. She seemed to be tied to whoever she was with. When we'd be talking with somebody else, she'd voice *my* opinions, and Gail doesn't do that hardly at all. She forms her own opinions and sticks to them. And I found that this really takes a great burden off of me in a relationship. And I don't have to be carrying the emotional stability, or the opinions, for two people. It's really like having a burden lifted off yourself when you're not living with a mirror image of yourself but actually another person. At that point I realized that for me Gail was another individual whom I did care for.

Later Dick talks about another issue.

DICK: Here is a problem that still gets to us, I think, and I think it originates with me. I don't . . . I'm not sure how these things arise anyway. But I think that I am *still* hung up about what *should* be and what *is*. It seems that all of a sudden I'll reach a threshold of Gail behaving in such a way that it just seems to me that it's *intolerable*. It should be *otherwise,* I think. But I get so *angry*. I guess that the reason I really love her is that she's her own person and yet because she is her own person there are things which I find *immutable*.

GAIL: I really can't be angry like Dick. I'm afraid to. I'm afraid he's going to beat me up or kill me or something, and he does get *really*, really furious and I get scared and I don't want to do anything that will make him any madder.

COMMENT. Some readers will judge Dick and Gail to be a very immature couple on the basis of their statements in this section. This judgment would probably be objectively true but it is of little help to us in understanding their situation since all of us have to change gradually from immaturity to a more mature behavior and it is only the rate that is different. Let me list some things which seem to be slow and gradual and difficult steps toward a greater maturity of relationship as they have described them in this section.

They were forced to face each other as persons and work things out rather than run away from them.

They were forced to face the difficulty of behaving differently in a real-life relationship.

They became at least partially aware of their deep fear of a real commitment which would be involved in such a phrase as "I love you." To say that they liked each other or even disliked each other at times would not be nearly so threatening.

Dick's real confusion about commitment is strongly emphasized when he says "I love you," just as he is walking out to join another girl.

Dick's learning about interpersonal relationships in other ways than intellectual is apparent. He realizes that though his new blond friend fulfills more of his intellectual list of demands, she is not nearly as satisfying to him as Gail. He respects Gail's independence of thought and action.

Or is this a deep respect for Gail? Part of it certainly is Dick's deep (and natural) fear of being responsible for another person and his dislike for another person being dependent on him.

Dick's hangup surrounds the word "should." Gail *should* be a certain way and when she is definitely and clearly not that way, Dick finds it intolerable and becomes furious. His explosions are so violent they arouse genuine fear in Gail. But this difference between his expectation of what Gail *should* be and his rage at what she *is* causes conflict in Dick because he realizes that it is her independence and the fact that she will not do what he thinks she should do which make her desirable. All this seems to me to be a part of growing up, no matter whether it starts early or late.

THE CHANGES WROUGHT BY MARRIAGE

GAIL: There was a more dramatic change when we got married than when we began to live together. There was to me.

ME: In what way? Why?

GAIL: Well, I don't know where all my ideas came from, but when I got married, I suddenly felt like my life was over. That was the end. I had nothing to do. I might as well lie down and die. There was no place for me to go, nothing for me to do. I had ceased to be a person. I could no longer be an independent human being or do what I wanted, even though when I thought about it, I couldn't tell why there had to be a difference between when we were married and when we were living together. . . .

ME: You felt much less of a person after you were married?

GAIL: Yes. I was really depressed and I am just now trying to pull myself up by the bootstraps. . . .

DICK: I don't know where my ideas came from either. They were just there. I thought, of course, that I wouldn't enjoy marriage and I would be tied down and I couldn't just really leave. My experience would be as Gail describes it. But it actually hasn't been. I am feeling like things are just starting and this is a surprise to me, a *real* surprise, and I can't account for it, you know. I just think that a lot of my attention toward other women as prospects is turned off. I don't have to go shopping any more. I've made a choice. I think the commitment has taken a lot of pressure off of me and left me feeling freer about actually going about the business of living.

ME: (*to* **GAIL**): What were your expectations *before* you got married?

GAIL: I talked myself into being very romantic about it and how nice it would be, and then other times I didn't want to be attached to someone, and other times I'd talk to myself and say, "Look, there's no *difference* between just living together and marriage—the only thing that changes is your name, and society will accept you," that kind of thing, but it does mean to be more stable.

ME: What were the reasons you got married?

GAIL: Well, I had kind of pushed Dick every once in a while about getting married. I'd say, you're never going to marry me. I'm never going to have any children, blah blah blah, but I wasn't all that serious about it. Then one night we went over to some friend's house and I was being kinda bitchy. I was in a nasty mood. Dick got mad afterwards and he kept getting madder and madder. We fought all the way home from their house, and it was a long drive, and we got ready for bed and we were still arguing and carrying on and then Dick told me to get out. He said, "You can pack your bags and get out." And I didn't want to and I said, "No, I'm not going to. I live here and I'm not going to go. I don't want to." Then after a moment, he said, "Okay. Then do you want to get married?" And I said, "Okay." It was almost like he said, "We'll get married or you'll get out." And I didn't want to get out. So I said okay. And then I was happy about it. It was nice to make this commitment.

DICK: It seemed to clear the air. It was obviously a resolution of something critical. Marriage did seem to resolve whatever caused this incident. Certainly the proposal of marriage at the time did seem to make a commitment one way or the other—either of dissolving the relationship or solidifying it. Also I think a large factor was to make everybody else happy. I knew immediately that it would clear the tension of our parents, on both sides, you know. . . . It was a legal thing and kind of a public commitment of what was already committed privately, and I had always thought that was what it was. And perhaps under ideal circumstances that's maybe what it is. But certain of these aspects did reverse themselves.

ME (*to* **GAIL**): Are there any other things that you think of in regard to your life since marriage?

GAIL: I found out that I had a lot of other funny ideas about marriage too. One of them, and I don't know where I got this, is that I thought you didn't have to be in love any more once you got married. And then I wouldn't have to be bothered with Dick and I could ignore the whole thing and go about my merry business. And none of them worked out. I can't go about ignoring Dick all the time and I still care about him, which is another shock. If you expect not to have to be bothered with that and you are bothered with it, it's a lot of work.

COMMENT. To me this section illustrates that when a person introjects a value or a social role from others without its being tested in his own experience, it has an incredible impact on his life and behavior. Gail had obviously introjected the notion—without being aware of it—that a wife is a nobody, a dependent person, unable to do what she wants, with no future. Quite naturally when she felt trapped in this introjected role—because it certainly was not something that Dick imposed on her—she simply felt that her life was over. In the final portion of this section some other introjected notions came out which seem most unusual. It would be interesting to know more of Gail's background, to know how she came to hold the idea that once one marries, love is no longer necessary. Also the belief that once married, a wife won't have to "bother with" her husband. She is now paying somewhat more attention to her own experience rather than to these introjections and she finds that she does care about Dick, that she is not freed from being "bothered with" her husband, and that maintaining the relationship is demanding work.

Somehow one effect upon me of this revelation is to make me very angry indeed at our educational system. Even granting the ineptness of most of the teaching and learning that goes on in our schools, even the crudest kind of education in the realm of inter-personal relationships would have spared Gail from some of these experiences. She would have learned that a woman's life, even in marriage, is in large part what she makes of it. She would have learned that love is a part of marriage. She would have discovered that one does not get married and live happily ever after: one has to struggle and work and build to continue to have and earn a satisfying relationship. It seems incredible that she could have gotten beyond the age of twenty-one without having had any *opportunity* to learn this.

Then there is Dick's introjected picture of marriage—that it would tie him down and make him unhappy. He too is learning from his *experience* that this is not the case. It is a relief not to have to be "shopping" for a prospective wife and it has given him a greater degree of freedom.

This section also contains two reasons for marrying which make the prognosis dubious. First is the motive of marrying to please their parents. While it is true that it did please the mothers and fathers, this is an unimportant element when two people are asking themselves if they can commit themselves to a permanent relationship. The other reason could be disastrously unsound, namely, to marry to resolve a crisis in the relationship. Clearly they were saying to each other, "We will either get married or split." The reason this appears to me a doubtful resolution is that there was no open facing of the very real problems of marriage or the difficult issues of their continuing relationship. Instead it was basically an appeal to magic—that deciding to get married would resolve things, would work a miracle. Their communication was very limited.

"A DIFFERENCE IN MODUS OPERANDI"

GAIL: When he tells me I have to change or be such and such, I believe it. I believe he wants me to be all different and then I'm stuck with either an unhappy husband or an unhappy self. You know, I want him to change too, but I have a different habit. I don't let it all bottle up and then explode. If he does something I don't like, I usually tell him at the moment. I tell you once, Dick, and then I pout.

ME (*to* **DICK**): How does she let you know when she's angry or unhappy with what you're doing?

DICK: Well, when the penny drops is when I first see her pouting. It seems like when you tell me, it kinda goes in one ear and out the other because I can't really remember that you tell me first and then get pouty. It kind of, it seems to me as though they are simultaneous. I don't say they are but that's the way I pick it up. . . . Of course, to me this is *infuriating*. I don't know why, perhaps it's just a difference in modus operandi. I prefer to bottle up, not for any moral reason; it's just my way. And I think, well, so she gets moody kind of, and since it's gradual, it seems to me to be all the time. You see, I forget the gaps when it's not like that. It seems to be all the time, and inside I'm going, "Why must I live with this moodiness?" and I think that accounts for when I ask her to change. (*To* **GAIL**) From my point of view your moods are like a wall I can't get through. Once telling me what you're feeling and then this pouting . . . I have a hard time dealing with it. I know my mother is a little like this and I have had just as much difficulty with her, and so I just tend to try to break it open, to burst through kind of. . . .

COMMENT. If you are observant, you have seen this kind of relationship between five- or six-year-old children. One demands that the other behave differently and throws a tantrum when this does not occur. The other pouts. To find "a difference in modus operandi" is not surprising. This we would find in almost any relationship. But to find it at such a level means that there is a great deal of growing and interpersonal communication necessary to build a solid relationship.

SOME PROBLEMS IN THE RELATIONSHIP

DICK: What we've been saying has regard to the marriage and not just living together. Living together was a very smooth transition. Gail met me in Boston and we immediately went about the business of trying to exist, though certainly we had conflicts and stuff. . . . One example, Gail, was when you would have a hard time letting me hold your hand sometimes.

ME: I'm sort of curious about this. When you would have trouble, Gail, letting him hold your hand, was that because you didn't like the physical aspect of it or was it just giving him a temporary message such as, "I'm not keen about you right now"?

GAIL: Well, it was more. It was, I think, this thing about commitment. It seemed more personal somehow to me to hold hands than just about anything else. You know, more personal somehow than making love. I never have been able to make a commitment without trying to wiggle out of it once it was settled that there *was* a commitment. And that's probably a bit of the reason I feel so upset about being married.

DICK: Getting married, to me, either was a resolution or it wasn't. . . . I tend to want things resolved immediately and without time being a factor, perhaps a simple decision. . . . *(Thoughtful pause)* Perhaps marriage only expresses an *intention* to resolve these things and not an actual resolution of itself. You know, an intention to say it's worth it if the two of us can come to an understanding and live together doing it. I think perhaps that would be a more realistic way of looking at it. It occurs to me right now that I might be able to live with that attitude a little better. An intention isn't a nothing, it's a something, and yet it does admit freely that what you're after isn't to be found right now, immediately, but is a product of something else, maybe work and time. . . .

ME: As you look back are you better at working things out in the relationship than you were in the early days, or is it about the same?

GAIL: Well, I'd say in some ways it's a lot better, but . . . I think it takes a while to recognize that somebody else is a person, for one thing. You know, it just has to be beat into you like learning to talk or something. 'Cause there's no reason for thinking that somebody else is just as human as you are unless you set out to do so. . . . After I started seeing that Dick really was another person with feelings that are just as valid as mine, then it was easier for me to really think about them and not think of him as an ideal, but to make allowances for a person.

COMMENT. Several things leap out at me here. Take Gail's statement that for her to hold hands was more of a personal commitment than to make love. This emphasizes how much each one of us lives in his own private world of perceptual meanings, which for him is reality. Her statement may seem unreasonable to the world at large, but it is the truth *for her*, and the only way I can understand her is to understand the world *she* lives in, not the one I inhabit.

Her statement about her tendency to wiggle out of any commitment has significance. A person who has been fortunate in growing up psychologically will not make a commitment without considering its consequences. He is unlikely to make any commitment for all of his life, because he knows he cannot predict himself that well. But when he has considered a particular situation thoroughly, he is able to make a realistic commitment and to hold to it. Gail is unable to do this. The hopeful element is that she has sufficient insight to recognize her tendency to escape any commitment and realizes that marriage has depressed her because there is no easy way of running away from it.

One fascinating bit of insight is Dick's dawning recognition that resolution of a conflict is not an instantaneous magic thing. He is beginning to realize that it may take "work and time" to achieve a better relationship, a more harmonious living together. Here is a man of twenty-four who has learned math and history and English literature and yet has scarcely a beginning knowledge of interpersonal relationships. How irrelevant can our education get?

The same comment would apply to Gail's learning that there is such a person as "the other." It was a great achievement for her to see that "Dick really is another person with feelings . . . as valid as mine," but it is tragic that this learning came not at ten or twelve, but at twenty-three.

SOCIETY'S PRESSURES

DICK: Can I digress for a second? About the effect of getting married. . . . All of a sudden I realized there is a price to pay for this social aspect of it, for making everyone happy, and that was that all of a sudden I realized the role that I as a male was supposed to be, and I have been reminded of it in no uncertain terms by the in-laws and my parents. . . . When Gail and I were living together, we were sort of equal partners in making the living, and if we were broke, nobody really took the blame for it; but when we moved back and came into such close proximity with our respective in-laws, all of a sudden it became *my* fault when we weren't making money and *I* was the bum who wasn't going out and looking for work or wasn't doing enough. . . .

GAIL: I know what Dick's talking about. I sort of had expectations like he did, you fall into a role even if you don't want to, which is *so awful,* of a husband is supposed to be this way and a wife is supposed to be this way, which is part of the reason, I guess, that I felt my life was over. . . . Dick is not likely to be a typical breadwinner husband and I'm not likely to want to stay home and clean house. So it put me in a big conflict because I'm thinking, "Well, I've *got* to be like this, I'm married, and I'm supposed to do this. . . ."

COMMENT is scarcely necessary because it is crystal clear that the role behavior expected by society of a man and a woman, a husband and wife, constitutes a heavy burden for the individual. The phenomenon is particularly interesting here, because it is evident that they do not impose these roles on each other. They are imposed by our culture.

AN ARGUMENT

They had been discussing the pressures put on Dick by both sets of parents and on Gail by Dick's sister, who lived next to them in Boston. What follows is a classic example of a marital argument.

43

DICK: But boy, no matter how much pressure my sister puts on you, you know. . . .

GAIL: You don't accept the fact that I can be pressured. . . .

DICK: I do accept that. . . .

GAIL: Or that it's intolerable for me. . . .

DICK: Well, you never said it was. And I defended you against my sister. . . .

GAIL: Not in front of me.

DICK: I did. I did behind you, and and I also. . . .

GAIL: Well, I did behind *you* and that's what you complained about. . . .

DICK: I asked you and you said you didn't.

GAIL: What—defended you?

DICK: Yeah.

GAIL: The hell I didn't. I did. I did plenty.

DICK: Well, this is news.

GAIL: It's not news. I told you. . . .

DICK: It's news. At any rate, if I don't make the money and if I don't pull things and if I don't find employment. . . .

GAIL: Except that I'm trying to find a job too, Dick. I'm anxious to get a job just as much as I was before. . . .

DICK: Yeah, but you're not expected to by anyone else but me. I really take issue with you on this. I think that pressure does come on me to get a job and be the breadwinner. You know divorces come about through this, "He's a lousy husband," "All he does is run around and play and do nothing. . . ."

ME: I get the feeling in this last bit that each of you is saying, "I'm more pressured than you are." "No, I'm more pressured than *you* are."

GAIL: I think that's true. That's why we can't ever talk about it because of that. Because it turns into "My lot's worse than yours"; "No, *my* lot's worse than *yours*," and so it really doesn't make any difference what's said. . . .

ME: One comment I would make is that when you are trying to tell each other what is true about the *other* person, that's when the tension mounts. When you say you *feel* pressure, I don't know how anybody could doubt that, because that's the way you feel. But when you say the pressures *are* greater on you than on Gail, well, who's going to decide that? She feels pressured also, but in different ways, and I just can't help but feel that the more you can work in terms of your own *feelings,* the more possible it is to reach some sort of an understanding.

GAIL: That's what makes me *so mad* at Dick. When we're talking, he tells me how I feel and then if I say no, I feel this way, he won't believe it. And there's no way I can talk to him. . . . At that point, when you're yelling at me and saying I'm this and that and the other thing, I'll say maybe, maybe. But I might have a small gram of truth in what *I* am saying, Dick, but you're not willing to listen.

DICK: I think, Gail, that my frustration on the other hand is that I find it difficult to talk with you. Getting a response out of you in the first place is extremely difficult and then even the response doesn't allow for sitting down. I would like nothing better than to sit down and say, "I feel this way. How do you feel? You tell me," and then asking each other what we can do about it. It really does seem to be preempted by your moods and somehow there's a block between us.

ME: You see, there too, you are telling her what the block is. Namely, it's something in her. If you could say, as you did a moment ago, "I have really tried to listen to you but it's tough because I don't hear what you're feeling," I don't think that has as much sting in it.

DICK: You're right. Yeah.

COMMENT. There are various types of fruitless arguments, but this is a common one. The outstanding quality, up to the point I intervened, is that neither is willing to listen to the other. In such a relationship, as Gail points out, "it really doesn't make any difference what's said." The failure to communicate is almost complete.

It would have been interesting to have stopped this argument at some point and ask both Dick and Gail individually to restate the meanings and feelings which had been expressed by the other. It is almost certain that they could not have done so. Instead, each is waiting for an opportunity to break in and needle the spouse, so that even the sentences are not completed. Yet the messages are quite simple. Dick is saying, "The pressure on me to be the breadwinner is greater than the pressure my sister put on you."

Gail is saying, "You don't believe I can be pressured. I'm not pressuring you. I'm trying to find a job too." Only the last statement is a cooperative nonattacking one.

It may be worthwhile to analyze the above messages and the dialogue itself in real detail. How did the argument get started? It took off when Gail told Dick, in a critical tone, what his belief or feeling was ("You don't accept the fact . . ."). This kind of statement, in which the speaker outwardly endeavors to tell another what is true within the other, and inwardly is feeling judgmental, almost invariably leads to trouble. She says, "You don't accept," and Dick says, "I do accept." Who can judge what Dick's true attitudes are? Obviously only Dick can discover the answer, and he is not likely to give an honest answer when he is under attack. This is the other feature of this kind of interchange—it usually carries with it an accusation, a negative judgment, and hence is apt to give a distorted picture.

Now note how just a slight variation of this kind of response makes a great deal of difference. I am not emotionally involved in the argument and I do want to understand what is going on in this interaction, so I come in with a statement about what I believe they are feeling. But my statement is empathic, not accusing; tentative, not judgmental; and expressed with a genuine desire to understand. This seems only slightly different from what they have been doing, but the difference in the attitude which is being expressed is profound. If one or both had said, "No, that's not what I'm saying," I would have immediately accepted any correction either wished to make.

This changes the tone of the dialogue. Once they feel that someone *understands*, even a third party, then they are both able to go more deeply and more coherently into the nature of their differences. Whether my rather didactic second response was helpful is hard to know, but I simply couldn't bear to see them arguing so fruitlessly.

In each of their next two statements one can see the seeds of further argument, although the tone of voice was much less accusing. Gail says, "You're not willing to listen," where the only truthful statement she could have made is, "I feel as though you never

Why are they empathic and communicative here and accusatory earlier? One could develop various speculative hypotheses, but frankly I do not know. But the difference in their attitudes toward each other in this area of sex changes the relationship for the better. I can only wish that this understanding attitude might spread to other areas.

It is interesting to think of the ease with which this portion of life, too, could have become a battleground. We can even see all the elements of the argument. Here is an imaginary dialogue:

DICK: You want too much sex.
GAIL: I do not. It's just that you're not very masculine.
DICK: I am masculine. The trouble with you is you're twisted and perverted.
GAIL: I am not, you're just weak.
(Et cetera,
et cetera, ad infinitum.)

The devastation which would have been wrought by such attacks is clearly shown by Gail's statement that Dick's *one* attempt to diagnose and accuse her sexually was *really* upsetting. Imagine what would have happened to the relationship if this had been a constant part of their lives.

A BRIEF LOOK AT THE FUTURE

DICK (*to* GAIL): Since we got married I really see you expressing yourself in different ways. Instead of expressing yourself only one way, and that's getting depressed, you're being hostile, or when you're happier, you're actually happier too, you know. I have a feeling of optimism about it, although, Jesus, it could go in any direction but I feel optimistic about you, you know, and your own feelings. . . .
GAIL: You really get tired after a while of making yourself not be depressed or making yourself feel something rather than just be blah. And it's very tiring. It's like exercising muscles that have never been used.

COMMENT. "It could go in any direction." It surely could! Here is a marriage with enough against it that only heroic and intelligent efforts on the part of both Dick and Gail could build a permanent relationship. I believe the weight of the negative factors—their inability to communicate in most areas, their immaturity in decision-making processes (their hangups about commitment), their introjected expectations of the role of husband and wife, their stormy relationship thus far—would all predict possible failure.

But I see three positive elements that provide a ray of hope. In their attitudes toward their sex life, one of the most important aspects of marriage, they are understanding and tender toward each other. If they could build out from this, it would undoubtedly help their marriage.

The second hopeful element lies in the statements just quoted. If Gail and Dick are becoming more accurately expressive of their feelings *as they occur,* then, as Dick says, it gives some basis for optimism. A part of this element lies in Gail's statement that a self-enhancing, feelingful relationship demands intelligent and focused effort. To the extent that they can progress toward a meaningful communication of the complex feelings which exist in the present—the tender and loving as well as the hostile and hurt —they increase the chance for living growingly together.

The third element I learned only by chance. After they left this interview they went to the home of a mutual friend, who told me that they were almost ecstatic about the experience. Someone had really listened to them and they had gained a great deal from it, they felt, for themselves. I am afraid that the first thing this shows is that very few people feel they have ever been heard, since this was an information-gathering interview and did not have a therapeutic purpose (though at times I could not resist the desire to be helpful). But it also shows how much they would respond to marital counseling if it were free (for they have no money) and if the counselor was receptive, understanding, and nonjudgmental—and if they could have the experience *now,* before their relationship deteriorates. I am afraid our culture does not offer this kind of service, and that only a minority of counselors have the attitudes which Dick and Gail would find helpful. So we will have to bid them good luck in their highly precarious marriage, which curiously enough may be less likely to be permanent than their uncommitted state of living together.

3 ✒ A "Now" Marriage

THERE IS A YOUNG COUPLE, Roy and Sylvia, who are in their early thirties. I have known them intermittently during the last ten years, and during one period, about seven years ago, I knew them very well. I was amazed at what I felt was their truly present-day attempt to make of all interpersonal relationships, including their marriage, a growing and creative experience. During that period Roy developed a real infatuation for Emily, the young, rather childlike wife of another man. This was, understandably to me, quite upsetting to Sylvia. But instead of divorce or bitter jealousy, they were able to talk out their feelings openly and to arrive at some kind of a new understanding (never made known to me) between themselves. The "other woman's" husband had learned of the affair and was *very* angry—at his wife, but mostly at Roy. Roy even planned for the four of them—the two couples —to sit down and talk out their feelings. Unfortunately, this attempt at four-way communication never came off.

Out of the talks between Roy and Sylvia and Emily came a recognition on the part of all that Roy had a deep caring for Emily, but that there was no reason why this should disrupt both marriages. It just seemed a natural thing that at times a man or woman might love or care deeply for more than one person. A short time later Roy and Sylvia moved away, so there was no thorough proof of whether this complex relationship could stand the test of time.

I think perhaps you can understand why, when I came to think of the relationships between men and women, I wrote to

Roy and Sylvia, on the other side of the continent, hoping they would contribute from their experience. They chose to write to me only about their present relationship, but to me it is valuable and I hope it will be for you.

One reason I wish to include this material is that Roy and Sylvia had, by the third year of their marriage, reached an open sharing and expressiveness which are almost unknown. I know that Roy had had experience in encounter groups and a year of psychotherapy with a competent, acceptant psychologist. Perhaps these factors help to account for the unusual openness in their relationship. I do not know. Nor can I predict whether their marriage will be ultimately "successful." But they are certainly struggling to build a richness in their marriage which would have been inconceivable fifty years ago. They are trying to be open, close to their own feelings, sharing, working the relationship through, rather than defensively glossing it over. The extent to which they share is, to me, almost incredible. Win, lose, or draw, they are pioneering new territory in marriage, a territory which is so important to all of us. I cannot predict whether you will see their relationship as ideal or will be repelled by it. I think you cannot help but learn from their experience. From this point, I will let them speak for themselves, only commenting from time to time.

THE RELATIONSHIP

Here are some of Roy's notes, often written in a kind of shorthand, but very revealing.

There has always been movement and development in our marriage but never like the last two years—moving from a small town to a large city, children both in school, women's liberation, sexual liberation in the youth culture—all have had a profound impact. As the kids grew, Sylvia increasingly began to search out her own identity. I really affirmed that. I wanted a stimulating relationship of coequals. Increasingly we spent time together talking—exploring wishes—my listening and drawing out her thinking about herself and what she wanted to become. It works. Now she does this for me too. It's great to have someone to help you explore your own mind.

We use words to get close. We have an understanding that we each strive for complete openness with each other—in fact I try to share particularly those things I don't want to, because they are usually getting in the way of our really being close and growing together. Like if I'm angry or jealous or strongly attracted to another woman—If I don't open up these things to her and they are on my mind we will gradually feel separate. I find that if I shut off some things I begin to build a wall—I can't cut the flow on just *some* things—without blocking *many* things.

High points and low points—they seem to come together in times of change in our relationship. The low times are core fears—fears of being ridiculed, maligned as childish, or impotent, or a drag, by her or by friends (tied to images of my father—his constant fear and insecurity). This fear is particularly strong when I feel separate from her —cut off—a loss of spontaneous affection—and I know she is expanding her world, in contact with other men. Such fears may be intense one hour or day and gone the next when we break the barrier and get close —sharing my fear—every last nuance—checking reality—what are her other relationships really like? Am I special? How? Are others special? How? Show every intimate corner of my thinking—risking every piece —this has been critical for me. Particularly sharing and exploring all my fears, however "childish" and "immature" I label them. Saying over and over again, first to myself and then to her—this is me—now—these feelings may never change. If you want me, you have to want these fears. I am vulnerable. I am threatened by your close relationships with other men. I'd say it took almost a year to feel free to express these fears when I felt them. At first I had consciously to force myself after internal "words with myself" to share these fears—to be openly as vulnerable and frightened as I felt.

Sylvia introduces her notes with a short but significant statement:

I guess I've been waiting to be able to write, "and we lived happily ever after." That will never happen. I've learned something. It has taken a long time to find the words. It has been good to get it down, though, for me.

And here is something of the quality of the relationship as seen through Sylvia's eyes in one particular incident:

We spent a weekend together at the beach just before Roy went away for a week. The trip involved a major responsibility for him and he had a lot on his mind over the weekend. I wrote this to him Monday morning, after he left:

I miss you

    I think about our weekend at the beach
        there were some nice things
        that fantastic place we'll go to
            sometime

but mostly we were solitary there
    I was alone
    you were alone
        and we were lonely. . . .

you were waiting for me
I was waiting for you

      and

I was waiting to feel like coming to get you
    and the time ran out
        the time ran out. . . .

Now you're gone
    I could have made you feel strong
    I could have loved you
        what a great way to go into your week

    but I waited until I felt like it
        and the time ran out. . . .

Her later comment to him about the poem:

I was jealous of your trip, of your stimulating job. I wanted to jet off somewhere, I wanted some of that excitement for me. Am I going to come to get you, to give to you—feeling angry like that? I didn't.

You were feeling guilty because you couldn't put the coming week out of your mind—you weren't really free to be with me. You had so much responsibility resting on you. And how can a person give to another when he's bound up with guilt and anxious over impending responsibility?

We could have talked about it then but we didn't realize what was going on at the time. It was still worth talking about later.

REACTIONS TO SEXUAL LIBERATION

They are experimenting with giving complete sexual freedom to each other. Not surprisingly, this has caused strain. Sylvia tells how it started.

Roy and I had been married ten years—we thought we knew each other. I had never had an orgasm—and I thought I was "just that way." Roy thought so too, but we never talked much about it. We could talk about everything but sex. Then I found myself really turned on by another man and I felt like making love to him—even though I didn't feel like making love very often with Roy. I couldn't believe I could really talk about this with Roy. I was afraid he would be hurt too much, that he would only be able to hear, "you're not satisfying me." But we finally did talk about it. At first it was awful—he was hurt and felt weak. That was painful—so painful—to know I was the cause of it. But he liked the new life evolving in me. That must be a good thing! I wanted that new life for me and for the two of us. He did too. It was important for me to see I wasn't "just that way," and exciting for Roy to see his woman in new ways. Roy said, "If you do make love to him, I want you to tell me—we have to know where each other is."

One day I did let that happen—and I told him. I took a risk. I took a risk. I risked that I would never feel like that with Roy—that I would always be dissatisfied and I would eventually ruin our marriage. That would have been tragic. Roy and I are basically a good thing—we have two children—we like living together—we love each other. But somehow it seemed that I had to do that. I had to bring that part of me to life—now that I knew it was there. It seemed that if this core part of me was freed, opened up, that I could then share that with Roy—the man who means the most to me. Sometimes that happens now. Sometimes Roy and I share our bodies in ways we never thought possible for us. I had always thought it should "just happen" between two people. If it didn't, I wasn't going to work on it—that didn't make sense to me. And besides, recently I was angry. Why should I have to *work* on being free sexually with Roy at this point when I just *felt* that way with someone else? That was a good question. The answer, I realized, was: "Because I wanted to be married to my husband—and I want to have that with him." This was a turning point.

Now here are some of Roy's notes on the same issue:

Probably the single most difficult change for me has been getting used to Sylvia's male friends—always comparing myself to them, fearing that I would lose her.

Seeing her physically aroused and feeling affirmed by another— feeling less power to sexually arouse her myself. I was scared and vulnerable and she was feeling angry at having been penned in with children, sexually repressed by her parents, not having been sexually freed up by me except sporadically. It has been a year and a half now since she demanded and took new freedom—and what she said to me about six months ago really makes sense. She said she really felt affirmed by some other men because they didn't have to affirm her— they were free to choose to be with her or not—while I had high stakes in making our marriage work and therefore it was harder to believe my affirmation. I discovered I felt that way too. Her developing other male friends, discovering what she liked and didn't like about them—led to awareness of what she liked about me and she began to affirm me— to discover what was unique about me—and I could begin to believe that, because it was based on real experience and choice.

My inhibitions relating to other women—working that through—needing this to allow her freedom—to understand her need for other relationships by experiencing my own desire for other relationships. Understanding my uniqueness for her by testing her uniqueness for me —through building relationships with other women. Relating my fear that she would be consumed in making love to another man (which is most intense when we are not grooving freely, sexually, with each other) to my fear that I might be consumed by another woman and that that would threaten our marriage.

I can't let her be free to be her feelings with other men and test the limits of what we can handle—without my freeing up with other women and testing the meaning of our marriage not through inhibiting restrictions but by choosing her in the context of a variety of relationships.

It no longer bothers me for her to have close friendships with other men—a year ago it frightened the shit out of me. In fact it's a freeing thing. I don't have to be everything for her. I'm free to be involved elsewhere without feeling guilty that she's left alone.

In fact, I'm convinced that eventually we will grow to the point that we can each make love to others without threatening each other. The key seems to be how strong we are with each other. When she has made love to another my reactions have varied from extreme anxiety and self-doubt to brief anger. If we can build a solid memory of beautiful times making love with each other, I think we'll be able to handle sexual freedom outside.

The other day I said to her, "I'm so sick and tired of being jealous and anxious, of wondering what you're doing with *him,* today, I just want to spew those feelings out—just rid myself of them—free myself —say, " 'Hell, when we're together, great! We'll build and grow and share—when we're not, we're free to enjoy whoever we're with.' "

THEIR SEXUAL RELATIONSHIP

The nature and quality of their sexual life together is conveyed, I think, by some brief notes from each.

Roy:

We've been married just over ten years and our sexual relationship is just beginning to get really good. We've always been more verbally than physically open. We both came from families who were very uncomfortable with sex. We've had good times sporadically over the years but only gradually have we freed up to really enjoy our bodies. Just lately we've had these fantastic sexy conversations when we go out to lunch—a darkly lit bar—talking about what it was like making love the night before—that's really been great for us.

Getting close with words is great but words get in the way too. The other morning—we hadn't been feeling sensual with each other for a while—we were talking and I just stopped, moved close and looked into her eyes—explored her face with my eyes. It was hard at first—it really cut through the words—no words, just look and touch. We just began touching each other and feeling the touch and opening up in a way words can never accomplish.

Being sensually close—touching, smelling, stroking each other softly, looking, exploring each other with eyes and hands from head to foot—with no demands that anything happen—just mutual pleasuring —I agree with Masters and Johnson that's basic to sexual response.

Sylvia's picture of the same morning:

One morning Roy stayed home from work and we had coffee in the living room. The children were at school. He looked into my eyes. He didn't say anything. He just kept looking at me. It was such a powerful thing. It felt new. It even made me a little uncomfortable—but I liked it. Then he touched my hand with just one finger and began to trace a pattern lightly. I felt it. It was almost as if he had never touched me before.

And Sylvia tells more about the developments for her:

We started reading about sex, all kinds of things. We read Masters and Johnson's second book and liked it. I even bought *Sensuous Woman*. That was a different thing for me to do. I don't know who enjoyed the book more—Roy or me—but he really loved it that I bought it. It was a new day—a new Sylvia—a new us. We went to a sexy movie and loved it—we could enjoy it together.

I began talking more about my family as I was growing up—specifically my Dad—and I discovered how angry I was at that kind, grey-haired old man for not showing me something of what it meant to begin to grow into a woman. My parents weren't comfortable with their sexuality—*that* I *had* assimilated, and I guess I was still angry about that. (I realize, however, that people can only teach and show something that they know about for themselves.)

Anyway—the night after I spilled out all of this anger a fantastic thing happened. When Roy and I were making love, waves began to overpower my body—and I let it happen—for the first time. I let go—and I will never be the same. What a powerful thing! This orgasm seemed to last forever. I had no control over what was happening to me—I just let it happen. I gave up control and this overpowering experience flooded my body. I wish I could let that happen every day—but I can't. I guess it takes a while to assimilate into who I am such new ways of being. All I know is it can happen with Roy and me—and I want to nurture that—I want to do what I can to let it happen.

Here's a note from Sylvia to Roy about a difficult time:

I'm thinking about when you feel like making love and I don't—usually that is a Bad Scene. I am closed—tight—and that makes me feel awful. How could I possibly give anything when I feel like that? Then one day I got a glimpse of something new—I didn't feel like making love but I was really caring about you—wanting to make you feel good. I lit some candles and put on a record we both like. I said, "roll over" and I gave you a fantastic back rub—pounding, caressing, letting my long hair trail over your bare back. I put my cheek on your back—my nose, my ear, my lips. I rubbed the tight muscles at the base of your neck. I traced a pattern there. How great not to let guilt—because I wasn't giving one thing—freeze me, make me cold, so I couldn't give anything. It makes sense that you would rather have a back rub freely and joyfully given than make love to a body without a soul in it. I must admit, a cup of hot tea (with honey and lemon even) won't always satisfy a man who wants to make love. But a funny thing happens, sometimes, when I am free to give what I want to give at the moment—it opens me up, makes me feel like a human being again—and who knows what might happen then?

A "DOWN TIME"

Roy encloses a note he wrote to Sylvia a year earlier than the other material presented here. It indicates so clearly that a marriage of this sort is never "stable," except in being a continual process of changingness.

I feel at a breaking point. We're both putting ourselves forth—demanding satisfaction of our needs. My need to be vulnerable, and to accept and value that me, seems to feed into your anger at impotence—you feel it as just plain weakness. Is it related to your father's weakness, to me in the past, or ? ? It's an erotic turn-off.

We could separate now and say—hey, we have some great things, but when it comes to sensuality—sex—eroticism—our past patterns, our childhood associations and deprivations, all those meanings are too much—better to take this knowledge and start fresh with someone else.

Or we can take the chance that we can build new meanings—new associations (can home be erotic? Hell, a nursing mother can be erotic), and find a third party to help us do it. I think it will take too long to do it ourselves.

We've changed many times, sexually and otherwise—yet in a brief slump, when it's a down time for one or both, we overread the signals in terms of the past—we expect the worst—we read too much into the signals. We expect the bad past and often fail to check our signals.

A few months later Roy expresses some of his feeling in a brief poem:

When out of caring touch
        I don't feel at home here
    my base is distorted
        together is gone

SOME GOALS—AND SOME DEEP THOUGHTS

Throughout Roy's notes there are significant expressions which look toward the future of the relationship.

The fact that we have lived together for ten years is powerful—the good and the bad packed together. Both the most restrictive expectations—seeing each other with old images—images of our parents—binding the possibilities of the moment with simplistic past images—the fantastic positive richness of exploring our subtle interdependencies—interlocking histories—why we were attracted to each other—what parts of each other's bodies we like and don't like—how we're the same and different from our parents—a million rich questions we explore as we try to grow and free each other and make a new relationship with each other—it's never ending.

Increasingly sameness is boring and boredom is less tolerable. Change is becoming the rule rather than the exception. In fact continually doing new things together is so stimulating that old patterns are boring. For example we've discovered that changing time and place of being together, being with each other in different situations, adds dimensions to our perceptions of each other—shit—this is too abstract—we move furniture—change our bedroom—spend time together in the morning—have lunch together—the point is that sameness becomes background. If we're always together at the same time in the same place perceptions and reactions tend to get fixed.

Lack of change and variety particularly kill sex—boredom is not sensuous and erotic. We will never be satisfied any longer with anything less than a vital relationship with each other that permeates the whole family. Our expectations are way up.

There seems to be no substitute for time together—relaxed—free to be defined in the moment—unpressed by work agendas—to share the same events, e.g., music, a movie, to dance together, to free our bodies—to explore our feelings, wishes and fantasies with each other.

A common growing, drawing vision that we share and continually expand is critical to positive satisfying change. A developing vision of the family we want to be, the house we develop for us. A flowing in and out of our wishes for ourselves individually and together. I want us to be two vital people creating the world we want out of experience that tells what we really value, what is life-affirming in society—the mutual exploring of our values, wants, desires, individually and with each other —while we are trying to act out pieces of that vision. I want us to be two living people, each with separate worlds, who have community with each other and basically come together because of that community, not because of the legal restrictions that make it difficult for us to part. I really feel affirmed when I know she feels free to be any way with anyone and she *chooses* to be with me.

The other side to this is that community takes work. I cannot always choose who to be with on momentary feeling, the current high. No lasting sharing and feeling of emotional depth comes from simply moving from one relationship to another—from what feels good to what feels good. Depth comes from commitment to working through even the most painful feelings—the ones that I want to avoid.

Sylvia voices very similar attitudes in her own way:

It seems to me that an important part of our story is that Roy and I try to work out a framework within which we will move and we try to be honest with each other. We trust each other. We care about each other and what we each need. We want to let each other grow—and yet we're only human. We have limits. We have to tell each other what those are—or *try to find out* what they are.

Given that we want to remain married to each other, what can we cope with in terms of freedom for each individual to grow? We have to be in touch with ourselves and with each other for this to work.

THE CHANGING QUALITY OF THE RELATIONSHIP

Both of them, at various points, make clear that it is an always changing, never static marriage, but perhaps Sylvia makes this quality most specific, giving some indication of the importance they attach to living richly. I think one statement is a classic:

"After all, we got married to *live* together, not because we wanted to pay bills and fix leaky faucets together!" No wonder their marriage still lasts.

Sylvia continues:

About three years ago—when I turned thirty—some new things began to happen in our marriage. We began to realize how *important* it is to have fun together. Roy was a golfer—I wasn't—but we both decided to give tennis a try. We really worked at it—four or five days a week for a while. I hated being a beginner at thirty—but Roy was patient and it was finally worth it. Now we sometimes have a volley of low, hard shots—and that is great. We feel alive.

We got bicycles and camping gear and began to really explore the outdoors, as a family and just the two of us. It's crucial, we find, to spend time together without the children. It is great to spend a morning at home—our children are both in school—and maybe go out for brunch.

Sometimes I go downtown and meet Roy for a drink after work. Why not? And maybe we go out on Wednesday and stay home Saturday. It's so easy to get in a rut. Sometimes the two of us eat late, with candles and wine and a special meal I have prepared. Sometimes we fix a pizza or try a new recipe together. A few times we have gone for a walk late at night—that's nice. Sometimes I write him a letter—when I'm at home. One of our best times lately was going to see a sexy movie. It was nice to be able to share it.

We enjoy music and buy records and really listen to them. Music, candlelight and massages can make a great evening. We spend about 5 per cent of our budget for entertainment and recreation. I used to think that was too much—but when it provides babysitters and experiences that help us be in touch, it's worth every bit of it. From time to time we try to cut down on this expense—see a matinee, eat at a deli, buy a long bread and some smelly cheese. . . .

COMMENT. When I was a boy, I loved to read stories about the early frontiersmen in this country, the hunters, the moccasin-shod explorers who ventured into the "trackless wilderness," crossed the Allegheny mountains, risking their lives, facing danger openly, far out ahead of the cabin-dwellers who would follow. I get the same feeling of excitement when I read the honest statements of Roy and Sylvia about their marriage. They are just as truly pioneers, exploring the far reaches of the relationship between a man and a woman. The risks they take are just as real as those taken by Daniel Boone. They live with uncertainty and at times with fear and doubt. They too have a goal which is both vague and definite. Just as the frontiersman kept pushing on, endeavoring to open up unknown territory, so these two are exploring the terra incognita which lies ahead in a modern marriage. I do not know whether their efforts will lead to success—who *could* know?—but they have my deep respect as they open new trails through the wilderness of human relationships. They have broken many of the conventional rules of "what marriage should be" and are striving, with real dedication to each other, to build a new model for a permanent man-woman relationship. It is built on continually growing self-knowledge, on a complete sharing of even the most painful and shameful personal feelings, on permission for each to grow and develop together or separately, on a commitment which is real but fluctuating, on a changing, flowing union which carries no guarantee except that of further change.

I find it especially meaningful to compare this marriage with that of Dick and Gail. The latter are ten years younger and have six years less of living together. Yet there are a number of issues which were faced in both relationships, and descriptions of their differing reactions may prove instructive.

DIFFICULTIES IN SEXUAL RELATIONSHIPS

Each pair has had some problems in achieving a satisfactory sexual relationship. Dick was occasionally impotent. Gail wants more sex than they have together and doesn't always achieve orgasm. Both feel there is something vaguely wrong with their sexual experience. Roy has felt inferior and inadequate sexually, and Sylvia had accepted herself as being unable to have an orgasm.

In this respect the couples show many parallels. Sylvia can't talk much about her failure to achieve a climax. Dick barely mentions his occasional inability "to perform." The major difference is that now Roy and Sylvia *are* taking the risk of talking very openly and freely about every detail of their sexual feelings—the dissatisfactions and the satisfactions. For Dick and Gail this type of communication is still very difficult. Yet in both marriages each spouse endeavors to be understanding and compassionate toward the other.

SEX WITH ANOTHER

Both Dick, in his relationship with Gail, and Sylvia, in her marriage, desired and experienced sexual and personal relationships with another partner. But their ways of approaching this potentially painful experiment were quite different.

Dick gives some confused negative reactions about his relationships with Gail, then says, "But I love you," and walks off to live with his blond girlfriend for a number of weeks. So far as one can get inside his feelings at that time, a genuine expression of them would have to come out something like this: "I feel a number of dissatisfactions with our relationship. I find myself doubting if it can last, even though I care for you very much. Painful though it may be for you (and perhaps for me), I'm going to try out a relationship with another girl to see if that can be better."

Sylvia, on the other hand, shares openly with her husband her feeling of being aroused by this other man and her desire to have sexual relationships with him. But she does this very carefully and caringly, because she realizes how easily her expressions could be taken as an accusation: "You're a failure sexually." Only after taking this big risk and sharing the difficult feelings which follow does she take the freedom which Roy has fearfully given her, and discovers that she is more of a woman with the other man. This, though exciting, carries the frightening possibility that she may break up the marriage.

In both couples the outcome is similar—they find that their

first mates are much more satisfying to be with, and they rebuild the relationship, having learned very significantly from letting themselves love another person. Certainly there is no guarantee that this would always be the case.

TWO CONCEPTIONS OF MARRIAGE

Perhaps nowhere is the difference between the two couples sharper than in their concepts of what constitutes marriage. To try to sum it up in one sentence: for Dick and Gail, marriage is a box; for Roy and Sylvia it is a flowing river.

Let me amplify that. All the pictures which Dick and Gail have of the marital state are static; these pictures change, sometimes drastically, but the new one is simply another still picture. For Gail marriage is a romantic box in which one has children and lives happily ever after; then it is a horribly confining coffin in which one's personhood is extinguished; it is also a trap in which one is snared by commitment; a framework in which one is enslaved to keep house and raise children; a sort of secure fence inside which a woman can reside, without having to care for or "bother about" her husband; perhaps most important of all, it is always a form constructed by others.

For Dick the enclosures are different, but always an already constructed enclosure. Marriage is a tight fence, limiting freedom; it is a roomy and comfortable box, giving more freedom than he had expected; it is a magic box, resolving the difficulties in their relationship; it is a box with shrinking walls, compressing him with, "Why don't you have a job?" "Why don't you earn money?" "Why don't you support your wife?" For Dick, too, the boxes are constructed by others.

Only very fleetingly does it dawn on these two that perhaps *they* are the ones who build the structure, and only through their own experience can they find the clues as to what the future of their relationship will be. Gail seems surprised as she says, "It's a lot of work." Dick says essentially, "Perhaps marriage is only an *intention* that takes time and effort to bring to fulfillment."

For Roy and Sylvia their marriage has, for a number of years, flowed as a part of a complex stream of experiencing. When Roy fell in love with Emily, the culture clearly said, "You love another woman, so you don't love your wife." But he said, through his behavior, "That's not what *my* experience tells me. I love each of them, in different ways, and for different reasons. I want this to be an open and shared part of my life." And when Sylvia wants sexual relations with another man, the culture says, "That means that you are an unfaithful wife." But Sylvia works it out much differently, by sharing feelings which are hard to express and may be hurtful. In regard to other aspects of their marriage, I can't speak for the partners separately. "We" is the only useful term. To put it in schematic form, "We want our relationship to be such that each is given freedom and encouragement to develop his (her) full potential." "We want our marriage to be an exciting exploration of new avenues." "We want to share so deeply that even the forbidden, the shameful, the jealous, the angry feelings that we have are as fully expressed and as much accepted as the tender and loving feelings." "We want our decisions to be mutual, to be based on this profound sharing." "We want our marriage to be full of surprises, of newness, of richly changing experiences, and we want to be imaginative in creating such newness." "We want to be the *complexity* of our feelings, which are by no means always simple and clear." So Sylvia can say, "I don't want intercourse with you now, but I do feel caring and I'll show it." And Roy can say, "I feel scared and risky and inadequate because you love another man, but I also feel daring and good about granting you that freedom."

A CONCLUDING LAST-MINUTE ADDENDUM

As this book was in press, I received an unexpected letter from Roy which demonstrates, more clearly than anything I can say, that when a process of change is initiated, in an individual or in a marriage, it tends to continue in growing directions. Here are the major themes from his letter.

Dear Carl,

In some ways I wish I were writing you now about me and our marriage, rather than almost a year ago. This has been a time of great self-discovery. . . . I have become more self-confident and less fearful. For one thing, I discovered that I had never trusted my own mind, or believed in my capabilities. And I have lacked the diverse life experience to push my thoughts to depth. Recently I have experienced for the first time that I can sit down for a week to think and write and my thoughts get better, more essential, less superficial, more in touch with experience.

Part of risking is self-confidence. But part is also believing what you say—having it grounded in, and tested by, experience.

Sylvia and I could write more now as our experience has changed and developed. We have not slowed down changing as persons, but we are more truly secure with each other. Our sexual life has stabilized in the sense that we consistently have satisfying times with each other and now have this as both memory and expectation. Also we have done considerable "unhooking" of our images and expectations of each other from those of our parents and thus we are somewhat more capable of contacting each other in the present.

We are learning to fight for communication and self-determination without all the destructive parental-judging overload.

It seems like my life has been a continual growth from concern about what others think of me toward security in feeling o.k.

Here's to growing up!

Roy

4 ✐ Marriage — Then

THIS WILL BE a very brief chapter. Its purpose is completely different from any of the other chapters in this book. I regard it as an interlude, but some of you will regard it as an interruption. If it troubles you or bores you, you can skip it without having missed any of the picture of modern marriages. But I should like to explain why I am writing it.

I find that I—and most of you—tend to think of the present as having lasted for centuries, just as it is. Intellectually we know better: we know that much change has taken place. But at some deeper level we feel—in almost every realm—that this is the way things always have been. It takes an occasional jolt to help us realize that this is not so. So my purpose in this small digression is to put marriage in at least some historical perspective, to see that change is not only taking place today, but is a part of history.

I will give three small examples of change, one from racial politics, one from marriage law, and one from the history of the family. Then I would like at a little greater length to picture marriage, not as it occurred centuries ago in some far-off place, but a few decades ago in our neighbor to the south, Mexico. Perhaps these few specific examples will serve the purpose much better than any broad world view, boring in its abstractions.

In 1934 President Franklin Roosevelt favored an anti-lynching law which was being proposed in Congress. Some people were shocked by the twenty-eight lynchings (twenty-four black) in 1933. His wife, Eleanor, strongly urged him to support such a law, which would give at least a primitive and fractional element of justice to the blacks. He refused, because he was sure it would have meant suicide for the many bills he needed to get the economy on its feet. So, without his support, the bill was never brought to a vote, and mob lynchings could still be carried on without any Federal interference (Lash, pp. 515 ff). Now in 1972, while there is still much discrimination and injustice, eight hundred black officials have been elected in Southern states, and a number of counties have county governments in which black officials are in the majority. There are black sheriffs and many black officers of the law. Perfection is far off, but the change in less than fifty years is almost beyond belief.

Or let me take another example, closer to our interest in marriage. For generations everyone in Connecticut was forbidden by law to use contraceptives. This applied even to married couples in the privacy of their own home (though it was rarely enforced in this respect). The law was abolished only a few years ago, in 1965. Now, by contrast, the Federal government is giving nearly $100 million dollars per year to support family planning, contraception, and research in these fields. In many states it is legal to provide contraceptive information to girls who are minors, without requiring parental consent. Such governmental actions ignore even the promulgations of the Pope—but not the wishes of the majority of Catholic people. So again, great changes have occurred in a decade, not centuries.

Or let us take an issue at the heart of our interest. Most people regard the nuclear family—father, mother, and several children—as being the unit of all civilization, as having persisted since the dawn of history. Nothing could be further from the truth. The nuclear family was forced into being not more than fifty or sixty years ago by the increasing mobility of the population. Prior to that the relatives, the "extended family," the neighborhood, the clan, the ethnic group was as much the unit of caring and support for the individual as his mother and father. The nuclear family is a very *recent* development—and it is working less and less well. It was born in changes which were unplanned and is disintegrating in circumstances equally unplanned—all within the course of much less than a century. So let us take a look at another bit of history.

Let me picture marriage in Tepoztlán in 1940. Why do I pick a Mexican village with an unpronounceable name? Because it has been thoroughly studied by prominent anthropologists and their data are trustworthy. Robert Redfield, anthropologist from the University of Chicago, lived in and studied Tepoztlán during 1926–27. The late Oscar Lewis of the University of Illinois, long a student of Mexican culture, restudied the village life from 1943–48 and again in 1956–57, spending almost three years in all. Insofar as any Mexican village is typical, this is true of Tepoztlán. The description I give is in general from the period of the 1940s. However, I can testify, having been in Tepoztlán twice as a visitor, that from what one sees in the market, the streets, the homes, the changes are not great and are slow in coming.

I will try to write of marriage then in a way that will permit you to think of yourself in this situation and to try to sense the reactions of the individuals, men and women, so different from anything you see around you today or that you find in this book.

If we begin with the marriage, you were married, if a girl, between fifteen and seventeen, and your husband was a couple of years older. The courtship had been very secretive, conducted often by letters, hidden to be picked up or to be passed on by a go-between. Though an elaborate asking for your hand was expected, the chances are one in two that you just eloped, lived together, and hoped that if both sets of parents approved, you would be married in church.

As a girl your mother had never given you information about menstruation, sexual relations, or pregnancy. She was sure you were completely "innocent" all through childhood. Even the information from friends and schoolmates (if you were lucky enough to go to school) was scanty indeed.

As a young wife you conformed to your husband's wishes, were passive and obedient, and submitted to his sexual demands. You tried to show no love or affection or indeed emotional expression of any kind. You were not lively and warm, but compliant and acceptant of your husband's domination of you. Like the other women of the village, your term for sexual intercourse was "abuse from the man." You tried hard to keep a good household, using all the skills you had learned from years of working with your mother. You took care of the children, went to market—or sent a friend if you were afraid your husband might be suspicious of having you out of the house. You asked your husband's permission before taking any action of any significance. Although most of the family income was in crops, if there was any cash income, you managed it, tried to save it, and must have had enough to give your husband when he went to the *cantina* or elsewhere.

Upon marrying, you gave up all your girlfriends, since conceivably they could lead you into bad behavior. If you were particularly unfortunate, you lived in your husband's home, where you became primarily the servant of your mother-in-law. She retired from many of her duties and you were forced to obey her and take them over, while she enjoyed being the "manager."

If you were the husband, you were perhaps eighteen when you married. You had had some affairs of a transient sort before marriage. You expected to continue this kind of behavior after marriage. Indeed, it was regarded as evidence of your manliness. You expected your wife not only to ignore such behavior, but not even to be curious or jealous about it.

Since your whole training up to this point had been to obey, submit, and learn from your father in the fields, you were often inwardly insecure about the role of complete dominance you were expected to assume. You were expected to support your family, but you were also responsible for the proper behavior of your wife and your children. This was a fearsome total of responsibility for you, since you had never carried such a burden before. Hence sometimes it took a few drinks at the *cantina* before you were bold enough to beat your wife for some real or suspected misbehavior or mistake.

In sexual relations you tried hard not to arouse your wife, since any awakening of her sexuality might lead her into infidelity. If she seemed passionate or sexually demanding, you knew you had married a girl who was *loco*—crazy—and this was most unfortunate. In any case you endeavored to keep her pregnant as much of the time as possible, since unfaithfulness was then less likely. Any sexual play or courting behavior was reserved for the women you wanted to seduce.

As the marriage continued, life fell into a routine. The husband went early to the fields to work and rarely returned until dusk. He avoided intimacy with his wife or children, keeping aloof in order to be sure of being regarded as the head of the household. He expected to be respected, obeyed, and served. Only occasionally, when a bit drunk and "lacking in judgment," would he hold his children or openly show affection or caress them.

Curiously, because he was so separated from the persons he supposedly controlled, he often inadvertently gave them the freedom they theoretically did not have. They could—and did—do things behind his back. When discovered, this put the wife on the spot. She was supposed to obey her husband and keep her children submissive to his wishes. Yet frequently she would try to intercede for them to prevent punishment from being too severe. She became a sort of mediator. This would often infuriate her husband. Since his security was tied up with his maintaining his authoritarian role, he often tried to make all his family fear him, his beatings, and his rages.

In this atmosphere the children were brought up to be as unobtrusive as possible, obedient and submissive as long as they lived under the parental roof. They were often severely punished, particularly between the ages of five and twelve. They were also controlled by fearsome stories of creatures who came out of the night to eat bad children.

As the children grew a bit older, they felt useful. The boy helped his father in the fields every day, and father became a careful teacher of skills. But the relationship was still one in which father retained his authority and position of respect. At home the mother and daughter became close, as they shared all the household tasks. But their closeness did not change the prudery which existed. No sexual questions were answered: it was all a taboo realm.

Godparents and relatives were of help in relieving the harshness of this family pattern. Though much of their relationship was with the parents, they also provided security, frequently for the child. The same was true of other relatives, although relationships with relatives were not cultivated.

As might be expected in such a rigid pattern of expectations, there were plenty of exceptions. Wives and husbands worked out partnerships which took some account of the separate individualities. In many families, too, a sort of unspoken compromise was reached to avoid continual conflict. They found some kind of a middle course. The husband gave up no whit of his traditional dominance, but in fact avoided being overbearing. His wife never challenged his absolute authority, but meanwhile would work out many ways of being somewhat independent of it. And of course the children could find many ways of defeating their elders without seeming to do so.

So without too much difficulty we can imagine some families and homes which were reasonably contented. Communicative? Absolutely not! Lies and deception became an absolutely necessary part of life, if one was to preserve even a vestige of individuality. Happy? I suspect this was too much even to dream of in the family, except perhaps for a mother with her newborn child, or during an occasional celebration. Happiness, or its counterpart, was reserved for the big fiestas, the playful, riotous, and increasingly drunken celebrations which brought the whole village together in a curious mixture of old Aztec and "pagan" dances, shows, and fireworks, with an overlay of "Christian" elements. Here was the outlet for fun in life, even if it ended in a hangover, the family money all spent, and acrimonious family arguments about behavior during the fiesta.

I hope very much that this account of marriage and family life in Tepoztlán helps to throw new light on the partnerships we have seen and will see in this book. If by some chance circumstance the couples who reveal themselves to us now had lived a few hundred miles further south and thirty years ago, this is the life they would have led. Indeed, we would not even have to cross the border to sense the depth and pervasiveness of change in every aspect of the relations between men and women in the contemporary United

States. The thumbnail sketch of village marriage in Mexico is not too unlike many rural marriages in this country a very few generations ago.

Perhaps we can conclude with the title of a recent article, which was addressed to women but applies equally to men: "You've Come a Long Way, Baby!" Indeed we have, and the partnerships we are examining have come a very long distance from those of thirty years ago in Mexico or sixty years ago in this country. We are out in new territory, and perhaps this brief chapter will help us to realize it as we proceed with our purpose of trying to permit real people, *modern* people, to reveal themselves in their fumbling attempts to establish a better kind of partnership. When, historically, we have come so far so fast, a few stumbles, some periods of feeling lost, and a few dead-end paths are not a matter for surprise.

To sum it up in a sentence: if we clearly realize that the marriage of Roy and Sylvia exists only thirty years later and a thousand miles away from the Tepoztlán marriage described, then we shall recognize that the difference is not in degrees, but in light-years! We are exploding into unknown space.

5 ⌽ Three Marriages— and One Growing Person

A COUPLE WITH SEVERAL children, living in another part of the state, came to my knowledge through several social contacts. My wife and I were impressed by the obvious congeniality of the couple, and with the open and spontaneous relationship they had with the children as well as with each other. It seemed to be a genuinely healthy marriage—something not too often encountered these days. Consequently, I was surprised to learn from a few casual remarks on the part of the wife that this was her third marriage, and that the first two had not been happy ones.

When I began to work on the chapters in this book, it occurred to me that if I could obtain an interview with this woman, I might be able to gain a few brief excerpts which would be enlightening. One reason for thinking of her was that she had seemed so very open and honest, a sort of healthily earthy person, who might be willing to talk freely about her experiences.

When I wrote to her, she was willing to be interviewed, to have it tape-recorded, and to have segments used for this book.

After the interview, as I listened to the tape, I found it so full of fascinating learnings—about marriage, about relationships in general, about sexual satisfaction, about the elements that change lives—that I simply could not take excerpts from it. I felt that it must be reproduced in full, with only the identifying details altered. So here is her account of her marriages. I believe it will repay rereading. At the conclusion I will comment on some of the psychological learnings it points up for me, but this by no means exhausts all its significant elements or the learnings it may stimulate in you.

As you will see, I spoke only once. From that point on, it is Irene's story.

ME: Tell me anything you want to about your three marriages, especially elements that you think might be of interest and use to young people. If you're sort of considering whether something is worth including or not, that would be the criterion, that if you feel, "God, I wish I had known of someone's experience like that when I was younger," then please include it. Not that you're talking *to* them—you will just be talking about yourself.

And include the mistakes, and the good choices and the good things you did, and the feelings in you in each situation, and whatever changes may have come about in you. Those are some of the things I have thought about, that I hoped you'd talk about. And then I have jotted down a few things which if you don't cover, I'll probably ask you about at the end. [They proved unnecessary.]

IRENE: You know, I was thinking about this appointment this morning, while I was sitting in the bathtub. *(Pause)* So, okay, starting with the kind of a person I was the first time, and reasons for being married.

Our family was really not a very friendly family. We had a lot of fun, we had a lot of problems, but we weren't very friendly, we weren't very real with each other. We didn't know much about that at all. There was great conflict between my mother and father and it sort of filtered down. None of us were very nice to each other. We didn't give each other room to be different, or to *be* at all. It wasn't a comfortable home to be in and the goal for most of us—there were seven of us—was to get out. That was the neat thing. And the only way to do that, that I knew of, was to get married. There wasn't money for college or anything like that. After we graduated from high school, we went to work. Anyway, that was my story. I did. And, I was anxious to get married, I wanted to get married and raise a family and settle down, and live happily ever after—storybook stuff.

You know, I think sex played an important role all along, even when I was very young. I was unaware, I was naïve, but sex was an important factor. There was never any discussion of sex in my family.

I remember once mentioning that a girl was pregnant and I was dismissed from the room for having used that word. So sex became something very interesting and very dirty.

I married probably, well, certainly, for all the wrong reasons. To get out of the house, and I not only really didn't know the man I married well at all, I didn't even know who *I* was. And so we really didn't do each other a favor. He didn't know who he was, and had had a very different upbringing, a very different family. He was very much loved and very sheltered and had always had financial security, which we didn't have. Those things were important to me, too. I thought, "Gee, here's a guy who has some money and a lovely family. . . ."

I was twenty-one, old enough to know better, but I was really like fourteen when it comes to understanding the world and me. Very naïve, and had had no sexual relations with anyone—had been terrified of it and fascinated by it all at the same time.

Another thing about my first husband is he had already been married once—this is an important factor—and divorced, and had had a child, whom he couldn't see any more. She was four at the time, and this really broke him up, a good deal more than I realized. His wife had threatened to kill their child if he so much as visited the girl, so he was not going to commit himself to marriage with the possibility of more children.

I wasn't tuned in to where he was, or who he was, or what was going on with him at all. It had been a terribly traumatic thing for him —he apparently loved his wife and loved his child. And she was sleeping with all his friends. He was the last one to find out and was divorced, and was terribly hurt by it, and felt really cheated, deceived, and didn't have a lot of trust. And I automatically assumed that that wouldn't apply to me, that I wouldn't be compared. I was a different person. But of course, I was compared. And he didn't trust me. I assumed a trust that didn't exist. He didn't want any more children, because he didn't want to lose any more. But very soon I got pregnant and we never really faced that. I know he was terribly unhappy about it, but we never really talked it out.

I really didn't pay any attention to anything he said, or any aspects of himself that he showed me that didn't fit in with some kind of stereotype I had for "my husband," you know, quote, whatever that is.

And "my husband" was going to be strong and capable and a good father and love children and provide for me and satisfy me sexually— a storybook kind of thing. Of course, he turned out to be a human being and not a machine, and couldn't produce for me like that.

Okay, I didn't have any experience sexually, which was a great problem to us. He was fairly inexperienced, too, and apparently had had no problem with his first wife, and assumed again that there wouldn't be any with us, and if there was a problem it had to be me. I assumed it must be he. Sexually, I never had an orgasm. I put the blame on him. I felt that it was his fault that I wasn't sexually satisfied. I always wanted sex, but it always left me completely unsatisfied.

I really had no idea what marriage was like. I had no idea at all, and jumped into it like we were playing a game—playing house. And, oh, another big factor I forgot to mention. Because he was divorced, my mother automatically labeled him unfit, and this was a big factor in pushing me to him. She liked him when she met him, she liked the kind of work he did, she liked his age, his appearance, all of those things, but as soon as she heard he was divorced, he was suddenly rotten, no good, bad, unfit, and it really rankled me. And marrying him was another means of defiance. By God, I was going to do this thing—and did, to my sorrow.

We had, as I said, serious problems sexually, and didn't know how to handle them. We'd talk about them in an accusative fashion instead of any kind of helpful way. I was ashamed of my inability to have an orgasm. It terrified me. It was, to me, a sign of not being a woman. And I blamed him as long as I could get away with it. And then I turned it inward on myself.

I'd never felt loved by my family or by my mother. I'd never had any real love from anyone. My mother told me when I was thirty-two years old, "I never loved you and I never can. I don't understand you, but I do respect you." I realized that she was really trying to give me something of a compliment, but my reaction was that I went to the bathroom and I vomited and vomited and vomited. That was just a terribly upsetting experience to know that not only had I *felt* that she never loved me, but she was saying *herself* that she never loved me.

I didn't feel worthy of being loved, just completely unlovable. And the sexual thing between my husband and myself just really validated those feelings. I wasn't worthy, I was not going to be able to experience this. But it was a terribly frustrating thing. I really let the sexual incompleteness get a hold on me and eat at me, and used it as a weapon on myself, and certainly on him, too.

It turned out that my husband wasn't a very strong man. He was an artist, somewhat effeminate and very sensitive, and as I said had been very sheltered and terribly hurt by his first marriage. None of these things did I consider. I expected him to be things that he wasn't, and he wasn't able to come across. So I hurt him, I did about everything wrong that I could, trying to work out *my* idea of what this marriage should be. It had nothing to do with two people trying to live together. I didn't even understand what *that* was all about. And he would—oh, he would start this project or that, spend money we didn't have, and not *finish* it. And I tried to support him, I thought, a good supporting wife, you know, "Honey, if this is what you want to do, why don't you *finish* it?" Not realizing that he was the kind of person that couldn't and that this pressure was ghastly for him.

And he wasn't a very sexy guy. He didn't need a lot of sex—he needed an occasional orgasm, that's all—just an ejaculation. He could have masturbated—I'm sure it would have been just as satisfying to him. He didn't like my body, he didn't like to see me without any clothes on, and I had a lovely way of punishing him there. If things didn't go well or I was mad at him, all I had to do was appear at breakfast stark naked, you know! He'd gag on his egg, and leave for work—I did just cruel things. I'd tease him. I didn't help him—I didn't help him at all. I just pushed him deeper and deeper into his own private little hell, I guess.

And yet everything that I did to *him* hurt *me*. I realize that now, but I was so little aware of my own feelings that I really was scarcely aware of it then.

We presented a beautiful picture of marriage to our friends in the outside world. People thought, "Gad, aren't they marvelous? Don't they get along well, and isn't everything just grand?" And it's a game a terrible game we played, and I think a lot of people do it. And we really could fool most of our friends, because they didn't want to know any more than that. We were fun to be with. Our home was a comfortable place to visit, and as soon as the doors were closed we began our own private *Virginia Woolf.* Yet we were both nice people. I think maybe we could have made it if I had had any of the understanding that I have now.

The children didn't help matters. I was pregnant all the time, had four children and lost two, even though I used contraceptives, and this was a responsibility he couldn't handle—an emotional responsibility as well as a financial responsibility. He just hated the thought of my being pregnant. He didn't want children. He didn't get any help from me on that, because husbands are *supposed* to be fathers, are *supposed* to love children, and all this nonsense. And sex was so awful, and became more and more awful.

This marriage lasted for eight years, and in the process I became really convinced that there was something physically wrong with me. And I don't mean physically, in the sense that it could be corrected surgically, or anything like that—that somehow when I was born, something was missing. I was beginning to believe that I simply could not be loved. This was a nagging thing with me. I had a lot of friends, but I sort of protected myself, I never really let myself get too close to people.

I even found myself holding back with my children. I would be uncomfortable if they wanted to, you know, really hold me or really get any kind of deep attachment. I didn't want that because I was just sure that if I allowed myself to love them and be loved by them, that they would find something out about me that they wouldn't be able to love. And I'd lose them, and so better not to love them than to love them and lose them. This didn't, of course, make it an easy time for my kids either, when they were little.

The whole household atmosphere was just ghastly. I thought I could live with it—be the martyr. I was the greatest martyr, I think, that ever lived. And I managed to go for eight years on that, with punishing and then consoling. I could just rip him to pieces, and then be his mother, and then criticize him for using me as a mother, and it was just a terrible, terrible thing. And neither one of us smart enough to know how to break out of this. We were really unaware of any other way of life, and stayed together mostly from pressures from family and society, and this silly game we played, not wanting *anybody* to know. That was very important.

Finally, as part of the sexual end of it—I don't know if you really want this, or not—but I'll tell you the point at which I felt the most degraded, the lowest, in our relationship. I used to want a lot of sex, because I just never was satisfied. I just needed more and more, and never got anything out of it, and I just drove him crazy, because he wasn't interested in it to begin with. And he finally told me that I was dull and uninteresting and I couldn't turn him on, and maybe if he had an affair with another woman, that would stimulate our relationship. And I even went along with that! He didn't want the responsibility of picking the girl, so I did *that* for him. And I couldn't very well punish him for something I'd set up, you know. It was just a sick, awful kind of thing we had going. I look back on that with a certain degree of horror.

I think that was a minor turning point. At any rate, I really took a good hard look at myself and what I was doing to myself. And to what end, you know. It was crazy, and I had thought I could live with it and I couldn't.

And his cruelty to my children—I mean, my husband really couldn't hurt me, he couldn't attack me, I was so well-shielded. He took it out on the kids, and so I could use that—that was my reason for divorce, he was cruel to the children. That was it. And I had the support of the whole world on that one.

I felt completely justified in the divorce. He just was not what a husband *should* be. I sentenced him and condemned him and I felt so *right* in doing so. I was a strong person, he was not so strong. I was just *right,* that's all, and he was a real bastard.

After the divorce I thought I was going to be in real good shape. I didn't have this worm hanging around my neck, and I could get a job and take care of things in a really super way. I had a lot of surprises in store for me there. I didn't drive, I had to learn how to drive a car. I got a job, a terribly dull job—office work in a factory, night shift. I had suddenly the realization of what it is to be alone. I had two children to raise. I was physically not well at all, recovering from a hysterectomy. That was another thing, in my decision to get a divorce, the timing couldn't have been worse. I was probably in the worst possible condition to make an important decision for myself. I was emotionally and physically just nowhere near tiptop.

I had to get a babysitter to watch the kids, and they were just running wild. My oldest boy was beginning to experience severe emotional problems as a result of me and his father and our marriage and everything. And I didn't know how to cope adequately with so many things at once. I was so, really, unfit to manage myself, let alone the other responsibilities— the kids and the house and everything else.

I guess at that point I really thought I could have a successful sexual relationship with almost anyone, and I had great need for this. So I found myself bedhopping for awhile. And to my utter amazement, it just wasn't any different. It didn't make any difference who I slept with— I still would just not be able to reach an orgasm. I'd go so far and stop. And I was so certain of my own worthlessness and unlovability that, for example, I never let any man know that I didn't have an orgasm. I put on a good show. The sexual excitement was real, I was sexually excited —but I'd also put on a good show of having an orgasm, just to make him feel better. I was just a complete shell. It was almost a driving obsession—if I could only have an orgasm, I would be a woman. It was so dumb. You know, that doesn't have anything to do with it at all, but that was it, and I wasn't measuring up, I just wasn't.

Working was a good thing. I met some new people and began to experience at least some sense of accomplishment, no matter how idiotic this work was, and easily moved up and began to supervise people, and that was a good feeling. But it was time-consuming.

I got into a little trouble with my neighbors. We lived in a tract area, we'd all moved in at the same time, and these people were all really my friends, I thought. But as soon as I was divorced, I found I wasn't welcome in any of the houses—that was a tough one for me to handle. I was a threat to all the women, I was after all the men—none of which was true, because I had a very strong moral code. A divorced woman is open for all kinds of things you just can't imagine until you're in that situation. It's like it's tattooed on your forehead, and you know, "Husbands, beware!"

Then I became involved with a man I worked for, one of the bosses. This was my second husband. He was twelve years older than I. He already had one degree, and he was working the second shift as well, because he'd changed his entire style of living. He was back in college, majoring in psychology. And he used everything he'd learned on me, and I was easy bait, you know, "Wow, isn't he marvelous!" A good-looking man, stable, quiet-spoken, gentle (so he seemed), very bright, and he was interested in me, which just seemed astounding to me. You know, what in the world was there about me that could catch the eye of so marvelous a creature? And I was foolish enough to think that it had an awful lot to do with *me*. It didn't. It was strictly a sexual attraction. And since I didn't place any value on my appeal sexually, it just didn't compute with me, so it *had* to be something else. And so our relationship began from two different assumptions, again. I just assumed it had to be something other than sex, and he assumed I knew it was sex—it was dumb.

And, well he was married also, so I had terrible guilt feelings about the time we spent together. Eventually he divorced his wife and we married. And that sounds very simple, but it was a complicated proce-dure. I didn't really want to have anything to do with him, but his attention to me was something I couldn't resist. I was just drawn to it. I needed someone to care about me. I really desperately needed it, much as I thought I could get along without it. And I could sort of cheat myself in a hundred ways, and rationalize it away, because of, you know, his attention.

I tried to stop that relationship over and over and over again and couldn't do it. Even, you know, "My God, why don't you just go away and leave me alone?" and the more I held him off, the more attractive I seemed to him.

He was beautiful to the children, or it seemed to me he was, and that was so important to me. However, he never fooled the kids, because they told me right from the beginning, "He's just dreadful, Mother, and don't have anything to do with him." And in my superior position of knowledge and age, and as MOTHER, capital letters all, I just put aside everything they said and told them *I'd* make the decisions for the family, and at any rate. . . .

I thought *I* had broken up his home and felt like a dog. But, hell, he was going to get divorced anyway. If it hadn't been me, it would have been any little chick who came along. I've learned that since, and I don't punish myself for that much any more.

At that time I was just no one. I was so easily persuaded, anybody could talk me into anything. I didn't know who I was, except that I was a nobody. And the thing that I remember with real shock is that even before I married him, after he did get his divorce, I told a very good friend of mine, "The only way I'm ever going to get rid of him is to marry him and divorce him."

That shows various things. I felt that he couldn't possibly be interested in me and that sooner or later he'd find I was no good, and so I went into it on a very cynical basis, feeling, well, he's so hot for this —he has money, he'll give the children a father, and I won't have to work. I was so tired, and physically exhausted, and ready to stay home. Then another thing was that he seemed to have an interest in my oldest boy, and of course my children really were desperate for a father. And he gave that as one reason for persuading me to marry him—that he would be a good father to John, my oldest boy.

Well, our marriage lasted one year, and it was perfectly terrible. It turned out he didn't have a dime, he couldn't handle money, he was in debt, terribly in debt; I ended up losing most of my possessions to pay his bills; I lost my car—well, everything I had that was of material value, and I didn't have very much. It was terrible! And all he wanted was sex, sex, sex. If I had been getting satisfaction from it, that probably would have been quite all right, but I wasn't. So, very soon, he became to me just a dirty old man. It was a ghastly scene.

Everyone was better off, really, when that ended. It's strange, too, because it's the part of my life that I recall the least. I find if someone says, "How long have you and Joe been married?"—this is my current husband—and I say six years, and my oldest child is eighteen, and they say, "Well, then, you've been divorced," and I always think only of two husbands. I never think of poor Ken, sandwiched in the middle. I really don't, very little.

I managed to get through it, somehow, but the important thing about this was that, again, I married for all the wrong reasons—I married so I could quit work and stay home with my children. I married for financial security which didn't exist, and I married for emotional security—the man was older, he seemed so capable, and wasn't. He was just a person too, like everybody else I know, and brought into the marriage his own problems and his own hangups, and I hadn't allowed any room for those. Once again I had had some nutty idea that as soon as we were married, then *my* idea of what marriage would be was going to happen, and, of course, it didn't.

Marriage was the one thing I really wanted, and failing at that *twice,* and so *completely,* was a very tough thing for me. I was at that time utterly and absolutely convinced that there was something about me that was unlovable, and I couldn't deny it any more. The pain of trying to love someone and trying to be loved, was really more than I could bear to try again.

I decided that I'd work and raise my kids and, you know, stay with them and do all those marvelous martyr things, and then I was going to kill myself. I had this plan all set up—that's the way it was going to be. And it gave me, oh, sort of an end to the misery, you know. I knew that eventually it was going to end. I wasn't going to have to wait through another thirty years of just terrible loneliness.

The loneliness would just eat away at me. And the knowledge that there was something wrong with me and that I wasn't going to be able to have any kind of sustained relationship—any relationship was going to be brief. And I'd make sure I kept it that way. Nobody was ever going to really know *me* again. I wouldn't show anything of myself, or darned little. Just as little as necessary. And learn to live without sex. I'd learned how to take care of myself. I'd masturbate and then I'd handle that guilt —just pile it on top, you know, one thing after another. Feeling guilty about what I'd done to my kids, what I'd done to two men, what I'd done to myself, and I could think two ways about that, either blame it on my mother—you know, poor old mother—or blame it on the fact that something was missing in me, which wasn't my fault, or I'd picked two peculiar men, which wasn't my fault, and half the time I could go that way and the other half I would just own it all, and, you know, punish myself.

I wonder sometimes how my third husband, whom I first met at a party and then at a meeting where we talked, ever managed to reach me through all of this stuff. It's kind of a miracle in a sense.

There were about three years between my first marriage and my second one, and there was about, oh, maybe a year and a half or two years between the second and the third one. Now in that period of time I really began to put aside my "shoulds" and my "ought tos," to put aside or somehow look at and own and come to peace with some guilt, by looking at the past and realizing, "It's past and I can't do anything about it, and I can really mess up my future if I mess around with the past."

So, first of all, I wanted to try to get acquainted with myself, and who I am and what are some of the things that cause me to behave the way I do—try to get in touch with some of my feelings, which were new things to me. I didn't think that anyone would care about those. Those had always been my own—and I guess those are some of the things I thought were the unacceptable things. If I felt suicidal or depressed, or if I felt unlovable, or if I felt any of the negative feelings I would have about myself, I must not let anybody see or anybody know about those things. It took me a long time to realize that those are the things that people can value and can care about. I wish I could remember clearly some of the process involved, and that's tough. I'm not very good at that. Joe had an awful lot to do with that.

Joe came into my life, and he's a man who has always been loved, knows it, accepts it without question, and I still feel in awe of that. He knows he has worth—that's something that is never questioned—and yet at the same time he could look at me, who had an almost exact opposite opinion of myself, and not be bothered by that or be put aside by that, and not encourage it either. He never confirmed my "sickness," he never confirmed my negative feelings about myself. He would hear them and accept them, and then, in his own way, say that they were kind of nonsense. "I realize you feel that way, but that's not the way you are."

And I began to try to look at myself. It was as if, just maybe, the way *he* sees me is closer to the way I am than the way *I* see me, and I began to sort of try that on a little bit. It's sort of an interesting thing. I found that it was a lot easier for me to put myself *down,* because then I didn't really have to perform. I didn't have to live up to anything. I was deprived and mistreated and unlovable and unacceptable, and *so* I didn't have to come out with any high order behavior at all. I could excuse myself for not coping, or not appreciating myself, or whatever.

I think if Joe had been fascinated by my horror story, I might have stayed in it a good deal longer than I did. He wasn't. He heard it and thought it was terribly sad, but he didn't want to hear it twice, and that was a little tough for me, because that was my ticket, kind of, with people—they'd be fascinated with anything ugly, and it would frighten 'em. I never frightened Joe. I could become so depressed, I'd sort of try on a suicide act. It would seem very real to me at the time, but he just never paid any attention. It just didn't exist for him, and it was, "Well, I hope you're over that now" or "My God, if you want to wallow in that, I'd better leave and come back when you feel better. Is there anything I can do to help you with this? I don't want to hear it again. If you want to beat yourself with your past, for the rest of your life, that's a trip you take all by yourself."

And a lot of it seemed kind of cruel, but it really snapped me out of it. I could go one or two ways. He cared about the person I was. He didn't give a goddamn about the person I had been or any of that. It was a part of me, true, but it was only a *part* of me. It wasn't all of me. And the more that I could look at myself through his eyes, the better I could feel about myself.

But an interesting thing about that was, I wasn't sure I wanted to. I didn't know whether I really *wanted* to be healthy, because there's a hell of a responsibility involved with that—just an enormous responsibility. I couldn't look forward to being a martyr, and dying in another ten years, and ending all the agony.

And I resented him, often, because still I believed, okay, buddy, you really care about me, but that's what *you* see. I don't let you see this little, black, rotten, ugly ball I have buried down inside that's really me, that's unlovable and unacceptable. And I was really terrified at that point in my life of attempting to—once again, you know—try to work on this exchange of love, the transaction of giving and receiving love.

I could maintain my status quo, you know, and feel sorry for myself, and put myself down and be a part-time martyr, and be safe, because it was known to me and I knew I could survive. It wasn't much of a life, but I was alive. Or I could really try once again to open myself up and let him see me and risk the possibility that that black ball inside of me really is so ugly that he's going to leave. And that's a terrible risk to take. For me, if I tried it again and failed at it again—and I'm not talking about marriage—I'm talking about a real relationship with another human being—I felt that I would go mad, that I *really* would lose my mind.

It wasn't worth the risk. But after a long time I realized that for me the greater risk—the greater risk was *not* to risk, and never really know whether I could be loved, and whether I could love.

I really had to reach that point. I held Joe off. I tried to shut him out every way I could think of. Joe was open, he was right there, he lived so much in the now, and I could find ways to criticize that. He was so very real it scared me. It fascinated me, I loved it, I really loved *him,* but I thought I knew how to do that and nobody else did. *I* could love; that was something I knew how to do, but nobody could really love me; there was going to be that terrible time.

But his interest in me did continue, and the relationship went on and on. We began to sleep together, and I got closer and closer to having an orgasm. And one thing was that Joe was never in a hurry. For me sex had always been a very quick thing. An ejaculation on the part of the man and that was it, and leaving me so frustrated that sometimes I'd go out and bang my head against the wall. And then I'd masturbate, and then I felt terribly guilty about that. I felt the masturbation was probably the reason I wasn't able to have an orgasm. So the whole scene was a very, very bad one for me.

But Joe was never in a hurry, and he was interested in what I enjoyed. What did *I* enjoy in our physical contact together? And I found that terribly hard for me to talk about. I just wasn't accustomed to that kind of interest and compassion. I really felt nobody could feel compassion for another person. But as I talked about it, and as we began to come closer and closer together, believe it or not, I began to have orgasms. And that made the whole relationship much more meaningful.

But I was certain that he would leave me just like all the rest. He'd get disgusted with me, he'd find out how unlovable I was. And so, for a while, I played the game of being attractive. I'd do anything in the world to please him. I never crossed him, never showed any negative feelings about what he did, because I felt I musn't lose him. If he ever gets to know *me,* he'll leave me, so I've got to play the game of being an attractive woman. The thing I didn't realize is that I wasn't fooling him!

But it's not possible to play that kind of a game forever, so I finally decided—it wasn't a very conscious decision, but a gradual one—that, well, if he's really going to leave, maybe it'd better be now, so I'll find out. And I would sort of reach down in and peel off a layer of my ugly black ball and bring it out and put it on the table, and I thought, "Now this one will drive him away, and it had better happen now before I get too deeply involved."

And it just never made any difference to him, whatever it was. He would acknowledge it maybe, or ignore it, or shove it off on the floor, or whatever, but he never got up and left. Sometimes he would be very angry, sometimes he would weep, sometimes he would laugh, you know, he would just react. I would get his reaction to whatever it was, but he never left. And I couldn't understand this, because it's all I had ever known. And I'd try another layer, pull another one up. And I'd get a *real* reaction from him, some of it good, some of it not so good, but he'd stay, and that was the important thing.

You know, after several months it was the children who moved him into our house! And for a while he would, in the morning, leap up and go and sleep on the couch, or leave and go home at four or five in the morning—park the car down the block, things like that. And the stronger and the more real our relationship became, the more courage we had to let the world kind of see us living together, and it didn't matter so much how they judged us, but how we felt about *ourselves.*

Then there came the real turning point, and that was a strange experience. We'd been living together for close to a year, which seems unbelievable to me. How that ever worked in that neighborhood I don't know, but it did. An awful lot of it had to do with how I felt about myself. And how we felt about ourselves. At any rate, Joe was out of town—he was away on business and I was home—the kids were asleep, and I was sitting in the living room watching television, which was across the room from me, and next to the television set was a window, a big picture window. Normally, I had the curtains closed, but I didn't this night, and so when I looked across at the TV, I could see my reflection in the window. And I kind of had a conversation with myself. It was very important to me, and I don't know if you can hear what I'm saying, but it was sort of like this: "Hello. Here you are, thirty-four years old, and how *differently* life has turned out from what you expected." I had always had a very unreal picture of life. I thought I wanted to get married, settle down, have six children, God forbid, raise the family, and live happily ever after. It seemed like such a simple reasonable dream. And it really hadn't worked that way *at all.* I'd found a man,

I'd loved him, I thought; I thought I was straight and open and honest, whatever that meant, and it really hadn't worked. There had been *so* much unhappiness. I'd had a lot of illness, I'd had so many problems with my children, I hadn't been able really to cope with life. I didn't know anything about it at all, it was really a devastating thing. Life had been pretty much *hell*.

I kind of talked to myself and listed all the things that had gone wrong. And then I began to wonder about some of the things that might be right. And one of the questions that came up—and, you know, these are questions from me to me—was, "What is it you really want? What is it that you're looking for?" And the answer turned out not to be a marriage, not to have six children, not to live happily ever after at all. It turned out to be that I wanted to learn how to love someone, just one person, and to be loved, and that's *all*. I didn't need the house, I didn't need anything else, but just really to know how to do that. To know how to experience that—both ways.

And my reflection in the window said, "Well, you jackass, what do you think you've got now?" And I sat there and thought, "Well, for crying out loud, you know, I really have a man I'm learning to love, and that means sharing myself. If that is my goal, to love and to be loved, I have it. Joe loves me, I love him, he loves the children. What do I want that I don't have?"

Up to that time I'd always had reservations about our relationship, because Joe had never seemed like he wanted to marry me. The piece of paper, that damned marriage certificate, was again my way of measuring his love, which is just dumb. He was living with me, he was sharing his life with me, he was marvelous with my children, very real with all of us. He accepted me just exactly the way I was, with all the crap, and I had exactly what I wanted, and I was denying it because I didn't have a piece of paper. I was cynical enough to be able to say, "Well, maybe Joe is just conning me, and what we have isn't real without a piece of paper." And I realized how *wrong* I was about that. And kind of a great thing happened to me, within me. I had a great talk with myself and felt a sense of peace that I'd never experienced before in my life.

I probably cried, I don't remember, it doesn't matter. But I also felt joy. Those were two things I didn't know anything about. I'm talking about a relationship with myself. I'd never experienced any peace and I'd never experienced any joy. And that was the first time, and it was all by myself. I hadn't needed Joe. I hadn't needed anyone else to do this to me or for me. It was my own private experience and it was great. I can't overstress the importance of this conversation with my reflection. It was a real turning point.

And when Joe came back from his trip, I didn't have a need to share it with him, it wasn't a great big thing that had to be explained. It was mine and it was private and it was healthy and it was beautiful, and along with it came a lot of responsibility that suddenly didn't scare me—no suicide or any of the rest of it.

And apparently, I lifted—Joe and I have talked about this much after the fact—I apparently lifted all kinds of pressure from Joe to marry. I didn't say anything, but just my attitude changed. Suddenly, from his point of view, I was completely with him sexually and totally for the first time in my life. The peace that I felt about myself and the good feelings I had toward me and my own private joy were obvious, and were transmitted to him, and apparently it was something he was waiting for. It wasn't a very cognitive process he went through, but I seemed very much present to him, and in two weeks we were *married,* which was really kind of astounding! All of a sudden, Joe was absolutely positive that we ought to—only I use that in the nice sense—marry; that what we had going for us was working. And that it had every possibility, from his point of view, and certainly from mine, to continue to work better and better.

And I wasn't sure I *wanted* to get married. It was funny, because I was experiencing good things and didn't want to spoil them, and I didn't need it. And I really meant that. I could have visited his parents, my parents, all of the people who had been so frightening to me in their judgment of me before—suddenly I could have visited them, without marriage, with great pride. At any rate, we were married.

And it's been great, it really has. It changes every day, it changes constantly. And I really don't know that I've shared the last ounce or pound, or whatever it is, of my little black crap inside. But I'm not afraid to, and usually it comes out sort of naturally. I haven't reached a goal or an end of anything, but I'm in the process of reaching it. And for me it's just *being,* and it's not easy to do. A lot of times it would be a lot easier for me not to share some of the things that are going on with me. I think, "Oh, God, that's going to trigger this, which is going to trigger that, and as soon as I do that, you know, I'm in trouble, and our relationship is in trouble." I've *always* got to remember to share what I am *right now,* which is just being, and it's the *process.* And that works, and it's the only thing I've found that does. And it has given me joy, and sometimes I look in the mirror and really think I'm pretty, and that's *really* movement!

It seems a shame to wait until I'm forty, after an awful lot of years, but really, I don't regret one single thing that's happened to me. I don't punish myself any more, I really don't. I see it, and I'm sorry about a lot of things I've done. I'm sorry about a lot of things I've not done, and the way I've been, but I really don't punish myself any more. And I'm learning how to live in the now, and I'm beginning to understand what that word means. Our sex is absolutely fantastic. I find myself getting quite courageous sexually, which is kind of marvelous. Joe thinks I'm simply beautiful. And half the time I think he's got to be *blind,* but that's all right too. I have a good relationship with my kids and they have with each other. The thing snowballs, it moves from one to the other and to our friends. I keep Joe honest, he keeps me honest, we keep ourselves honest. No tricks, no games, and it's so wonderful to be able to live— to be just exactly who I am all the time, or *most* of the time, and find out it's okay. I really don't have to hide anything, I don't have to try to figure out what anybody wants and try to give it to him, in order to make friends or—It's *nice!* I'm sure I'm not that way twenty-four hours a day, by a long shot, but it's building, inching along, and it's kinda neat. And I'm glad to be alive. There aren't any guarantees, but I'm glad to be alive.

And you know, I've found that the little black ball inside of me is the most lovable part of me. The part of myself that I thought was ugliest is the most beautiful, because I've learned how to share it.

MEANINGS I FIND

A whole book of personality dynamics could be based on a study of Irene's life as she reports it. There are learnings about child development, about parent-child relationships, about the creation of one's self-concept, about the elements of bad relationships and good relationships, about the factors which make for personal change, about the sharing of oneself, about sexual adjustment (bad and good), about rationalization, and so on and on. At first I thought I would organize some of the meanings I find in Irene's experience under such headings. I came to feel that it might be more helpful if I simply listed some of my learnings, very briefly, in the order in which they occur in the interview. In that way you can check back to the document to see if you agree or disagree, and whether these suggest other elements to you. So here is a partial list.

The effect of destructive family relationships on the child and young person (p. 80).

The influence of early inhibitions regarding sex (p. 80–81).

The incredible gap which occurs in a relationship based on rigid expectations of the other and not on understanding (pp. 81–82).

The disastrous effect which a failure to achieve a satisfactory sexual relationship can have on a marriage (pp. 82–83).

The lasting influence of severe parental rejection (p. 82).

Some of the elements which can go into the building of a negative self-concept; maternal rejection (p. 82); sexual inadequacy (pp. 83, 86); failure in two relationships (pp. 88, 89); husband's dislike of her body (p. 83); etc. Some of these elements occur primarily in others, such as "I never loved you." Others are experienced: "I've never had an orgasm." But when the person introjects the negative perceptions of others and values his own experience in terms of others' expectations ("I've never had an orgasm, so I'm not a woman"), then indeed the concept of self can become very negative.

The rising spiral of cruelty in a relationship based first on role expectations of the other and second on accusations for failing to live up to those expectations (pp. 82–83, 84).

The strain of maintaining a mask in public which is totally different from the private reality (pp. 83–84).

The fear of relationships which is based on the belief that

deep within the self there is something unspeakably awful which must never be revealed to others (pp. 84–85).

How a complete lack of experiential knowledge of living in a relationship with another, separate person can destroy a marriage (p. 84).

The bizarre behaviors which can gradually grow out of mounting frustration (such as soliciting another woman for her husband, p. 85).

The ease with which we adopt comforting rationalizations: "that was my reason for divorce, he was cruel to the children" (p. 85).

The difficulty of coping with the real world, a difficulty never realized until experienced (pp. 85–86).

The delicate complexity of a satisfactory sexual relationship between a man and a woman (many references, but especially pp. 82–83, 86, 88–89, 92).

The need for attention and love which, when strong enough, distorts perceptions (pp. 87–88).

The guilt over being a homebreaker, which added to her black self-concept (pp. 87–88).

The weakness which grows out of the lack of any firmly grounded, positive, picture of oneself—the effect of being a "nobody" (pp. 87–88).

A catalogue of dubious reasons for marriage: exhaustion, readiness to stay home, financial security, emotional security, good-looking partner, providing a father for the children, sexual attraction (on the part of the husband). Also rebellion against mother, wanting a home and children (pp. 87, 88, 89, and also pp. 81–82, 84).

The way in which we suppress unpleasant memories (p. 88).

How life can become so unbearable, and how one's self can seem so awful that suicide and the destruction of the self seem desirable (pp. 89–90).

The first dawnings of psychological health—looking at oneself (pp. 90–94, also pp. 85, 86).

The ambivalence each of us feels about growth and health.

They involve risk and responsibility. It is easier to be a martyr or a suicide. (pp. 90–91)

The strain that can go out of a relationship when one is being *real* (pp. 94–96).

The unimportance of social expectations and judgments, when a relationship is real (p. 95).

The meaning of life and relationships as a *process* of living, rather than as sets of role expectations (pp. 95–96, compared with all of the first two marriages).

The enormous value—and the risk—of openness in a relationship (pp. 94–96).

The overriding importance of the self-concept as the guide to a person's behavior. Compare the open, sharing behavior of a lovable, sexually adequate, non-guilty, "pretty" person, with beauty at the core (pp. 95–96), with the behavior of an unlovable, sexually inadequate, fearful, unloving, basically defensive and ugly person (pp. 80–91). To be sure, many influences help to account for Irene's gradual change in her perception of herself, but it is not until she *does* gradually perceive herself differently, and has a different picture of herself which she accepts, that her behavior actually changes.

These are some of the meanings I find in Irene's experience. They seem rather pale beside the interview itself, but perhaps they will provoke some thoughts in you. I hope that her story has spoken to you in many personal ways, as well as provided food for thought about broader psychological principles.

6   Black and White

HAL IS A BLACK MAN whom I first met when we were both on the staff of a large workshop in the Midwest. We became rather well acquainted, and I was particularly interested to learn that he had married—and had been divorced from—a black woman by whom he had two sons, and that he was now about to marry a white woman. I also learned that he had spent his childhood in an urban ghetto. Consequently, many months later I wrote and asked him if, while I was on a trip to the Midwest, I could tape an interview with him about his marriages. He readily agreed.

Hal is slight, almost fragile in build. He speaks very softly and courteously. He has completed his doctoral degree in one of the social sciences. He is teaching and has also organized a free clinic for people in need.

In the interview he spoke freely, but I believe he is not a person who reveals his feelings easily and at times one must "read between the lines" to get the full meanings of his experience.

It was my intent to focus this chapter almost entirely on his relatively new marriage to his white wife, but I found that Hal cannot easily be understood without a considerable presentation of his unusual background and first marriage. Much of this material is presented in excerpts, but the content is not changed.

HIS RELATIONSHIP WITH HIS MOTHER

Well, I was born and raised in Chicago. My mother worked hard, and we had enough money for me to live pretty well. But being in a segregated community, we had to live among Italians and blacks and some Polacks. But most of us were all black and there were all socioeconomic levels. There were some very, very poor in our community and then there were some people across the street who were wealthy. I never wanted for anything. I have always had everything I wanted—four bicycles at one time, a suit almost every payday from my mother. My mother never bought herself anything. It was always for me—overcompensating.

Now, I guess, the real problems that I begin to recall is that I have always been a very demonstrative person, I guess, very cuddly, and, well, I never had this as a child. I never had anybody to love me and care for me, but my mother always worked for me to make sure I always had enough clothes, enough money. Being an only child, and not knowing my father, lots of uncles and aunts sort of took the place of a father, due to the family relationship that I had as a child.

I never knew my father. But we never made an issue of it, because I always had the things that I needed, and nobody ever talked about it, and I never had any reason to ask. I never felt like some people say, well, you didn't have a family, you didn't have a father to take you to baseball games and other things. I went with so many other people that it never dawned on me that you had to have a father to enjoy these kinds of things, so it was never a problem to me. I never wanted for a father.

I never remember my mother ever reading to me or reading with me. In fact, I have only kissed my mother twice, I think. We had a relationship like a brother and sister. As I would leave in the morning —I would get up in the morning and iron my shirts, and my mother would be asleep, because she didn't get home from the post office until about two o'clock in the morning. So maybe she would wake me up or bring me something and I would eat it and go back to sleep. Nobody ever cooked for me. I had to cook for myself or she always left two dollars every day to buy myself something to eat. So the only time we would eat together would maybe be on the weekend when she was home after church. And then she went to one church—she was a Baptist and I was a Methodist—so we never did anything together. My mother and I *never* did anything together. The only time we had any close relationship was after she married my stepfather.

ME: That really astonishes me, that you don't remember kissing your mother more than once or twice. Did she show affection in other ways? How about embracing you or putting her arms around you? Was there any of that?

HAL: I never ever remember being really embraced by my mother. I embrace her now, and put my arms around her. But I knew she always cared, because she always gave me things I needed to have. But also she was very strict. I didn't fear my mother, but I knew if she said something, she meant that, and I knew she would smack me or spank me if I didn't do it. . . . I remember once my mother wrote me a letter when I was in high school and she told me how proud she was, and how hard she had worked for me, and those kinds of things, and how glad she was that I seemed to be happy and that I was making it in life. This letter was very meaningful to me—I don't know what happened to it—it really hit me. She showed a lot of caring in that letter. She always thought I was a baby, Carl, for example. That was one problem we had in our marriage, my first marriage, that she would always send me clothes, you know, even when we were married. And she gets very hurt, for example, if I tell her that I'm not going to do something. Or like raising the kids, sometimes I say, "Mother, don't treat the kids like that. I would like to treat them another way." Then she reminds me that she raised me. But I still have to call home every week, even now. If I don't call home, she's upset and she calls and wants to know how we are.

HIS BACKGROUND AND NEIGHBORHOOD

The atmosphere and behavior outside of his home was very different indeed from the indulgent but well-behaved manner inside the home.

I remember I started drinking when I was about seven years old. I was sneaking drinks. And then I remember in elementary school we used to drink all the time. We would go out and buy bottles of wine. We would go to the grocery stores and since I was the smallest they would kick the bottle of wine all the way down to the end of the door and I was so small I could grab it and run around the corner with it. We used to do that and sit out in the backyard and drink the wine. Then I recall we always used to have somebody in the neighborhood buy a half pint of Hill and Hill whiskey before we would go to a party, and we would always be drinking something.

Then I remember the kids in my neighborhood were on drugs at a very early age. In *elementary* school I remember the kids taking pills and smoking marijuana. And most of the kids in my neighborhood were on heroin at an early age. And there was lots of prostitution going on in the community.

There was lots of gang warfare in my community. We used to have to pay protection dues to adolescent gangs just to come out of the house. If you didn't do this, you would be beat up on and you couldn't go to school. . . . And I was sort of one of the fastest in the neighborhood, and I was a good boxer, so I would always be the collector of the money. This other fellow we called "Honest John" I ran around with. He was the worst person in our neighborhood. So it was my responsibility to—if the fellow would say, "I don't have the money," then he would say, "Hit him, Hal," and I would hit him and then I would jump back and they would jump on him and take the money from him. I had to do this or I couldn't come out of the house. So in order for me not to be a coward, I had to run along with them. But I never had a fight, one to one, with anyone in my life.

So learning to drink at an early age and having been exposed to narcotics at an early age—I recall my mother remarried, and my stepfather, who was a minister, he told her that I was a wild man. Because when they got married, I wasn't even at the wedding. I was about eleven. They just didn't know where I was. I was gone someplace.

I was never a child. I never knew what it was like to be a child. At the age of seven I was able to clean the house. We had a rooming house with twenty-two rooms in it. We rented the upstairs out. And all the basement was mine. I had . . . my mother bought me a bed for down there, weight-lifting equipment, a pinball machine. I had a regular-sized pool table. I just had all those kinds of things at an early age.

He describes how he was active in dramatics, went to concerts, and had a very considerable cultural education, ". . . but when I would leave that kind of thing, I would come back into the community where I lived and would take on a hoodlum role again. You had to have this, because if you were ever seen as not being a part of it, well, then you were ostracized and ostracism meant that you would fight every day!"

SCHOOL

I never learned anything in elementary school. I remember that the teacher would send me to the store to do her shopping for her—to go downtown and buy her stockings for her, things like that. I was always such a good little man, 'cause my mother trained me to buy her stockings and to do the shopping. I ironed my own shirts, I cleaned the house. I did everything like that. I just knew how to maintain myself. So they thought I was being a nice little man when I should have been in school learning with the other kids. So as a result of that I didn't really start learning until I got in college. I had to go back and relearn all the things I should have learned in elementary school.

HIS FIRST MARRIAGE

Hal reflects upon *why* he married his first wife:

I guess the first and most important thing that I can recognize is that I got married out of loneliness, having been raised as an only child and having had not very many close relationships with people, and not having done lots of dating in my life. I went into the service after spending two years in college, where I met my wife.

The thing that I can remember about the relationship was people saying that she would make me a nice girl. She was a very quiet person, a churchgoing person. Her family didn't drink or smoke, and she was a very Christian person. But our lifestyles were so totally different.

But people said she would make me a nice girlfriend, and then I was most encouraged by a friend of mine—a fellow that I had much respect for—that she would be a good person for me.

After a period of some dating, Hal left for his stint in the Navy, and didn't even write to her. However, a chance circumstance started up their correspondence, and just before he was discharged, they were married. He was twenty-three. They were a very inexperienced couple, sexually and in every way, "inexperienced about just living."

I was still thinking about not being the best student in school, and I felt with a wife like this who could complement me when I had my weaknesses, that she could help me get my papers out on time and those kinds of things. But after a period of time I found out that she was unwilling to give me support, or unable to. An example is that I would write a paper—and I would ask her to type it for me right away, because I didn't like to wait. I always liked to get my stuff in early. Well, maybe some days she would wait until the day it was *due* to type it, and I would be very upset and angry and nervous.

He feels that the great differences in type of background and of lifestyle, the fact that she was very uncomfortable with his friends, especially those he was meeting professionally, were additional reasons for growing more remote from each other. But there were other factors.

I think one of the things that really hurt me was my being cuddly and needing love and caring—but it didn't dawn on me then that I didn't have that in early childhood and that there was a need for that. I remember once I reached to kiss her and she moved away from me. I never forgot that. It was very hard for me to show affection anyway. I would always think that people would reject it because of my stature —I was short and I never thought that anybody would really like me in any particular kind of way, other than my money. It was sort of like buying friendship. Then when somebody that you think you are finally able to relate to sort of moves away and rejects you, I think it was just a little too much for me.

I got through school in *spite* of my wife's lack of effort and interest, anyway I did. And I wasn't sure whether there was sort of a jealousy or what, but it seemed to me the more I would go up the ladder, the more resentful she would become. She never really voiced resentment but it was just the way she would do things. For example, I would leave for school in the morning and maybe come back in the afternoon and she would still be in bed. Or I remember the fellows used to tease me about my having to wash my own clothes and having to clean the house on Sunday. And so these were some of the things that were irritating to me.

The sexual life wasn't a good one after a while. I really didn't enjoy it. And I wanted to leave several times. One time I remember that I did move out and then I came back . . . I was gone for about a day. And then I thought, "Well, this is no way." And we laid in bed and cried about how sad it was, and we shared that together. I felt better, but I guess deep down I knew that it wasn't going to last.

ME: You mentioned that sexual relationships became less and less satisfying as the marriage worsened. Had they ever been satisfactory to you, and especially had they ever been satisfactory for her?

HAL: I think there were several times. I would ask her if she had a climax and if she enjoyed it and she said she did. But other times—I can also remember sometimes that I caught her masturbating. My sexual patterns were that I was much better in the morning and I liked to have sex in the morning. And she would like to have sex in the evening. Well, sometimes I was able to. Other times I was just *tired,* just physically exhausted. Exhausted. I was working sixteen to eighteen hours some days, and when I would come home, I was just *too* tired. I would have one can of beer and fall asleep. So those were bad times for me and so I would try to help her understand. . . . I don't remember having an awful lot of enjoyable sexual experiences with her. There were times that there were physical releases, but I was always conscious of a woman being satisfied, and I have always worked hard at that, to make sure that she did, and I tried not to be selfish about it.

He understood that she wished he was in business rather than professional activities. So he went all out in a variety of simultaneous business ventures, which left him exhausted, as he has mentioned.

With all her skills and talents I thought that she would certainly want to help me do these things, but it ended up that I did all of them myself. And so this kept me out of the home quite a bit, trying to run the businesses and keep things up, and for us to have enough money to do the kinds of things she wanted to do.

By this time they had two children, so the problem of supporting his family was real.

THE BREAKDOWN—AND BREAKUP

The element which finally brought a separation was quite different from anything thus far mentioned, one in which he did not see the warning signals.

She had a habit of getting up late at night and driving away, you know, down to the lake. It never bothered me at first when she would do this. I felt that she needed to get away. I worried about it—it was late at night sometimes—and I didn't quite understand this.

And then sometimes she would take off and go home [in another city] without my knowing it. I remember once she left me. I took the kids out riding and came back and she was gone and didn't come back for several days. I didn't know where she was. So I called her home and found out she was there, and I had to be very angry and tell her the kids were sick and she should be at home.

Then later on she had a . . . a nervous breakdown, I guess it was. This time it sort of bothered me, because she went to a friend, and this friend called me and said she was on the couch having hallucinations . . . saying she was dying and very fearful of this. And she would start writing notes—typing things on the typewriter which I found later—which were incoherent. I didn't quite understand it.

I remember sometimes she said she wanted to talk to me but I never knew it was that serious, you know, and sometimes it seemed there wasn't much to talk about. Then I would plan some days to come home and be very kind to her and do things that I thought a wife would like, you know, buy her flowers and bring her things. That was okay for a while, but it seemed to be something in our communication, that we just didn't talk enough, that we always waited until a crisis happened.

Eventually she had to be hospitalized, and much trauma was associated with that. Some time after she was home from the hospital Hal received a good job offer in another city and they moved there. Her sister came to visit.

I left going to work that day, and when I came home that night, she had completely moved. All the furniture, everything was moved out. The only things I had left was a rollaway bed, my clothes, and my clock radio. Everything was completely stripped by the movers. They took everything out. So it was hurting and sorta sad, but there was a great relief I felt. Because, you know, I didn't have to make the decision, she made it. But I felt more pain about the kids than feeling sorry for where she was psychologically.

ME: You commented earlier on what must have been her feelings of fear and so on, but what were *your* feelings at the time of her breakdown?

HAL: Well, my feelings were . . . I was very hurt. I wondered if I was the cause of her breakdown and what role I played in it. I was sort of upset that I hadn't taken time to listen to her, not knowing it was that serious. And I felt bad because working so much with other people, I didn't see the indications at all that she was sick. I knew that she had these migraine headaches all the time. I knew this. And I knew that she was, well, I know sometimes she seemed to be depressed. So these things I reflected back upon and I felt very bad, not knowing what my role was in her being ill.

But the thing that, I guess, really helped me not feel too bad about my responsibility for her being sick was that the psychiatrist told me that he didn't think it was my fault, and that she was schizophrenic, and she probably would be that way, and it was just a thing that happened, and that it wasn't my fault. And he said that these things were probably there a long time ago. The thing that helped me in relationship with her family, too, was that they made comments to me like they were surprised that the marriage lasted so long. They had often felt that there was something wrong with their sister, that she would often go into her room and stay there for a week by herself and just wouldn't come out. And she always had the headaches, and this type of thing. They said that it always seemed like she lived in a world of fantasy, even as a child. But these things hadn't dawned on me, but it sort of helped me to feel better about it.

ME: Did she ever talk with you as to why she left home?

HAL: No. She never has. We never really talked about it. . . . It was just sorta that she was glad that she was away and out from under the stresses. I guess I was so glad in a way that she was gone and the pressure was off me, that I never asked.

After the separation, one time I went to do a workshop and I called my kids to see how they were doing, and she asked me to come and get the kids. So I thought that was sorta . . . well, it bothered me for a mother to say, "Come and get the kids. I want you to keep them." I didn't think much of that, but I did go and get the kids and they lived with me for a year and a half before I got married again. That meant that I was mother and father. I had to cook breakfast, and iron, and my oldest boy being asthmatic meant that I had to keep his room very clean. He couldn't drink milk and eat chocolate things and it was sort of tiring on me, with me still going to school to try and get my degree.

COMMENT. My comments on Hal's first marriage can be brief, because the roots of its disintegration stand out so very clearly. There was first a lack of real acquaintance before marriage—some dating, a considerable period of no interchange at all during his first period in the Navy, then correspondence, then a marriage before he left the Navy. They had really had no opportunity to get to know each other well.

The reasons he gives for his marriage are his loneliness, the fact that she was a quiet, religious girl, and perhaps most important of all, the advice of his best friend and others. None of these represents a very solid basis for a partnership.

Then there is the almost complete lack of any real sharing

during the marriage. He *suspected* a jealousy on her part of his academic and other achievements, but they never explored it. He *thinks* she was resentful but it was never voiced. He must have had reactions to doing the washing and housework, but they were never stated. It didn't "bother" him when she took strange night trips, but "this time it sort of bothered me" when she was hallucinating and showing obvious signs of disturbance. But he learned only much later that her strange behavior went far back into the fantasy world of her childhood. He sums it all up when he says, "it seemed to be something in our communication, that we just didn't talk enough." The height of this barrier between them is shown by their never having discussed together her leaving of the home, involving her final separation from him.

During the period of the separation and the divorce, Hal was working on his doctoral degree and engaging more and more in encounter groups and other intensive group experiences. I see a real difference in his relationship with his first and second wives, probably due in large part to this kind of experience and training.

THE PERIOD BETWEEN MARRIAGES

During the year and a half between marriages, Hal was actively seeking a new partner:

. . . I decided . . . after the separation and divorce . . . that I am just not a person to be single. I don't find any fun in being a bachelor. I have often known that I like family life, and I just like being married. And so I was just dating several girls and then it dawned on me that I should be starting a weeding-out process . . . *(laughingly)* and begin to see just who I would want to be serious with.

He ran into various problems. "Some of the problems I found, Carl, in dating, were that some of the black girls I dated felt very insecure." He felt that they were uncomfortable because most of his friends were professional people, and the girls felt inferior, though actually they were not.

They really should have no reason for feeling insecure around my friends. And this happened not only with the girls that I knew that were professional or semiprofessional, but just all of the girls that I went with and dated. They just didn't feel comfortable. Some of them would say that I was just too ambitious, or most of them wanted me to spend more time with them. Like devote all of my time to them—be accountable for my time—and they gave me no breathing ground. . . . And then many of them I found to be so very *insecure* that I would have to leave work and have to do counseling with them, so there was never any basis of developing love or understanding. Some of them hadn't been able to identify with their fathers because of a divorce situation; or some of them were trying to raise their brothers and sisters or . . . there were just lots of things that happened that didn't allow for a good, warm, caring relationship. Then one of the girls I went with whom I really would have married, if she had wanted to at the time, wasn't able to be with my kids in the right way. For example, she would want to discipline them, before showing love to them. And I think you can't discipline kids until they know that you also love them. So we had some conflicts like that.

I guess the things that led to me marrying Becky was . . . I met her in Kentucky when I went to do a workshop on school integration problems and . . . Becky happened to be in my workshop. And at that time she was married and going through some divorce processes. I never really noticed her except that she was one of the prettiest girls in the group. But I didn't really pay much attention to that. I was really concentrating on leading the group. And then we went to a party, and she asked if I had a ride, and I said, "Well, I don't know. I don't think so." So she said she would give me a ride, but she was hesitant, because she thought that two of the black women maybe wanted to give me a ride, and they may have felt embarrassed or not feel too good toward her if she offered to give me a ride—one of the cultural and racial things was coming into it. So then I accepted a ride from her and we went to the party and we danced and talked and had a good time. So we just sort of met like that. Then we talked coming back, and she told me about some of the problems in being separated, and this type of thing, and the possibility of her getting a divorce. And then we became very close to each other and we embraced and then. . . . I was leaving the next day, and I didn't know she was having these warm feelings about me this way, though we felt very sexy and attracted to each other and loving toward each other. So, I went back home, and later she called and said, "This is Becky, and have you forgotten me?" I said, no, I hadn't, and then she began to talk and asked me if I would be free if she would come out and visit me that summer.

So Becky did come out and spent a weekend. She revealed more of her current marital problems but Hal felt "I didn't want to be a part of a divorce thing, so then she assured me that this had already taken place and they were already in the process before, and her husband wasn't living at home half the time and lots of things like that. So then we began to correspond quite often."

During the weekend Becky told of a good friend of hers who had been divorced and who decided to try a new life. But by the time she felt ready for marriage, the man she wanted was no longer available. "Becky said that this woman told her that if there was anything she wanted, it was best to go after it."

MARRIAGE TO BECKY

After they had corresponded for some time, Hal began to weigh his feelings toward her.

There were just so many things after a while that I came to like about her. She had the kind of things that I wanted in a woman. She was very warm, she was very motherly with the kids, and they really liked her. And I liked her son and I saw how she treated him. She just really complemented me. For example, her being raised on a farm, she was more down to earth. She faced things more realistically. She worked hard. She loved to cook. She loved to take care of the house. You know, all the kinds of things that I like to have done for me and with me. And she showed lots of compassion and understanding and she didn't want me to give up anything for her. She liked the life I like, and she was very aggressive, you know. And she said, "All right, now you get through your doctorate program, and then I'm going to do my master's, and eventually I'll go back and get a doctorate." She just really was feeding the intellectual environment I needed, plus the warm caring as a person.

I just felt that we sort of complemented each other. Also she sews a lot. And if I come home and something like the toilet is broken, she has fixed it. She doesn't have to wait till I get home—it's already fixed. And the thing that she explained to me is that her other husband wouldn't do those things and so she had to learn to do that, and she hoped I wouldn't feel bad if she did the things she thought a man should do. And I explained that I didn't have any . . . any problems with that, and that people do the things that they can do best.

So they were married in the presence of black and white friends. Though the marriage is less than a year old, Hal says, "We have just been very happy and we haven't run across any serious cultural differences."

The thing that makes me very happy is the way she relates not only to our kids but the kids that she teaches. She spends lots of time with them. She goes home and makes sure that the mother knows why they were on detention or why they are not coming to class, and those kinds of things, which really is something that that community hasn't had. Then our two boys really like her now. They call her mother now, you know. She and the kids have worked through that, they really have gotten to know each other better. And I think one thing that helped us was this summer when we took a four weeks' vacation. Living that close together in our camper, together with the kids, we really got to know each other well. We went fishing with the kids, and we went hiking, and picking berries and things that *I* had never done before either. So it was a new experience for me. Like digging bait to go fishing, just a warm kind of thing. So now I am beginning to do the kind of things that I had never done before. Buying the camper was an attempt for me to get out and see more of the world. The thing that I like about it in comparison to my other friends and their wives is that they say we always seem to have a better relationship. We talk through things. When she gets upset sometimes she'll sit and I'll sort of help her bring it out. The only problem we have had for a while is her kid not being with us. We have to go to court now with the case to get her kid. Her ex-husband doesn't necessarily want the boy but he doesn't want us to have him, because of the interracial marriage. And that has been one of the roughest things for her to go through.

And sexually she's much freer than some of the girls that live in the city. She hasn't got the sexual hangups, for example. She has seen cows, and she has seen calves being born and horses being born. And her whole attitude is more healthy than most people. And so that helps us to relate better because she is freer. And she is not wrapped up with the city accomplishment type of thing. Like, for example, clothes. She would rather make her own clothes than spend the money for buying things like that. So as we come together, we share my background and how I respond to things differently, and she shares how she responds to things differently. And so I think that is helping. But here's the thing. We *do talk* about it.

Another thing I might add, too, is that she is not trying to make me white and I am not trying to make her black. We're not imposing our values on each other. We just recognize and know that and just keep on going. If there is some conflict, we deal with the conflict then, without trying to say, "You have to do it my way" or "This is the way I think it should be done." There's lots of give and take.

ME: There is one thing I wondered about when you were talking about it. In a sense you are both quite career-oriented, aren't you?

HAL: Yeah.

ME: Frequently when a husband and a wife are both career-oriented, then the question of who is moving up the fastest or who is getting the biggest salary can cause difficulty. Do you have any comment on that?

HAL: We have talked about that. Like, we want to have some children, and so we are going to have one or two children, and then after the children Becky wants to go back to work if she can. But she is not so career-oriented that she *has* to do that. She is just saying that she would *like* to do that, time being available for us. And I'm saying, good. Because if that's what you want to do, I would be very happy with your doing that. We don't want to smother each other. We don't want to stifle each other's growth. Because so often that is what really happens in a marriage relationship. Plus our marriage gives *me* freedom and *her* freedom to each develop our own life, you know . . . develop our own interests and grow. And so we have discussed that, I think, to where we are very comfortable about her going on and continuing her work in school.

THE DIFFICULTIES IN AN INTERRACIAL MARRIAGE

Up to this point, Hal had mentioned few troubles resulting from this being an interracial couple. So I raised the question.

ME: From your own point of view, it sounds as though the interracial aspect hasn't made any particular difference at all. But what about your life among others in the community? Do you get lots of flak or very little or what?

HAL: "Well, sometimes I get a little flak. At our clinic . . . we have some volunteer workers. And first of all some of them couldn't cope with an interracial couple working in it. And part of it was because of things like . . . well, some of the black women still think that a black man should be with them, you know. And I shouldn't be a part of Becky. And then they didn't trust that she was really as actively concerned with the community as we said we were. And some of it is plain jealousy and envy. We have gotten there. We have started our community clinic. We haven't asked anybody's support. All the money has come out of our own pockets. People are used to seeing people come in and asking everybody else to help and soliciting for money. But we haven't done that. We said that when we decided we were going to do it, we were just going to start it, and not be relying upon anybody else.

Then some of the people I meet really admire us, the way we are. They have seen that for the short period of time that we have been married, we have done lots of things. Like we invested in property and we save money and we just do lots of things together. We work out in the yard. You'll see Becky cutting grass, painting the house, you know. It's sort of like the other women are now trying to come out and trying to do more, because their husbands say, "Well, why don't you do things like Becky does?"

Sometimes people will do the staring type of thing. Some of the people at the university are shocked when we come there, who didn't know that she happened to be white, you know. But we really haven't experienced any difficult things. We thought at one time that the kids might experience it, but . . . so far they haven't come back with anything. For a while, Jerry, my youngest, didn't know how to tell people that Becky was their stepmother. He hurt Becky one time. She overheard him say to one girl, who asked, "Is that your mother?" he said, "No, that's our babysitter." And that sort of hurt Becky. But now with them it's just all "Mommy." Because they have needed the love and attention and caring and they really get it from her. You know, she spanks them, she disciplines them, and they accept it. It's not the same way as I would do it. Like yesterday she had to spank Martin, and I didn't spank him, so she did it, and when it was all through he was just back hugging his mommy.

I remember the other day I went into her class to tell Becky that I was going someplace else before I came home and then one of the kids in class, one of the black kids, said, "Mrs.————, is that your husband?" And they were talking—you know how kids will talk—and most of them were shocked to find that I *was* black and that she had married a *black* person. So lots of dynamics go on in the community. . . .

Some people are watching to see how we will react . . . what we are going to do and how we do things . . . but I don't think she has felt too much about it. She says some of the black women look at us and that she can feel sort of jealous. She gets sort of jealous if they get too close to me sometimes, because she thinks they look prettier than she looks. And so we have had to work on those kinds of things. Sometimes I feel overprotective of her because she doesn't know the community and sometimes this community can play lots of games. And if you don't know the games, you can get trapped in them. Uh, they say some things that they don't mean all the time, but they bait you in and check you out to see if you are really real. So I am trying to get her to know about the subculture and know what it's really like.

ME: You haven't mentioned whether there have been any of these problems when you are mingling with white groups. What about the situation there?

HAL: Well, I watch white men, particularly how they test you. We were at a party and one fellow came over and when he first came in he walked up and grabbed Becky's hand and kissed her on the hand and was carrying on . . . we hadn't met him before. But we were sort of special guests at the party. Eventually he finally got around to asking her why she loved me. You know, what was it in me that she liked. So you see these kinds of things, and you can feel the tension that goes on, because they still . . . smile as if they like you, and . . . but they still have all these concerns in their head . . . about the differences . . . and they really want to know. I don't think it is necessarily bigotry or racism. Some of it is just being curious. But some people still feel very uncomfortable. For example, we are members of the church and we go out to certain occasions now because the kids are all active in church, and we are active in church, and I can just see the tension. We go to some of the cookouts and the wives don't know what to say. They, they . . . start talking. Usually most of the men would come up to me and talk to me and talk to Becky and then the minister would come over and talk, but rarely do the women come over. I have noticed that. I haven't really talked much to Becky about it but I really notice this. So we keep right on going, and because Becky is so outgoing, she is busy meeting friends and mingling and she is not aware of how people are standing there and staring. I usually stand back and watch it. And sometimes I really shock them and ask them what they think about our relationship, you know. And then they say, "What do you mean?" And I say, "What do you think about this interracial marriage we have?" And then . . . then they fumble around very clumsily and don't know what to say, and I say, "You must have felt something about it, you know." Then one time I went to a party and a fellow just stared at us and I said, "Gee, I wish you wouldn't stare. Is there something you would like to say to us, or make us feel comfortable, or what? There must be something on your mind." Then he got offended when I asked him that. And then he didn't want to talk about it, you know. So I do sense those things. I am very careful about where I go to parties. I go out to have a good time and not to go to be the show or to be the press agent.

ME: You may notice that people are shocked or staring or jealous . . . but does that affect your relationship with Becky very much?

HAL: No, it doesn't. Uh . . . there are times . . . I guess I am suspicious of whites. Basically I am that suspicious. And I want them to accept us the way we are, but I have also found out after a long time that I don't worry . . . I don't waste time worrying about it the way I used to, about being accepted. So we keep on going and the stares and the comments that people make—well, I just keep on going. At a football game or a basketball game, somebody, I remember, said something about us and made some remarks about us. Then the people, when Becky is out with the kids, I notice how people look at her when they call her "Mommy," and those types of things. But that really hasn't affected us because we are so wrapped up in each other and we feel secure in ourselves, I guess. But for people who aren't secure, and who don't have as much to work with as we have to work with, it would be a tremendous problem. You know, interracial marriage per se is a very rough and difficult thing. Well, just *marriage* is a very rough and difficult thing. And then compounded with the interracial thing, people may *say* there is no problem but there are problems that develop, you know.

THE RELATIVES

Another thing I have noticed is how *my* relatives have come around. Now they just really love Becky. Like my uncle calls her his niece and he says, "Well, come on to my niece's house. She cooks the best food in the world." They just feel warm and she is just a member of the family. And I think she feels sort of bad because *her* relatives didn't accept me the same way, and I know that has been a problem.

But her mother is now coming around, who opposed the marriage at first, who didn't understand it, and didn't want to have anything to do with it, and now her mother is saying . . . now she knows it's going to work, and so it's okay and she's happy with it, but it just took time to believe this was the right thing. So now she might come out this summer to visit us, so she is understanding that our marriage is based on sound things and we are really doing okay. Becky is teaching and I have the clinic and teaching too. And really it's a good thing.

THE RELATIONSHIP IN THE FAMILY

I was thinking that when Becky first moved in with us, my . . . my oldest son . . . needed so much love and there was a conflict between him and me for the need of love, and I would become angry sometimes because I thought he was taking up too much of her time when *I* needed that much time. And then we were able to work that out, or *I* was able to work it out. I really began to see that he really needed love. He never had a mother to love and care for him. *I* hadn't either. So then it was sorta like *I* needed a mother, too, that type of thing. And she was able to love me, and cuddle me, and care for me the way I needed and the same thing I found in my kids, and particularly the oldest boy. He needed it as much as I did. But the youngest boy just sort of sat back, but he also needed it. Then it dawned on me that what was happening in the relationship was that all of us were so starved for love and caring that we sort of had to take our time, and share it in a different kind of way. And so now the oldest kid is just not craving for it as much. He is getting it more and more and he is getting it in different kinds of ways, like getting it from me and from Becky and that's maybe a better way. And I think that since we have been married he hasn't had any asthma attacks at all. He wheezes and we put the vaporizer on and then he is okay. But before he was always—oh, maybe once a week I would have to take him to the hospital, up to the clinic. And so I think he is getting his need met, and I think we have all benefited greatly by the marriage in that way.

COMMENT. Many things stand out for me in this second marriage, and the events which preceded it.

I note first of all Hal's selectivity in his perceptive evaluations of his dates and of Becky. Here is a much more mature person than the younger Hal, who married a woman because his best friend thought she would be good for him. He was in the difficult situation of any man with two children and he tried to choose both a good wife and a good mother, and he was sensitively discriminating in the process.

Becky surely deserves comment. One of the fortunate aspects of the increasing liberation of women is that Becky found the man she wanted and could go after him. The fact that he was black seems to have made no difference to her. But it takes only a little imagination to guess the courage it took on her part, facing the opposition of society, of her family and his, to pursue a potential husband of a different color.

Some men would have resented being pursued. But Hal did not, and Becky knew not only what she wanted, but also what Hal needed. He was fortunate in finding a woman who wished to be his mother, which he desperately needed, and wanted also to be his wife, a companion not only in his activities but in his dreams. She is a giving person, not a demanding one, and this is priceless for each member of the family.

But Hal has learned enormously since the time of his first marriage. Most important, he has learned to communicate. In this respect the change seems incredible. He and Becky talk things out, including such touchy subjects as her quick jealousy of black women who appear to be getting too close to her husband. They have worked out, at least for the present, their possible educational and professional competitiveness. They took a month-long camper trip, in which all four came really to know each other and close communication was a part of each day's living.

As I listen to the interview and read its transcript, it is, in fact, difficult for me to believe that the Hal of the first marriage is the same person as the Hal of the second marriage. Certainly part of this change must be credited to Becky, who is much more outgoing and communicative than the first wife. But Hal's experience with various kinds of intensive group experiences demonstrates conclusively that a person can change, can learn to communicate his feelings and can listen—really listen perceptively—to the feelings of his spouse.

An aspect of marriage which we have not encountered before in this book is the change in Hal's method of working for success in marriage. In his first union he hoped that a successful relationship would come through his *doing* things—the housework, the washing, his business ventures, his achievements in school. If he worked hard enough on doing all these things, surely his marriage would improve, and he worked himself to exhaustion in this attempt.

In his present marriage he is devoting himself first of all to improving the process of their relationship by sharing—his feelings, the relevant information about his community, his ambitions —and it easily becomes a two-way sharing. Doing things is secondary, grows out of the relationship, and is composed of *joint* efforts. They improve their home, they save money, they encourage each other toward professional achievements, they establish their free clinic and work together in it. Actually, as I know from other sources, what they are accomplishing is outstanding in meeting all kinds of psychological needs in the community through their clinic.

Somehow for me two of the most impressive signs of the healthy process of their family relationship are these: Hal's open recognition of his jealousy of his sons as all three of them compete for Becky's love, and his insightful, maturing, cooperative handling of this problem; most striking of all is the end of serious asthma in the oldest boy, which can only indicate that he has found a family climate in which he can relax in a caring relationship.

I am impressed that this is first of all a partnership between two *persons* and only secondarily an interracial marriage. Yet this latter is not to be minimized. They are surrounded by stares, by shocked looks, by the silence and avoidance of white women which spells hostility, by the jealousy of black women, by vulgar remarks at sports events. Hal's deep suspicion of whites is natural and is clearly present. Without any doubt Hal and Becky are "freaks" to the people with whom they mingle, both black and white, educated and uneducated, in professional situations and at church suppers, to his black family and her white relatives. Yet they go forward, which is possible only because their relationship is presently a source of great security to each.

Hal sums it up well that any marriage is a rough and difficult thing, and interracial marriage simply includes a fresh crop of difficulties and problems. I certainly would not venture a prediction, but I admire the way in which thus far they are facing the problems not only between themselves, but between them and their various subcultures. Particularly I admire the fact that he is not trying to make Becky black, nor is she trying to make him white. If they can continue this understanding and acceptance of their very real differences, as well as of their unusually complementary strengths, then the prognosis is indeed favorable.

7 ⊘ Communes as Experiments in Human and Sexual Relationships

ONE CANNOT WRITE a book on modern marriage without discussing communes, which often provide alternatives to conventional marriage. Yet I approach this chapter with an uneasiness based on several facts and feelings.

1. The two-to-three thousand communes and intentional communities in this country—the number is only a combination of estimates—keep growing, changing, closing, and starting, with a rapidity which immediately outdates anything which can be written.

2. The variety of communes is so enormous that any general statement one might make is simultaneously true, for some, and false, for others.

3. A number of excellent books have recently been written about communes, and it seems presumptuous to write only a brief chapter about these diversified groups.

4. Most important is the fact that I have not lived in a commune and hence lack the basic inner experience which I can bring to writing some of the other chapters. To offset this, I have been helped by two people, Natalie R. Fuchs and Robert J. Willis, who served as eyes and ears for me.

THE HUMAN RELATIONSHIPS AS FOCUS

Naturally I will make no attempt to cover all aspects of these communal groups. There is the economic problem—how to survive. There is the ideological flavor—mystical, behavioristic, wilderness pioneering, an emphasis on women's lib, the search for a higher consciousness, for nonviolent revolution. There are various degrees of organizational philosophy, from wildly hippie to philosophical anarchism to quite strictly ordered. There are a variety of problems in relating to the neighboring community, whether the group lives in an isolated forest or in the heart of a large city. None of these will I touch on, though the references in the bibliography will help those who wish to explore further.

My interest will be, in keeping with the purpose of this book, to explore the ways of coping with marital, sexual, and other interpersonal relationships in the communal groups. I shall do this in a way which I believe is not identifying of any particular person or commune. Most of it I can do on the basis of taped interviews or from observations by persons whom I know or trust or from letters and reports written by participants.

SOME GENERAL REMARKS ABOUT COMMUNES

Before I begin this undertaking, I should like to clear away certain misapprehensions which may exist in the mind of the reader.

In the first place, communes are not gathering places for "hippies," as that term in understood by the public. They *are* an attempt to live with a set of values different from that which exists in the ordinary community, and frequently this is apparent in their unique and different clothing. But the people quoted in this chapter come from groups made up of people like these: a former industrial engineer, a social worker, a corporation executive, a research scientist, a clinical psychologist, a former computer programmer, a divinity student, a former CIA agent, a person skilled in data processing, a carpenter, an artist, assorted graduates of Radcliffe, Swarthmore, Harvard, and other colleges. Here is a fraction of our intelligentsia, trying to create a revolutionary new world in the midst of the "Establishment" world. They are to be viewed in this light.

A second comment is that most present-day communes—not all—lean toward some degree of an anarchistic philosophy. Since to most people this is synonymous with chaos, lawlessness, and terrorism, a word might be said as to its real philosophical meaning. It rests on a base of self-determination. It involves the rejection of all forms of coercive control and authority, whether governmental or religious. Bertrand Russell caught its spirit when he said of another, "He was inclined to anarchism; he hated system and organization and uniformity." Many commune members would subscribe to this.

In many ways they are, in their philosophy, not unlike the early Christians as described in Acts 2:44–46: "And all that believed were together, and had all things in common; and sold their possessions and goods and parted them to all men, as every man had need . . . and did eat their meat with gladness and singleness of heart." Not all communes give up property to this extent, but many of them go a long way in communal sharing, as one other indication of the fact that they have turned their backs very definitely on the materialistic, competitive culture in which they were raised.

Perhaps the best brief definition comes from the *Merriam-Webster New International Dictionary* (an older edition): "In its more practical forms anarchism . . . [has] for its ideal the formation of small autonomous communes, the members of which respect one another's independence while they unite to resist aggression. At its best it stands for a society made orderly by good manners rather than by law, in which each person produces according to his powers and receives according to his needs." I believe many commune members today would subscribe to this as a goal, while admitting they often fall far short.

In this respect they are very different from the Utopian communes of the last century in this country, in which there was usually a unifying religious ideology, a strong and charismatic leader, and a group of followers whose lives were regulated. In an interesting study of these older communes (Kantor, 1970) it was found that certain items separated sharply the more permanent from the less permanent. (Obviously permanence is not the only criterion by which they might have been judged.)

The outstanding difference between the more and less permanent was that the first practiced either free love or celibacy, while the less permanent did not. In other words, in the lasting communes sexual behavior was clearly decided either by the members or for them. Ranking after these as characteristic of the more permanent were no compensation for communal labor, communal work efforts on a daily routine, daily group meetings, and celebration of special community occasions. It may be of interest to bear these in mind as we examine today's communes.

NINE BRIEF EXAMPLES

I should like now to plunge you into some of the variety which exists. Let me try to give some feeling for the great diversity of groups which are classed as communes by describing a number of them in one brief paragraph each. I have purposely omitted the names of the groups, so that instead of immediately categorizing them, you will be more inclined to imagine what it would be like to live in such a group. All of them are real communes which exist or have existed until very recently.

1. There is a rural commune of eleven adults and six children which functions pretty much as a family. The work gets done, purposes get implemented without any particular organization, just as in the average family. It is not self-supporting and some of the members work for short periods in the city to help balance the budget. Food stamps are also used. No one is in authority. The children are cared for unevenly, but have the advantages of an extended family. The adults are mostly paired, but sexual relation-

ships outside a pair are not prohibited. Interpersonal difficulties are worked out (usually) by very frank interchanges in the group or between the parties involved.

2. One commune "family" is composed of about a dozen professional men and women (and one child) living in a house in the city. They are remodeling the house to give every person more privacy. They all—with the exception of the man who is remodeling the house—hold jobs in the city. They share the communal work. The couples are paired, but there is experimenting outside the pairs, with the knowledge of the group. Encounter group procedures are often used in the handling of interpersonal tensions. Nearly all have had some experience in such groups. The neighbors, at first suspicious, have become much more accepting.

3. A semirural commune was open to anyone who wished to come or stay. Individuals could do whatever they wished in the way of work, or nothing. Drugs were heavily used. The living and sanitary conditions became impossible, and it was eventually closed as a public health menace. The community was enraged by it.

4. There is a coed house near a college, its dozen or more inhabitants mostly students, which has lasted eight years. It has been agreed that all members find their sexual companions outside the house. All work is shared, cooking, etc., regardless of sex. The relationships are similar to brother-sister ties. The aim is to learn to live with one another as human beings. Because these are students, there is considerable turnover, but a great loyalty develops. Meetings are held to deal with tensions which arise. They make much of occasional celebrations or house "rituals," which seem to promote closeness.

5. An urban group is one of those trying the experiment of group marriage, with three men and three women involved. The house is efficiently run. Some work in the city. All come from educated, mostly WASP backgrounds. The group sexuality brought problems, and they finally developed a chart, which shows which man and woman sleep together each night. (The sleeping does not always involve sex.) There is one night per week "free." For some

reason the interpersonal interactions, though intended to have an encounter flavor, are often biting and cynical and are aimed at the other person's weak spots. It is far from being a harmonious "marriage."

6. A large group of related communes, with a history going back more than four hundred years, are all farming communities ranging from fifty to a hundred and thirty members in each. Monogamy is the definite rule. Pacifism has been deep-seated as a policy over the centuries. Religion is a unifying force. Higher education is scorned. There are two leaders in each commune, the preacher and the work boss. Both are elected. I am sure they would be shocked to be included in this list, but they are definitely communal, eating all meals together and sharing all goods in common. They have separate homes or apartments. They have a deep-seated belief in their permanence, strengthened by the fact that they have endured, though expelled from one country after another (including for a time the U.S.) because of the refusal to serve in the armed forces.

7. Another is a clean, orderly, highly organized commune, numbering thirty men and women (only two children), in which everyone must earn a certain number of work credits per day. In order to get *all* the work done, more credit is given for the jobs which people tend to avoid. Some members are also employed outside for two-month periods but they tend to dislike this. Their aim is to build a viable alternative to capitalism (an aim which they take very seriously) and to alter their personal behavior in ways they desire. At first, three planners made all the significant decisions, but gradually the group is moving toward operating by consensus. It started with a small number of individuals (ten) with conventional marital standards. Now nearly every member has a roommate of the opposite sex. An important concern of the group is sexual freedom. Good order is the hallmark of this commune.

8. A sizable number of communes, mostly urban, scattered throughout the country, are bound together by three strong threads: a highly charismatic leader; frequent ideologically based group sessions whose purpose is to attack each person's defenses; and the fact that they have all been drug addicts. The organization

is definitely hierarchical and rules are strict. Members are promoted to more responsible posts when they have, in the view of the group and the officials, earned them.

9. A rural commune, limited to twenty-five, is bound together by a combination of Eastern mystical beliefs. Unlike most communes, they focus on the individual rather than the group. There is a great deal of silent meditation and contemplation, though each week there is an ecstatic ritual dance. Work is shared, each member signing up for six "chores." Individuals are a bit remote from each other and any problems are worked out individually. Some members are married, some not. They draw on a number of gurus, but depend on no one guru. Each summer they import a number of these leaders, to absorb their teachings in two-week sessions.[1]

INTERPERSONAL PROBLEMS

Naturally, no group of human beings live together without all kinds of differences, frictions, jealousies, angers, and all the emotional disturbances which can upset the sharing of lives. And when the group is composed of men *and* women, all of these may be magnified. It may be useful to see how these have been handled in specific instances, recognizing that they are just that—specific instances, from which one generalizes with caution. I will begin with some issues which involve simply people, without any special focus on sex.

One of the problems faced by many communes is the problem of membership, of numbers. Can anyone come—and stay? Is membership a limited thing? If so, on what basis? Robert Houriet (Book IV) describes vividly how one commune met this problem.

[1]For those who must know the sources of these descriptions, here they are: (1) High Ridge Farm, described by Houriet in Book II; (2) an East Coast commune, visited and information supplied by Natalie Fuchs; (3) Morningstar, now defunct, described in Gustaitis, Chapter 8; (4) in the Northwest, visited and information supplied by Robert J. Willis; (5) Harrad West, from Houriet, Book VI; (6) the Hutterites, described by Allard; (7) Twin Oaks, modeled after Skinner's *Walden II*, from Houriet, Book VII; (8) Synanon, perhaps best described by Yablonsky; (9) Lama, from Houriet, Book VIII.

It was a farming commune, wresting a meager living from the soil. But more and more visitors came. They stayed. Some caused problems in the commune, some with the neighbors. But nearly all members had come initially as visitors, so there was no group of "old-timers" to settle the issue. Little by little the meager resources were being drained as the group grew to fifty, until complete failure seemed to be the only possible outcome. Yet there was one faction whose philosophical views dictated that everyone who wished to come should be accepted and should be able to stay.

The matter was settled in a dramatic fashion. A big strapping man, Big David, called a meeting—a permissible procedure. Many people, visitors and those of longer vintage, had to be practically pulled from their rooms to attend. When the meeting opened, the big man spoke:

Look, I'm a desperate man. There's a problem here. Too many people. Now this place can handle about twenty-five. Few of us did anything to build this place. People like myself who came last fall and helped with the harvest—we don't want to kick anybody out. That's the scene we left. You're all brothers and sisters. But all of us *can't* live here. And you have as much right here as me. But there's not enough food, not enough space on the floor. So how do we decide? I've been on the run all my life. I've never had a home. I've lived on street corners, in a different pad every night. This is the first place I've wanted to call home. And now I see it being destroyed. My old lady and I have been out on the highway, and we know what it's like. We're going to have a kid, and I don't want to have to leave. But unless some of you people split, you're going to force us to go back on that highway. That's why I am a desperate man. (Houriet, pp. 159–160.)

After much argument and discussion, pro and con, with many arguing for cutting the number, Big David spoke again: *"Who's going to leave?"* Slowly, to everyone's surprise, about twenty people stood up, leaving about twenty seated. Within two days thirty had departed, including the philosophically minded anarchist who had wanted to accept everyone. Big David put up a sign at the gate saying, "No visitors, unless on business." In its unique way the commune had settled the issue and was again a self-supporting group, through modifying its philosophy.

In another commune a problem arose which involved the relationship with the neighboring community. Peter was concerned about the issue, but he put his concerns abstractly, using phrases like these.

PETER: "It might be wise to contact a spokesman of the straight community"; and he dropped phrases like "anticipating their objections," "appointing a committee that would embrace a spectrum of society," etc. . . . His choice of words angered both Claudia and Elaine.

Claudia screamed, "It's not what you say, it's *how* you say it that makes me so mad."

Then Elaine took over. It was as if she were peeling an onion. "All the time I've known you I've had the notion you were trying to keep things from us . . . as if we were children and you were trying to spare us the pain of knowing all the cares that weighed on your shoulders. . . . It's a kind of insidious paternalism, and you're the leader. You had the foresight to press on and buy the land when everyone else was holding back. But now you try to influence us just by the tone of your voice. . . ." Elaine halted. Silence.

"Go on," said Peter.

CLAUDIA: "Why don't you come out and tell us how you feel instead of using all this formal shit. I've very, very rarely seen you express the real *you*. The other night with the record player was one time. You were passionate, angry, frustrated, but it was you."

PETER: (*meekly*): "This has been a very helpful conversation."

CLAUDIA: "Fuck! There you go again. By the very *tone* of the words I can tell it hasn't sunk in."

BILL (*who has been reading a how-to book on raising earthworms*): "What are you all talking about?"

PETER (*angry at last*): "Why don't *you* get your head out of the sand? Why don't you ever say anything?"

CLAUDIA *and* **ELAINE:** "That's more like it."

ELAINE (*to* **PETER**): "For as long as I've know you, I've thought you were always judging yourself and others. Every time we make music together (she plays the guitar, he the recorder) I can feel you criticizing. . . . It destroys it for me. It makes me feel very unhappy. Why don't you throw away the report cards you're always keeping? Take a vacation from school and teacher's dirty looks? Once I came into the kitchen when you and Claudia were talking, I don't remember when or about what, but I remember the tone . . . it was like hearing an interview between a social worker and his client. . . ."

PETER: "Well . . . thank you." He tried to say more, but Elaine hushed him with a kiss, and Claudia hugged him. (Houriet, pp. 65–66.)

This is an excellent example of the kind of feedback and forthright expression of real feeling which, for many communes, as well as other groups, appears to constitute the best means of bringing out into the open and resolving simmering negative interpersonal reactions. It might of course have been a dialogue taken from an encounter group, except that this is not an artificially organized session and its members will continue to be together day after day. When the feelings really *have* been expressed, as they seem to have been here, the result is the transmutation of negative to equally real positive feelings, as symbolized by Elaine's kiss and Claudia's hug.

Not all interpersonal problems involve the whole commune. Many are simply the frictions which always occur when people live closely together. Perhaps a very minor example from another commune, taken from a taped interview, will illustrate what I mean.

SALLY: When I lived in my own apartment, I liked to play my record player *loud* if I was housecleaning or something. And I'm one of the people who will play it *very* loud when I am working on art stuff. And in the next room is Ned. His bedroom is next to my workroom and he is a writer, so he wants it quiet. So when I play it loud and he wants me to turn it down, that's a violation of my privacy because I like it loud. That's a hard thing. You know, it depends on where people's heads are at, because he and I can work it out just fine, but not by making a rule that we will have the record player on only at certain times, but just by saying, "Boy, it's really important to me today to have it loud." And I'm important to him so he gets behind that, *or* vice versa, you know.

Here they simply adjust to each other's moods, not by rules or principles, nor in response to authority, but in a highly existential consideration of each other's needs at this moment.

Not all such problems are so easily worked out. Here is Sally again:

INTERVIEWER: How do you solve things like jealousies?
SALLY: There's different kinds of jealousies. There's jealousy about, like I'm a pretty central person here in the house. While I am not taking on so much of a leadership role, just by who I *am* I have a very central relationship here in the house. I probably have more close relationships with more people here—not because I am better at it than anybody else but because that's more important to me than to some other people. Some of us spend more time on that or working things out, or talking to people or *enjoying* people. That's like a number-one activity for me. I really enjoy that almost more than anything else. And I know that people feel jealous or resentful that I have that centrality. And that's hard, very hard for me because I feel I don't need to change. But this has always been an issue in my life; I just don't feel good if there is anybody around who is at all jealous of me. And then I turn around and degrade myself and point out all my mistakes, which doesn't do any good at all . . . just fucks it up even worse, you know. And this thing of having been a group leader. When someone has a problem here, more than likely they come to see me about it. And I know a couple of other people say, "Why is it *you* that people come to? Why do they always go to Sally? I would like to be used too." That's a very uncomfortable issue for me.

It is clear that this is an unresolved problem which neither she nor the others has as yet brought into the open or worked out among them. It is to be hoped that it will someday be the subject of an encounter which might resolve some of the feelings.

Even in the coed house (No. 4 in the initial nine examples), interpersonal frictions naturally arise. They have endeavored to solve the sexual problems by ruling that each member find sex companionship outside the house. Yet all the other problems exist and the main complaint is that they don't get together enough to talk about things that are meaningful. Deep communication seems to be avoided, and there appears to be a certain superficiality about their intimacy. The group members are very loyal to each other, however, and members make statements such as "Good vibrations around the dinner table"; "I've been able to trust and know people"; "It's a help in standing up for myself relative to the world." One woman member adds, "I use my sex as a complement to the guys in a sensible way."

It is interesting to note that, like some of the last-century communes, they have coped with the sexual problem by making a rule which keeps it out of the commune as a difficult subject. Perhaps because of this, one has the impression that it is more of a "happy family" no doubt than the "straight" community, but perhaps lacking in deep intimacy, confrontation, or communication.

RELATIONSHIPS INVOLVING SEXUAL PARTNERS

Because many communes are departing most sharply from societal norms in the area of sexual relationships, it is not surprising that some of the most troubling problems arise in regard to partnerships, triads, and other arrangements, whether temporary or more lasting.

It would be possible to give many examples of different individuals with different sexual and partnership problems. Yet so much is contained in an interview with Lois, a member of a city communal group, that I believe it may be more profitable to see many facets of these issues through her eyes, as she has *experienced* them in her own relationships. It is interesting that in spite of all her experiences, she thinks of herself as quite "straight." For the next several pages I will let Lois speak for herself, with no interruption except subheadings to indicate the topics to which she addresses herself.

Lois is about thirty years old, professionally trained, from a middle-class background. She has been married and divorced and has one young son. She has been in encounter groups and has led them. She was part of a summer community group which was something of a preparation for her life in the commune. After her divorce she was threatened by deep commitments, and though she felt very close to Boris, a man who was much involved with her, she did not want to commit herself. But she and Boris entered the commune together, where they have lived for a year with approximately fifteen people. The interviewer raised the question as to whether jealousy was ever a problem, and Lois's initial denial led to a deep exploration of the many aspects of man-woman and other relationships in the commune.

JEALOUSY OF PARTNER'S "AFFAIRS"

LOIS: Male-female jealousy? I don't think that is much of an issue here. I am trying to think . . . I certainly feel jealous when Boris makes love with somebody else. I am really perverse in this sense, in that I would rather know about it and I would rather know *all* about it, including the details, and somehow that makes me feel better, if only in the end I am reassured that he loves me more and he would rather make love to me. But if I know about it, I am more reassured; it's funny though, he's just the opposite. But such things are pretty open here.

INTERVIEWER: Is that part of the group norm that it's open if there's any change in male-female relationships within the house?

LOIS: Well, just let me say, we are definitely middle class. We're not like hippie freaks at all. We're much closer to the monogamous and cheating couples in the suburbs. For example, about a month or two ago Boris and I decided we had been monogamous for a long period of time, but it was becoming sort of destructive and we were taking advantage of each other and feeling obligated to each other, and it wasn't feeling good, and we decided we were going to end, at least for a while, the monogamy of our relationship. And we talked about it in our house meeting. Particularly since he really felt like going out and balling some chicks. Picking them up and balling them, and that was his thing, but that's just not my thing at all. I'd rather make love to somebody that I am close to, so that likelihood was much more for me in the house, you know. So we talked about it in the house meeting, and the main question that came up was, "Well, you know, are you going to be mad?" If Enrico said, "Well, I'm going to make love with Lois, and, you know, you better have those feelings about me." Well, it wasn't like the minute that the door was opened everybody just rushed around, you know, and reshuffled themselves.

THE HURT INVOLVED IN SHIFTING PARTNERS

We're pretty straight. There is a norm that you can sleep with anyone you want to here in the house. In fact, I can't think of anybody who at least intellectually speaking doesn't agree with that, but what makes me laugh so is that people think there won't be any problems about it. That you can take on a norm like that intellectually and say, "Oh fine, this is just what we happen to do." There is a problem every time. Someone feels hurt or someone feels threatened or someone feels less important. But I have never once felt it has produced a bummer, you know, or it has set people far, far apart.

INTERVIEWER: Somehow you have managed to work most of that out . . .?

LOIS: Yeah. It also isn't all that frequent. Most people here, when they're in a relationship, they're in that relationship, or they are being single and they are making it with everybody or anybody, you know. It's not like after dinner—you know, I think people sometimes fantasize that after dinner everyone looks around the table and says, "Well, I guess I'll sleep with so-and-so tonight," and just trundle up to bed. It isn't like that.

THE POSSIBILITY OF AN ORGY

We've always talked about having an orgy, you know, just a big group thing, but we've never done it yet. I'm sure we probably will. We've had things that verge on it, but we've never had just a big group with everybody screwing everybody else but we probably will, because there's enough in everybody's head and I think it would be fun, you know. Especially being a girl. I think that would really be nifty—all night long, you know (*chuckling heartily*).

LOVE BETWEEN FEMALES—AND JEALOUSY

Well, I'll tell you one thing that's different, and this has to do with the only time I have really felt jealous, since living here in the house, and that's intimacy. That's a thing. You know, you become closer and closer to people and it's more and more natural to make love with them to express it physically and I've felt that with women here in the house and particularly one woman—I'm very close to her—and a couple of times have made love with her and another guy—once because I was a little drunk and another time because I really wanted to do that with Boris—I mean he didn't have any idea this was coming. We just sort of decided to go to bed together and we went and got into Boris's bed. That's been probably the newest and most exciting sexual experience I've had here, in really feeling very much like wanting to express myself physically to another woman. It's just amazing, you know, just the experience of rubbing another body like your own. It's not a heavy thing, but it freaks me a little bit.

That one night I discovered an awful lot about it. I could tell Jan really wanted to sleep with me. I literally locked myself in the bathroom. I just couldn't decide, you know, whether or not that felt *safe* to me. And I took on this very passive role, which I don't like to think of myself as doing. It was really interesting—it turned out to be just like a male-female relationship, you know. Then at other times I've been more aggressive and she's been more passive. It's really sort of an interesting experience and then you get into jealousy. Like one time I thought maybe she had made love with another girl and I really felt bad. And then it turned out she hadn't, but it was a funny feeling to have.

JEALOUSY OF CLOSENESS

The other thing is Boris. He has some interesting feelings about that, like *really* being turned on by it and enjoying it. It's sort of like being a masturbatory fantasy thing with him, feeling not jealous of the sexuality between Jan and me but the *closeness*, and his feelings are resentful of that. Jealousy has been a hard thing in that way too because he's felt a lot of times jealousies of my relationships with someone else. He's sort of possessive, and he's gotten jealous of the closeness of other people too, when I like to spend time with them, instead of just spending all my time with him. But we've worked that through pretty well. I *think* pretty well.

WAYS OF DEALING WITH SUCH PROBLEMS

INTERVIEWER: You've worked that through mostly by yourselves, or in the group . . .?

LOIS: Well, I like it better to work it through ourselves. I don't really have any belief at all that anybody in this house understands my relationship with Boris. I really don't, you know. I have this feeling people don't know him very well, and that he is the kind of person that is there on a one-to-one level because he is so sort of involved with me. He has sort of focused all his attention and energy on me and he hasn't gotten to know other people that closely. Therefore people haven't gotten to know him that well either.

I think people misjudge our relationship a lot. We fight a lot and we hit each other and we scream and then we make up, you know. That feels really good to me, but there isn't anything else like that going on around here. That sort of gets it out for me, and then I feel good and loving. But I think it really sort of frightens other people. They don't understand that and don't know what's happening in our relationship. I think we're better off working on it by ourselves or by getting another couple, or a few other people who are close to us, to come and work it out with us.

I don't have a sense that the group is in fact very helpful to us as a couple. I have more of a sense that it is destructive to us as a couple and that there are even some people here who feel that it might even be better if everybody wasn't a couple. They do as much to put in misinformation between us as helpfulness. I really think that's true, sad as it may sound. Especially it has been true I think when for a while other people felt possessive of me. At least two or three other people would have as soon had us split up, 'cause they resented Boris coming up to me and saying, "Lois, come on, I want to be with you now," and me getting up and going, and they'd make trouble. Like Robin would tell me something Boris said to Tommy, my son. Then I'd get mad and then of course I'm mad at Boris, and sometimes she has been absolutely right, and that's exactly what happened, but it was a funny thing to do.

THE LIBERATED WOMAN

INTERVIEWER: There are . . . what . . . three couples in the house?

LOIS: There's one married couple, Robin and Ben. They have changed an awful lot since moving into the house. They were monogamous completely for seven years, since they have been married, and when I first met them three years ago, Ben wanted to get it together with some other girls and Robin was *terribly* threatened by that and terribly upset. When I first met her, she was afraid Ben would get turned on by me and she just didn't like me in the least and just thought I was awful—and I wasn't in fact at all interested in Ben. But that's a sample of how completely freaked out she was by it.

Then last summer he did have an affair and she was *really* upset and I spent time with her that day. It's funny. I wasn't threatened by that situation. I mean someone had to do it for me, when Boris turned around and made love with someone else. I spent the day with her, sort of saying, what did she really want? Like she had an empty space and she could paint a beautiful picture in it, or else she could just get so focused on this, you know, act resentfully and sort of dejectedly, and not have what she wanted in the first place. And as a result of that their marriage has really opened up, maybe even more than any couple in the house. Robin has more affairs and more dates and more going out and doesn't spend too much time here in the house. She does more of that than anyone else in the house, including the single men. And I'm not sure what I think about that, I guess it's not the kind of relationship I'd want—I *know* it's not the kind of relationship I want. But it seems to be making her really happy right now, to be doing that. I guess part of my resentment about it is that she's not around enough because she's always out on some date. But I also worry, like, that maybe Ben is lonely.

I also worry deeply that it's not *really* what Robin wants to be doing. You know, maybe she feels that she *should*, because that's the new social code. I'm not really convinced at all. She talks a lot about wanting to have a baby. They're two very different things. One is running around all the time and the other is tied up to a baby. They're *very* different things.

MY REACTIONS

There are a number of things which strike me about Lois's account. There is, for instance, the complete intellectual commitment to open sexual experimentation, though this is not, in many instances, backed by an equal experiential commitment. Boris and Lois, Ben and Robin can choose to try other than a monogamous life for a time. The single members can try out various relationships on a temporary or more lasting basis. Lois and Jan can experience a homosexual relationship with no feeling of guilt. Lois is even gleeful about the possibility of a sexual orgy in the house. In short, one of the elemental facts about many communes is that they are experimental laboratories where—without guilt, without public knowledge outside of the group, without a commitment to any one mode of behavior—a variety of sexual unions can be tried. What is, for many people, a fantasied variety of sexual experiences is here brought alive in reality.[2]

But all of this experimentation is not without cost. The senses of loss, of hurt, of jealousy, of self-pity, of anger, of desire for

[2]It is of interest that, as far as I am aware, relationships between man and man are much less common in communes than between woman and woman. I was unable to obtain a satisfactory *inner* account of such a union, though I know that they occasionally exist as part of the experimentation in communes. Somehow male homosexuality seems more threatening to many persons than female homosexual contact.

retaliation are experienced time and time again by those involved in the experimentation. No matter how "modern" the person's point of view, or his or her intellectual commitment, someone is hurt in one way or another, as Lois makes clear, every time partnerships shift. And jealousy does not necessarily relate simply to sexual behavior, but to such things as a loss of closeness, such as Boris feels about the relationship between Lois and Jan, even though he also finds it exciting.

But the laboratory has its curative elements too, to assuage these hurts. Lois helps Robin in her jealousy and pain, just as someone helped Lois previously in a similar situation. And the impression, from her account and from other experiences, is that very frequently these hurts are also moments of potential growth. It is impressive that Lois believes the experimentation has never once "produced a bummer" or "set people far, far apart." Undoubtedly this is too sweeping a statement, but the fact that a person experiences unpleasant hurts is certainly not synonymous with saying he or she has been permanently damaged.

Another element which needs pointing up is that the group has both its constructive and destructive possibilities. This was mentioned in the brief earlier account of the acrimonious group marriage. Lois makes it more specific by stressing the group's lack of understanding of her stormy but vital relationship with Boris. And, as in any group, there are those who are quite capable of causing trouble through inputs of inappropriate information, whether accurate or inaccurate.

Here, as in so many situations, we have the knowledge which would improve such situations, but we fail to utilize it adequately. A facilitative person, if he is at the right place at the right time, can help to resolve hurts and jealousies and backbiting. But we are far from such a millennium.

One note which strikes me in Lois's account is the vital necessity of knowing, accepting, and trusting one's feelings. Is Robin really blissfully happy in her carefree sexual life? Lois questions this and so do I. Her behavior sounds too much like retaliation, which in turn is a cover for her hurt. Here again she almost certainly needs facilitative help in discovering, beneath whatever defenses she may have, her true feelings. Then she can act as a unified and real person. Whether she will wish for or find such assistance is an open question.

Another element which seems clear from Lois's statement and from much other knowledge, is that most people have a continuing need for a secure relationship. When Lois points out that experimentation "isn't all that frequent," and that most people when they are in a relationship value that relationship, she is expressing something which is, I believe, very widely and profoundly true.

ANOTHER EXAMPLE OF EXPERIMENTAL RELATIONSHIPS

Sam is thirty-eight, divorced, and now married to Rita. There are two sets of children. They moved from a suburb into an urban commune because, as Rita says:

I was very isolated. When Sam went off to work, unless I had a particular thing to do or to go to, I just felt very isolated, in a house very separate, you know, from the people across the street or the neighbors. And here people are going in and out—it's just a world by itself.

Later Rita describes the man-woman relationships:

We don't feel that we have to have sexual relationships with every member in the house. The fact that we are nonmonogamous is the fact that we are open to other relationships with other people, but if there were people in the house who felt very strongly that they *were* monogamous and that is something they really believed in—they could probably make it work. . . .

SAM: . . .This woman the other night expressed it in this way. She said, "Well, I don't have the idea of coming into a commune with the expectation of having sex in the house, but if something developed that might be nice. And I wouldn't want to encourage her nor discourage her. . . .

Rita and Doug, another house member, are involved in a sexual relationship, and this has not been easy for Sam. One senses tension in Rita's relationship to him.

INTERVIEWER: How do you handle the jealousies and the feelings? Or have you managed to relieve yourselves of these feelings . . .?

SAM: No. We are still handling them. At a meeting one night the chairwoman said, "If anybody has had nonmonogamous relationships and has worked them out, will you please tell us." So Doug, who lives in the house, said, "Has anybody worked out their whole life?" So, we're still working it out. And from my point of view in terms of Rita, Doug, and myself, one of the things that makes it easier for me is that Doug tries to be a friend to me as well as to Rita and we do consider each other friends. And his relationship with Rita—it isn't meant to cut me down or push me aside or to make me feel bad, but it is just another thing that has a validity all of its own. I have to keep telling myself that, especially, you know, during the time when they might be having an upswing in their relationship and I'm more or less alone.

INTERVIEWER: That sounds like it could be very hard to handle . . .

SAM: Yeah, and when you've had years and years of conditioning . . . a sort of romantic complex, you learn you don't play around or whatever. But the other side of the coin is that I've never met anybody who didn't spend at least some energy in having fantasies of a relationship with someone other than his or her spouse. So I think what we save is a lot of energy from playing the fantasy game and in our actual relationships working it out, and also it's pretty open, which I think is a *far* healthier thing. Better than sneaking off and pretending we are not having a relationship when we are having one. In some ways I think it made my relationship with Rita probably better than it was . . . I can see my relationship better than it used to be at any point. Better now. Then I think that the fact that she developed this outside relationship has helped. I think it has helped her to feel more worthy as a person, and curiously, it has helped *me* to think of her and to feel about her as being more worthy.

INTERVIEWER: Is what he said true?

RITA: It's not the way I think of it.

Rita doesn't explain this contradiction between them, but goes on to talk about some aspects of sharing, which leads Sam into that topic.

SAM: Yeah. I don't like to go for walks very much. But Rita likes to walk and Doug likes to walk, so some people like to go for walks. That's fine. So, some people who like to walk probably need some walking. So, people who like to sit can sit.

INTERVIEWER: It doesn't put the pressure on to be everything to one person. . . .

RITA: Yeah.

SAM: Yeah. I have a relationship with another woman that doesn't live in the commune and it's not a terribly good relationship and it's a person who I don't think I selected as carefully as I might, but I went into it at a time when I was feeling half lonely after this relationship between Rita and Doug started. But it's fairly good. I guess I'm envious that I didn't start a relationship with someone else living in the same house. Because it's very hard for me to sustain this relationship with this person that is just more than an occasional sexual encounter. If I really spent a lot of time with her, well, I feel that whether Rita is explicit about it or not, she knows the answer. And you see, it's easy to spend time with someone you care about who lives in the same house without making a big deal about it.

At a later point Sam adds, speaking of relations outside the partnership, "You can run a risk when you do this sort of thing. But you run a risk when you get married."

If there is any comment to be made about Rita and Doug, Sam and his outside girlfriend, it is simply that there is always a price to be paid for experimentation in the forming of sexual relationships outside a partnership. But as Sam wisely points out, there is risk in marriage too. And the outside relationship does free each spouse from trying to be everything, to meet *every* need, of the other.

A TRIAD IN FORMATION

Here is an account of a groping threesome, Clyde, Libby, and Myra, which ends with a temporary sexual triad. It is told with great frankness by Clyde in a confidential letter. I am grateful for his permission to use portions.

The initial circumstances were unusual in that his commune had invited a second group to come as visitors for a week. From this point on excerpts from his letter tell the story.

... Here is my now-family: George—artist, farmer, metaphysician; Libby—George's legal wife, the woman whose bed I share, weaver, gardener, mother; Minna—George's bedmate, also weaver, gardener, and especially breadmaker; Gregory—my 10 year old son, a boy who loves to touch and be touched by other people; Ruthy—George and Libby's 9 year old, a beautiful being to live with and one of the strongest reasons I know to be where I am. And now enters Myra, very open to new experiences, warm and "touchy," bi-sexual or perhaps better described as all-sexual.

We are living in the country. Snow is thick. Ruthy floundered, leapt, and tunnelled to reach the mailbox. Except for a couple of incidents, everyone was constantly buoyed up by the group—the feeling of being supported was hard to resist—and individuals, including our many visitors, found themselves accepted as some of them never had been in their lives. Libby and Minna performed miracles in feeding 21 people lunch and dinner that week and the food was stupendo!

Myra and I were immediately attracted to one another, having something of that "prior understanding" that always seems to exist when I meet someone with whom I might have a deep, meaningful relationship. And too, there was something dark in her which called to my darkness, i.e., the still-present desire to possess and be possessed.

He tells how he and several others took a walk, and "by accident" he and Myra were left alone. They made love, albeit not too satisfactorily.

. . . When we walked back I found Libby in the road crying. I was overwhelmed with remorse and guilt. I had to tell her, then and there, what had happened. It was a hard, hard, time, made harder by the fluidity and *strength* of all the feelings that were flying around that week. She had been feeling very low, the result of being overworked and not participating in any of the group activities, plus the two of us not taking time enough to be together. Now, as she said, this was the icing on her cake and *she didn't need it!* We went to bed, talked a while, then fell asleep—mainly from exhaustion, I think!

Myra and the others left, but later Myra returned for a visit of several days.

. . . About two days before Myra arrived, Libby went into isolation. It was a separation from me and us, in all but a physical sense. She felt jealousy, possessiveness, distrust of Myra and hated herself for being in a state of unlove. . . . But this was a time of more than usual clarity for me, and I was able to stay with her, a fact she recognized, even in moments of deepest isolation. I felt calm, loving, and completely with her.

When Myra came the three of us spent hours together. Libby felt that Myra posed a very real threat to our life here and said she couldn't understand why I didn't go and live with Myra. She was so ambivalent about this suggestion that it was hard for her to hear me when I said I didn't want to leave our place and live with Myra. Libby said she felt Myra wasn't interested in anyone but me, and wanted to separate us. Myra said that as well as she knew herself she *did* want to know all of us, but particularly Libby, to whom she had been attracted.

. . . At this point we separated, it being the quiet hour. Libby and I stayed outside and walked and talked. Myra went into the house. At the end of the quiet hour we went toward the house and Myra came running out saying, "You were right! I discovered that I *did* want to separate you because I can't get to know either of you this way." Which was certainly true, but for Myra and I to have a one-to-one basis of communication was a "bad" in all our minds, upsetting the seemingly stable pattern of Libby–Clyde, that was and is so sound and beneficial. But it isn't and can't be *stable*.

That night Libby and I went to bed late, exhausted, but not sleepy. We began talking again and I said, "I wish Myra were here, because we're talking about things that involve all of us." Libby said, "I sort of wish that too." Then I got all weak and watery and I asked her to make that decision. She decided "yes" and I went and woke Myra up. She came and we spent the rest of the night in our bed, talking and making mutual love. There were only a few moments when I felt the three of us were truly together. I found out I have definite limits to be with two other people so intimately and intensely. I think we all reacted quite similarly. The experience wasn't orgiastic, deeply giving—or negative. We all shared the learning that being three together in lovemaking wasn't a deeply satisfying experience. Fine.

Next afternoon Myra left. . . .

Naturally her leaving did not settle things. Clyde was next to be "down," and felt self-pitying and frustrated and furious because usually when Libby wants something fixed, he can fix it. But here was something he couldn't "fix." After his self-anger ran its course, with Libby being the compassionate one, they had a dramatic reconciliation. End of story—for now! Clyde still writes to Myra.

SOME SIGNIFICANT ELEMENTS

I have previously commented on the hurt and jealousy which arises in any change or even potential change in partnerships, so further comment seems unnecessary, except to point out how strong it was in Libby.

I am struck by the helping capacity in each individual. Clyde, during Libby's blackest hours, was able to be "completely with her" in the most restoring, the most curative way he might have been. He did not try to reassure or console. He was simply inwardly with her in her isolation, jealousy, and self-hate. It makes no difference that she did not respond. She simply "recognized" his deep companionship in her private isolation. I know from long experience as a therapist that this is definitely the most helpful attitude he could possibly have held. Where did he learn it? How did he know? It simply confirms my belief that many, many people have an intuitive capacity for helping—a capacity which equals that of the best-trained therapist—and can release it in a climate in which they feel freedom to act spontaneously. The same thing shows up at the end, where Libby was a compassionate, understanding, helping person for Clyde. There can be no doubt that the freedom of the commune enabled each to release the helping person in himself.

The second element I see in this situation has even more profound implications. We have seen it—and its absence—in other chapters. It is the unspoken determination to live one's feeling life openly—to expose one's real self, real attitudes as deeply as one is able. It shows up in many very specific ways in this incident. Clyde tells the crying Libby that he has just made love to Myra. Then he can be more free, open, and helpful in dealing with the very painful hurt. It shows in the hours the three spent together talking, during which Libby is open about the threat she feels from Myra. Clyde is open about both his feeling for Myra and his desire to live with Libby, and Myra, "as well as she knew herself," expresses her attraction to both of them, not a desire to separate them.

Then, an hour later, Myra has discriminated her feelings still more accurately. She *does* want to separate them, at least enough so that she can get to know each more deeply. Clyde is open about the fact that his relationship with Libby is so beneficial, but that it *cannot* be stable.

Finally the openness of feeling in the night discussion, and the honesty of Clyde's statement that mutual lovemaking for the three of them was not very satisfying. In every one of these situations something has been learned. There is pain, distress, shock, surprise, caring, loving, and black despair. But none of these is final, nor are they *finished* experiences. They are part of a *process* of living, loving, learning—all of it open between them.

I speak of this at such length because I think it is not sufficiently recognized that this is an almost completely new mode of life. The sharing of bad feelings as well as good, of pain as well as loving, of looking inward to discover what one is *really* experiencing, is very literally a new pathway. These young people have not seen it in their parents, their schools, their ancestors. They would not find it in Oriental cultures where "saving face" is so important. They would not find it in European tradition in which, especially in matters of love, deceit is the rule.

No, young people and others are today trying out a genuinely new way of living. To me it is refreshing and hopeful. But I am sure that I am not enough of a prophet to say that it will be the way of our culture tomorrow. All I can say is that this open, sharing of *all* of one's self nearly always, in my experience, leads to personal growth. I can also add that I believe it is very rare that a person who knows this way of living prefers to go back to living with the façade, the armor, the self-deceiving and other-deceiving "front" which characterizes the great majority of the people. So we cannot know what the future holds for Clyde and Libby and Myra, except that each one is likely to grow as a person.

WHAT DOES THE COMMUNE MEAN FOR CHILDREN?

Few communes have, as yet, many school-age children. Hence some of their most difficult problems are still to arise.

So far as the young child is concerned, he behaves much as he does in any home, enjoying himself at times, feeling hurt at times, fighting with other children, testing limits. In the commune these experiences have a somewhat different flavor. No longer is there just one person—his mother—who must handle all these "crises," important to the child if not always to the adult. There are a number of paternal persons, men and women, who take a hand in or purposely ignore these situations. The child may be scolded by one of these parents, temporarily overindulged by another. He does not receive consistent treatment, but he lives in a world of real adults, to whose idiosyncrasies he must adjust while finding psychological room for himself, his desires and his activities.

One aspect which is actually quite natural will seem surprising to many readers: young children accept quite readily the fact that their parents may at times be sleeping with different partners. Children accept their world as it is, especially if that world is acceptable to the others around them. On the other hand, an adolescent who has spent most of his or her life in the ordinary community and has absorbed its norms may be very much troubled or conflicted by the "bad" behavior of his parents.

In the rural communes there are two other things to be said about the young. Children have more room to roam and play freely with one another, without the dangers of traffic hazards, an overabundance of toys, or the bullying of some organized gang. The realities they must deal with are mostly the hard realities of nature itself.

Furthermore, the rural communal child has a place in the group life. As soon as he has the physical strength for it—certainly by age five or six—he can help in the never-ending tasks of a rural existence. He feels himself *useful*, an experience so rare as to be almost nonexistent in the suburban or urban child of our present-day culture.

But what will they do about school? There are groping experiments already underway. The depth of opposition to the "Establishment" is shown by the non-registering of births in some communes. Hence these children are "non-persons" as far as the state is concerned. Parents are experimenting with educating their children in ways very foreign to those of the public schools.

Possibly one straw in the wind is this: during the days when Haight–Ashbury was synonymous with "Flower Children" (and not with drug-pushers, murders, Mafia, and the like), one "free school" was established there; now there are said to be sixty such schools in the Bay Area. This represents a very small percentage of the children, but a decidedly potent force.

This seems to be one of the many evidences of the truth of a statement by one of the early inhabitants of Haight–Ashbury, now living in a commune: "I can change the world by changing myself. I can't change others." The establishment of a "free school" was simply their own way of meeting their own needs and those of their children. There was no effort to have an impact on schools. Yet a few years later others are doing the same. Living one's values does have an impact. As Lao-Tse, the Chinese philosopher, said centuries ago, "He who imposes himself has the small, manifest might; he who does not impose himself has the great, secret might." I believe there is much in the way commune members are living which is a demonstration of the truth of this ancient saying.

THE "MANSON FAMILY"

If we regard the communes as experiments, then it is inevitable that many fail. Certainly the best-known commune in the country today was a most frightening, horrible failure. The "Manson family" has received thousands of pages of lurid publicity, while the rest of the communal experiments have, by choice, received little or none. So the public image is apt to be grossly distorted. Hence some comment is required.

I know no more of this notorious group than any reasonably well-informed newspaper reader, so my comments are remote from direct experience. But I would like to point out a few obvious facts. It is curious that the group fulfills two of the characteristics found by Kantor (1970) to make for permanence in the last-century communes. There was a charismatic leader—no one can doubt that—with an ideology, no matter how warped or twisted. Also sexual behavior was regulated by the leader, with members having little or no choice. In this case the girls—with or without their acquiescence—were available for sexual intercourse with Manson or any of the men in the group.

These may be some of the elements which led to the amazing tenacity and loyalty of the group throughout the long, long murder trials. We have also discovered, to our sorrow, that a charisma developed in jails and prisons and the most degrading institutions our society can devise can lead to senseless murder, bizarre or sadistic behavior, and incredible violence. It shows too how heavy drug use of all kinds can combine with this charismatic—some say hypnotic—leadership to dull all of even the most common social sensitivity, tenderness, and feelings. It was without doubt a horrible, frightening story, and the more the details were revealed, the more horrible it became. Particularly saddening to me is the fact that—contrary to news reports—some of these girls grew up in concerned, intelligent, middle-class homes.

Yet it is important that we not be deceived. There are thousands of communal groups who have won the respect of their communities. They are experimenting with a new way of life, but idealism—not sadistic, meaningless murders—characterizes their group living. Their ways of behaving may be a shock to many accustomed to the traditional ways, but they are not antisocial, even though they are anti-Establishment. It is most unfortunate that the worst of the groups have occupied the front pages of our papers for weeks on end.

SOME OF MY OWN PERSONAL LEARNINGS

Let me conclude this chapter with some of the ways I have benefited. I have learned a great deal from my contacts with prospective, present, and former commune members, and especially from the diligent study involved in drawing this chapter together. I am convinced that these strange offshoots in our culture will have a great influence on the economic, ecological, educational, technological, and political aspects of our time, and on the future. I am tempted to expand that statement but refrain from doing so for two reasons. First, it does not fit the purpose of this book. Second, I believe these implications should be—and are being—spelled out by those who are much more closely involved in these developments and much better informed than I. But there are still an ample number of personal learnings which I should like to explore.

The first is that I can understand the growth of communes, and the burgeoning interest in them, only as part of a true revolution. Here in a culture which is deeply (and seemingly wholeheartedly) committed to improving any and every technology; committed to materialism and "success"; completely committed to violent force—whether military, police, or criminal—as the ultimate solution to problems; committed to the authority of the great and strong and influential over the weak and small; committed to the denial of human dignity in everything from our schools to our welfare systems; committed to permanent marriage and the nuclear family; especially committed to the belief that we can do no wrong, thus promoting enormous "credibility gaps" and hypocrisy everywhere—in spite of all this, a quiet revolution is taking place.

Here are groups of nonviolent people, using very few words, with no striving for power, completely rejecting all of the values I have mentioned above, and trying to create and live in a totally new society in the midst of the old. With few exceptions, such as some of the religious groups, they are not trying to persuade us or to "sell" us something. By and large they have pretty well given up on the political system, which they see as corrupt. They do not stand out as reformers, nor are they trying to do us good.

They are instead attempting something much more difficult: they are trying to *live* a new culture, to *be* a new set of values. This accounts for their tremendous appeal to young people, who are very discouraged by a society which in countless ways says one thing and does something which is not only different, but different in ways that are awesomely destructive of persons, of the environment, of human dignity, of honest relationships. So young people are interested in those who have formed laboratories of their own, human living experiments, in which many, many mistakes are being made, and some very hopeful beautiful things are occurring.

The communal movement seems to me to have its own trends, which from my limited knowledge and experience I would like to put forth for consideration.

There is, I believe, a trend toward inconstancy and change. A commune opens and fails, or changes its ways, or gives some structure to its nonstructure. To many older people this must seem to be an indication of great weakness, of confusion, of lack of clear goals. But it is the weakness of the sapling, not of the dead tree. As I have known people who have left communes or have rejoined the "straight" community or have joined a new commune, it is my strong impression that they have moved *on*, not backward. Even those who rejoin the usual community do so in most unusual ways, still living their own values. These are not, and in my judgment will not be, the stockbrokers, business executives, or politicians of tomorrow. Or if they do take up these occupations, they will give them a completely new form.

The trend is obviously toward living in small groups. Even the urban communes are not a real part of the impersonal, robot city. In these small groups intimacy, contact with others, with nature, with oneself, with relationships of all kinds, even with the cosmos, is possible.

The trend—and here I speak very tentatively—seems away from radical activism, from violence, from hard drugs. Marijuana yes. LSD occasionally, but more and more rarely. "Speed" and heroin no. These groups are learning to "get high" on nature, meditation, Zen, yoga, ritual celebrations, a transcendent higher consciousness. They are learning that life can be rich in many ways, without the stimulation of drugs.

WHY JOIN?

But why do intelligent, educated, sophisticated individuals, with all the opportunities ahead of them which our society offers, join communes? Let me try to set down a few of the motives which I believe are operative.

One is to escape the increasing alienation and individual isolation in our society. They long to escape from punch-card dehumanization to a place where they can personally *belong*. Big David's speech is an extreme example of this. They desire to be a part of deep, sharing relationships, which, as we have seen, can occur in marriages as well as in communes.

Certainly another reason is that communes offer an opportunity to be the whole self in a unified way, a very rare opportunity in modern life. All aspects of the person tend to be valued—physical strength, occupational skills, parental aptitudes, intellectual ideas, feelings and emotions, ideals and religious or mystical interests, can all be lived simultaneously. Life is much less fractionalized. This can happen in marriage, as we have observed. It can, to a limited degree, occur in encounter groups. But a commune is another—and perhaps more difficult way—of trying to achieve this new expression of the whole self in a unified life.

Frequently a prominent reason is to find a sanction for all kinds of sexual relationships: in marriage, in partnerships of varying durations, in all kinds of combinations—man-woman, woman-woman, man-man. This experimentation is simply not freely possible in the ordinary community. In the commune it usually finds a supportive climate and can be carried on without guilt—though not, as we have seen, without pain.[3]

Another motive which is perhaps gradually discovered by the person is that the living group is, whether consciously or unconsciously, an experiment in some philosophy of social organization (or nonorganization). Free of the "rat race," it is a chance to build a functioning group in which things get done. So from anarchy to controlled behaviorism, a whole crop of new societies is germinating, each different from the other. The group must wrestle with problems of survival, of authority, of work distribution, of the management of interpersonal differences, of relationship to a very different outside world.

This leads to another realization: that this is not a closed-end experiment, but an opportunity for *learning.* Here is an opportunity for a changing personal development—an opportunity which by no means always occurs, but which stands as a hope.

Finally, there is great drawing power in the dropping of roles. Early in the chapter I mentioned the many backgrounds and work experiences from which these persons are drawn. But in a commune a person is not primarily a Radcliffe graduate or a computer

[3]The sexual experimentation in a commune is vastly different from that of a group of "swingers." Evidence shows that swingers try to avoid anything approaching deep involvement or more than casual relationships.

specialist or a psychologist or whatever. A person is a person. A man is a man. A woman is a woman. There is a basic equality which makes movements such as women's lib obsolete, since each woman—and each man—can carve out the personal niche she or he desires in the group. (Interestingly, the women very frequently opt for "feminine" functions.)

All these motives sound appealing. Yet people leave these groups, communes fail or become destructive or fall apart. Why?

One of the most prominent reasons, I believe, is that they have frequently given insufficient thought to the ways in which interpersonal conflicts and hurts and cross purposes may be handled. We have seen in this chapter that they can also excel in a curative function, but this does not happen necessarily.

Frequently they have simply failed to solve the problem of self-support, but this is a bit outside the realm of this chapter.

Jealousy is often an underestimated problem which can undermine a group. Indeed, I wonder whether jealousy is something simply conditioned by the culture or actually has a basic biological foundation, like territoriality?

Related to this is, I believe, a similar underestimation of the need of each person for a reasonably secure, continuing, one-to-one relationship. This need seems to run very deep and may be considered too lightly.

It has been borne in on me—by material I have gathered, by the reading I have done, and by the very intimate accounts in the following chapter—that it is far more difficult to sustain a healthy and satisfying relationship in a triad or a group marriage of four or more than it is to sustain it in a two-person marriage (as if that were not difficult enough!). Consequently, communes have fallen apart because of the inability to resolve the problems of highly complex relationships.

Sometimes there is a failure to recognize the great need of each individual for privacy. This can be provided in a commune, but sometimes it is not, with very negative results.

Often, in my judgment, there is no recognition that an anarchistic philosophy, beautiful though it may be, can operate with some degree of success only when the group is composed of people with a high degree of psychological maturity. Hence the attempt to live anarchistically, when the group is made up of individuals badly warped by family and society, can be a resounding flop.

There is sometimes failure to recognize that all ideologies are greatly modified in practice. Thus, Twin Oaks, fashioned on B. F. Skinner's theories, is no longer run by three planners but largely by consensus. The environment is no longer set to condition certain behaviors, but the individual *chooses* which behaviors he desires to change and *chooses* the rewards which are meaningful for him. All this has little resemblance to *Walden II*, Skinner's fictional utopia.

So communes have their full share of problems and failures. But they are process failures from which one can learn. They seem to be performing a most important function in our culture. They are, at little psychological or financial cost to all of us, conducting the laboratory experiments to determine what place marriage, partnerships, interpersonal relations, technology, and social organization may have in the future. Our culture, in all probability, cannot continue as it is. The flaws and fissures, the injustices and hypocrisies are too great. What, then, *will* it become? Communes, with all their mistakes and privations and failures and regroupings, seem to be exploring the way.

A TRANSITION

I considered making the chapter on communal groups the last major chapter in the book. But it is my strong feeling that great numbers—probably a vast majority—of young people, interested though they are in communes, consider marriage to be their goal.

So we move on now to the last account of a marriage—one which has been fantastic in its variety. In it we will meet all the issues we have found in communes, as well as many new ones. It is a marriage which simply defies the old saying "You can't change human nature." Here are two natures which have changed so greatly that their present selves scarcely seem like part of the same psychological universe as those with which they entered their union. I hope it will have the fascination for you that it does for me.

8 ✍ Fifteen Years of a Radically Changing Marriage

THIS INTERVIEW WITH Eric and Denise is the last one in the book, because it includes about as many problem elements and joyfully strong elements as could ever be expected within a fifteen-year relationship. Married at twenty-one and nineteen respectively, they were bound by expectations; after five years Denise had a "mental breakdown" and the relationship was extremely cold and unhelpful; therapy helped build Denise as a person and for the first time she really fought in marriage; marijuana changed Eric from a highly rational intellectual sort to one who appreciated his whole self—feelings and natural rhythms —to the great strengthening of their marriage; on the other hand there have been many times when the marriage has seemed on the verge of a split; each has experimented sexually outside of marriage (and shared the experiences) and, interestingly, has become more monogamous in the process; they are about to embark on a completely new life in another country, with some of the apprehensions one might expect. Even to state this "bare bones" description of their experience is to indicate something of the tremendous variety which has entered into the process of an exceedingly enriching marriage of two now highly independent people.

I would like to say a word about my contacts with this couple. I first met them socially ten years ago, and would, had I been asked, have predicted that their marriage—already a failure—

would end very soon. (So much for the gifts of prophecy and diagnosis!)

Following that first contact, I occasionally met Eric professionally and once we worked together very smoothly on the organization of a small conference. There were many seeds of possible disagreement in our work together, but I found him brilliant, reasonable, ready to seek workable compromises, a pleasure to work with.

In recent years our contacts have been social and very occasional, but I have been deeply struck by the changes in both Eric and Denise. If our meetings were a year apart, as they often were, it seemed to me that both were almost completely different persons than they had been the year before. This process of—to me —surprising change was what led me to write to them to ask if they would be willing to be interviewed. To my delight, they agreed, but I was quite unprepared for the richness of the material they were willing to give so freely and revealingly.

In other chapters I have frequently done a good deal of editing—putting together elements which belonged together, even though they had not been spoken in consecutive order. I have also frequently interrupted the interview to make comments. With Eric and Denise, however, the material had such a natural flow, and moved so readily from one aspect of their experience to another, that I have done almost no editing except to change identifying details. I have simply introduced headings to indicate where the topics change, to make it easier for the reader to look back and find material which has meaning for him. So, without more introduction, let me permit Eric and Denise to speak for themselves. My personal comments are reserved for the end.

THE PIONEERING MOVE

ERIC: It just occurred to me, Carl, flying in here today, that we're doing this interview with you on what's essentially our fifteenth anniversary, next month, and also at a time when we're dissolving all the structure of our marriage. We're selling our home, we're selling all our properties, we're leaving our friends, our jobs, professional positions—we're leaving the country we were married in, and we're starting in a completely new way with, really, just ourselves and our children, and a few of our very elementary personal effects. So what seems to me to be one of the most important aspects of our marriage, and the way it's developed to this point, is the fact that it has not become more integrated into a structure of an area, of possessions, of long-term friendships, and so on. Instead, we've taken that growing structure and now we're dissolving it and we're going to start something completely new. A whole turnaround in our way of relating to the world around us, as a couple.

ME (*to* **DENISE**): That really hits me, and I'd like to know your reaction to what he said.

DENISE: I hadn't thought of it that way, but one of the scary aspects of the move has been the fact that we are going to get down to just the very elementary nuclear family and rely on nothing but the interaction between the four of us. We cannot be helped out by close friends. So it feels pioneering in that sense. And I hadn't thought as far as the marriage went, as specifically as it affected the four of us as a family—that what we're doing is taking a leap, without knowing quite what we're getting into.

ERIC: We've never had a tranquil marriage. We've always fought a lot, we've always had a lot of conflict—very intense conflict—and during the last few years we've learned how to accept that, as a positive thing, which promotes our growth, which in a sense keeps us from getting bored, keeps us from taking each other for granted —so that the conflict that used to be very bitter has now taken on a kind of a sense of humor to it. But one of the reasons it's taken on a sense of humor is because we always knew that we had a lot more to our lives than the marriage relationship. That is, if I got really mad at Denise, I'd split for a week, and she would do the same thing—split from me for a couple of days. We'd go see friends or we'd turn our attention to other things.

Now over the last couple of months, when we look at it we say, "In two more months we're going to go off to the end of the world, practically—a place where we are isolated from everything we know —and what we have is each other and our children." And then when we get into a fight about something, or Denise acts in a way which is upsetting to me, and I get angry at her, my immediate reaction is, "My God, do I want to go off with this woman and live out at the end of the world somewhere?"

In a sense, the city, the urban life, the professional life, the web of friendships here provide an escape from the pressures of the marriage. And when you begin to realize you're not going to have that escape— at least not for a while—when you're going to a place where you're a complete stranger, where you're not acculturated, and where there are very few people, and when there are very different kinds of people than we're used to knowing, then the marriage kind of closes in around you.

For example. There are two kinds of fights, that we have at least, and I suspect a lot of people have. One of them is just where you get really bitter and angry with each other and you're pissed, you know, and you hate each other. And all that anger comes welling out that's stored up from all kinds of things. The other kind of fight we have is one where something makes one of us so just kind of alive and assertive— genuine, authentic, and what we are, what we want, what we believe —that we don't want any longer to tolerate the simple façades, or the dishonesties, or the lack of fulfillment that goes on from day to day. And we say, "I will have that, and I will not put up with less."

And that's what's starting to happen now, you see, where we are saying, "By God, this has got to be right, or it's going to be deadly for us. Here is our last chance—this is an overdramatic way of putting it —to decide whether we have any problems so great that we shouldn't be living together. Because we're *really* going to be living together now. We can't play games with the marriage for the next two or three years. We're going to be absolutely stuck with each other in a way we never have been in the past. That's what I'm saying.

ME (*to* **DENISE**): What's your reaction to all this?

DENISE: I agree with him. I guess I had not thought of those terms myself, on my own. Some of this is familiar because we had a recent fight, and he said some of these things, but I hadn't thought in these terms—of the way it sounds so final.

ME: Spell that out a little more.

DENISE: I didn't think of it as a—like he said, this last fight got him all in the middle of thinking this way. I reacted to it, but I didn't instigate this. He is the one that thought of it. I anticipated it being harder, but

I didn't think of it as being in terms of making the marriage tie or bonds weaken at all, or any more than anything else that's happened to us. That's the difference. It doesn't seem like it'd make us split up any more than anything else. We've been through so many trials by fire, you know, as far as the tie dissolving or not, that this is tame.

ERIC: Well, the reason it's important to me—see, I think there's a difference in your going to another country and my going to another country. You are pretty sure of what you want and you're pretty sure you're going to find it there. You're going to be able to have some open land, you're going to be able to be a potter, you're going to be able to do some of the natural things you've been dreaming about doing very much. And those things are focused in on the family. And you feel very comfortable with that.

Okay, I'm going with quite different professional kinds of feelings. For me a lot of my excitement and a lot of my personal challenge from day to day has been with the really groovy, challenging friends, professional stuff, running around with my students, and what-have-you. It's been because I really like the social milieu in which we move here. And I don't think that's going to be the case there. For a while, at least, we are going to feel very alien in a new country. I'm going to feel very lonely, in a kind of an intellectual, professional, social sense. I mean, I don't think these are going to be the kind of groovy people that I can swing with, frankly. I think it's going to be a very faltering, very difficult way of establishing friendships, of building relationships, very slowly, across quite a wide bridge. Which means that I'm going to be turning more and more for my sustenance to my home—to you and to the kids. And so I look at that potentiality and I say, "Wow. This had better be good. Because if I'm going to be angry and frustrated and unfulfilled at home, that's going to be hell." That's what I was saying. I can't turn somewhere else like I do here.

THREE PHASES OF THEIR MARRIAGE

I had one other thought when we were flying in that I thought I might try to give. It occurs to me that we've moved through, I think, three major stages in our marriage.

THE PERIOD OF SOCIAL "OUGHTS." It's very clear to me that the first part of our marriage was one in which most of our behavior, most of our expectations, our ways of relating to one another were determined by sets of predetermined social rules. I mean, we went into marriage with whole ideas about how we ought to act toward each other, how we ought to feel toward each other, how we ought to act towards each other sexually, how often we ought to make love. You know, we'd been taught, not only by parents, but by the whole culture, that a man who is a stud screws a lot, and you know, all the ways you relate to others. And we lived within that structure of social rules as a kind of template for our marriage for about five or six years, until it absolutely collapsed for us. It proved disastrous for us. And that's when Denise ended up with a breakdown, and I ended up agonizing and miserable.

THE SENSUAL PERIOD. And we deliberately threw that out. I mean, there came a time when we were both healed enough from that crisis, where we sat down and very calmly said to each other, "This crap we have been told should be the basis for our marriage does not work. We've got to find another way of relating." And it was at that time that we really got into things like basic encounter groups; into things like drugs, to some extent—grass, LSD; into things like experimenting with relationships with other people outside the marriage. Saying, "Let's allow ourselves to open up to whatever relationships occur, and see if we can integrate those." And that became kind of a sensual period in our marriage, a time of opening up to what our senses, our perceptions told us was the right way to live, as opposed to the sort of social template.

LIVING BY INTERNAL RHYTHMS. And I think now we're going into a different phase. The sensual being is the kind of thing people ordinarily talk about when they talk about sensory awareness or increasing your perceptivity—you know, that you learn how to slow down, how to really get into things more. Heightened sensitivity, heightened awareness. I think we're going out of that sensual phase into a phase which is really a following, in our behavior, in the way we pattern our lives, of the natural, internal rhythms of our bodies. That is, so that we—even things like eating, now. We tend to eat now when we get hungry. We don't eat at breakfast, dinner, and supper. Sometimes we don't eat anything, sometimes we gorge ourselves all day. And we tend to make love more on the basis of a sexual buildup and desire, rather than, you know, "It's night now, we're alone, let's now screw" or "We haven't screwed for three days, let's screw." And the way we tend to relate to our children is more authentic in terms of organisms, of what's going on internally in us. I don't know why that's happened.

Well, sure, it's happened partly because of bioenergetics and yoga, but more and more we have gone away from tapping into the social structure for our structure, and through the period of the sort of chaos of opening all the senses, and now, tapping individually into our own organisms and whatever our own biologies tell us, for the structure of our marriage and our relationship with each other. I think that's true, don't you, Denise?

DENISE: Yes.

DENISE'S BREAKDOWN—AND HER LACK OF SELF

ME (to **DENISE**): I don't know whether you regard his three divisions as sound ones for you, but I would like you to comment some about the early part of your marriage, where it did seem as though you were living by rules.

DENISE: My breakdown occurred on the fifth anniversary of our marriage. And up to that point I was living in kind of a naïve fog for a good deal of this time. I did not understand why he was unhappy the times he was unhappy, why we weren't getting along, because a lot of the time I was satisfied with the status quo. That first five years is so long ago, it's hard to bring it back, but I remember the discrepancy between your reaction and my reaction, when we got into the big thing—the fifth-anniversary thing—and the talks during that period of time. I hadn't had the memory of the amount of unhappiness that you had been living with. Because for me, a baby, having Alan the second year of our marriage—a lot of my focus, and natural rhythm of my day, was being satisfied.

But I agree, as far as this business about social norms. I remember reading books and trying to—expecting life to follow these norms. What is normal and average, that's what should occur. I remember reading Spock for having Alan. I followed Dr. Spock very avidly. So that breakdown was a division for me, and after the therapy and getting into that next phase, I agree, that went on for quite a while.

ME: I want to ask one question at this point. You felt sort of fulfilled and that you were living a normal marriage—sure, with troubles, but reasonably satisfied. How do you reconcile that statement with the fact that you had a breakdown?

DENISE *(pauses):* I imputed more maturity to myself then than I had at the time, that's for sure! When you think back, you can't remember how *juvenile* you really were. I remember that I thought I was a lot more mature and could handle things when I got married than actually was the fact in the ensuing years. And I think that was apparent to me—that I wasn't as grown up as I thought I was. And I wasn't able to handle the crises between us. We didn't make any headway. I cannot remember what it felt like, though, when we had a real marital crisis those first few years. I can't remember—I can't bring it back, what it was like. But I'm sure there must have been some indication there, that we were in some kind of trouble. Because when I made the suggestion, on our fifth anniversary, I said, "Well if you're so unhappy, maybe you ought to divorce me." Something had led up to that, but I can't. . . .

ERIC *(breaks in)*: And I said, "A great idea" *(laughing)*.

DENISE *(continuing)*: But it wasn't only the marriage. It was religion, a religious quest, and not being able to be understood by my parents on this quest. There was that, in addition to the marriage. It wasn't just the marriage.

ERIC: As a matter of fact, I think the marriage was secondary as a cause of the breakdown. I think it was triggered off by the religious thing, and she focused. . . .

ME: You came from pretty conservative. . . .

ERIC: Fundamentalist background. Denise went through a long period of feeling very guilty, because she rejected that under my influence but really didn't have much to replace it with. I don't believe, you know, that it's sinful to wear lipstick and things like that. And then her parents would push her, "Well, what do you believe? What have you sold out your birthright for? You've really sold it out cheaply. Eric has no coherent philosophy of life," etc.

Eventually she got to the point where she started reading a little bit, and thinking a little bit, and she could talk a little more intelligently about what some of her beliefs were. So after a period of this, you decided, "Now I can tell my parents, and I can get together with my parents, because I now have something to share with them that comes out of me." Of course, when she attempted to communicate with them, it was a disaster. There was nothing.

ME: I recognize what you're saying about the religious aspect, and yet I was interested in your remark that it was when Denise said, "Well, maybe you should divorce me," and you said, "Good idea," that that really is what brought the crackup.

DENISE: This all happened at the same time. The talk with my parents, and the anniversary all happened within two or three days. But I wanted to get into what we both realize too—that that breakdown saved our marriage. Because it put us into two totally different people—it was just amazing. After I got myself back together, it was as though now we really had a chance to make something of our marriage. Before that, as he said, we would not have made it, for sure.

ME: Who were you before that? You say after that you really became a person and there was a chance of making a marriage out of it. Who were you before that?

DENISE *(long pause)*: Nobody's ever asked me that before. I've never had to put it into words. I certainly was a neat creation of my parents. That's for certain. I really dug myself in a lot of ways, but in a lot of ways I . . . I mean I didn't really love myself. But I felt I was a good person.

ME: Partly because you fitted pretty well the parental model?

DENISE: Yes, I was the yes girl. Who was I? *(Pauses and hesitates)* It's hard to know. I agreed with what people said I was, and that's why it's hard for me to answer from this viewpoint now, because I took *their* model of myself for my *identity*. First my parents' and then Eric's. And when that came into conflict, then, five years later, that was it.

ERIC: Denise had very little identity except what other people had imposed on her. Her parents had imposed one, I imposed one, and they were absolutely in conflict, and it tore her apart. She had schizophrenia imposed from the outside, in a way. Something had to give.

MARRIAGE SAVED BY ITS CRISES

You know, our marriage, Carl, has always been saved by crisis. If you were to take the most destructive, horrible things that could happen to a marriage, and enumerate them, they have happened in our marriage and they have been the points at which we have had our great breakthroughs, to a different level of being together and relating to each other. And it's almost as if it's at those periods of crisis where you become so alive, so energized, and so desperate, in a way, that something happens. The rest of the time you just tend to go along and adjust.

ME: There are times when you have to face things.

ERIC: When she had the breakdown—the old order passed away. And everything had to be started over again. All the old assumptions didn't work, so we had to find new assumptions. Then, when we were in the period I was mentioning earlier, when we were dealing with other people, we entered into a relationship with another couple, which escalated into a tremendously dramatic and demanding thing. That too furnished the basis for our having new kinds of concepts of one another. And also a new level of honesty for us.

ME: And a new type of crisis.

ERIC: It was certainly a crisis. It was a crisis that threatened to tear our marriage apart. But out of that came a level of honesty in our dealings with each other, in sharing with each other our fantasies, our fears, our dreams about other people—love affairs and what have you—that just totally changed the basis of the relationship. And then there were others, real crisis situations.

DENISE: I think the reason that the crises worked in our favor was because we really were *strong* in *wanting* it to work—we really *worked* at it. We stuck through the hardest part—we didn't turn tail and run. We didn't chicken out. And a lot of times it would be very easy to run. Like Eric was very tempted to run when I had my breakdown, he once told me. And I just about turned tail and ran a couple of times, through these other affairs he was talking about. Running from the pain. Now if you can stick through the pain level *long enough,* you get the rewards. But something's got to be strong there to begin with or you wouldn't stick through it. It's got to be strong between you. You have to fight as strong as you love.

THE UNDERLYING LINK—DIFFERING VIEWS

ME: What do you think accounts for that underlying commitment that it sounds to me like you're talking about? When it has all gone to hell on the surface—you've cracked up or the marriage is in a crisis with another couple? Why do you care enough to keep *working* at it? As you say, you *have* worked at it—that's been the thing that has impressed me, just from the outside—and why?

DENISE *(laughing)*: Karma. I'm sure we're karmically bound. I don't have any doubt about it in my mind. If anything would make you believe in it, this would. That's a facile answer, but I've recently been getting into reincarnation, and it certainly could explain a lot of what we've been through. We certainly owe a lot to each other.

ERIC: I think one of the reasons is a very simple sociological one: that we both come from fundamentalist backgrounds, we tend to be the kind of people who are committed to stuff. Divorce was unthinkable in both of our childhoods, absolutely unthinkable. And we grew up with that, and that gets very deeply into your value system, so there is a kind of a commitment there.

The second one is that we really dig each other sexually. And both of us have had enough sexual experience with other people to know that that's not naïveté, that there is a real special quality to our sexual relationship.

And for me another one which I have tried to say, sometimes, and which is hard to put very clearly, is I spend a lot of time with some very exciting people—students, colleagues, what-have-you, but all of them bore me sometimes. Every one, without any exception, I just get tired of being with someone and would rather be by myself. I've never felt that way with Denise. I have never been bored with Denise, in fifteen years. I've hated her, I've been furious with her, you know, I've thought she was evil and destructive of my—I've never been *bored* with her.

And that's not only in terms of thinking, you know, "I've really been bored the last year," never that. Never has there been a time when

I wanted to be somewhere else rather than with her, just because I was bored. There have been times when I wanted to be somewhere else because I was angry, or something like that, but not out of boredom.

So, you know, you start putting things together and way down at some deep level there's a real tight link between us. Also I happen to believe, at the same level Denise does, in karma. I think there are mysteries in our biological structures that we don't know very much about. And I think that when two people get linked through children, that is a real linkage. It's not an abstraction, it's not a social concept, it's something that really happens to their biologies. Because you start relating to one another through that third person, who is a combination of your genes and your biology and your production.

DENISE: Then you think you and I are different now than when we were first married?

ERIC: Very different. And for me, now, a new reason for us to stay together, for any couple to stay together, that has children, is that I think you're doing a real violence to something terribly, terribly deep in the way you respond to the world when you break up a relationship which has children involved in it.

So that has been one of the things which—as a matter of fact, the last time we had a really severe crisis, I was about to split, to run off. In agonizing through that, it was very apparent I firmly believed and felt that kind of connection. That was not something that I was willing to rupture for what seemed on a conscious level, you know, the best of reasons. I think both of us are getting much more mystical, but we're going in slightly different directions in our mysticism. I'm going toward kind of a biological mysticism and Denise is going toward an astral mysticism.

"HOW DID YOU ACHIEVE PERSONHOOD?"

ME: This is really fascinating. Now I'd like to return to the other question that I had on my mind. (*To* **DENISE**): You were, as you say, sort of a person that was created by others, until your breakdown. You mentioned having therapy. Is that what gave you a separate personhood, or did you work it out between you, or how did you achieve a person-hood which was quite different from what you started with?

DENISE: Various forms of therapy, starting with—well, that isn't the only answer, but that's the first answer. I was in straight psychotherapy for several years, with two different men. And then there was a year and a half with no therapy. And then I got into bioenergetics with the second therapist, who had since taken on bioenergetics and was doing both—it was six months of bioenergetics therapy with him. That was the capstone, that six-month period. I went deeper, and more completely than the two and a half years of therapy I'd had with him previously, and just became completely my own person. And, I want to add, reading your book. This was before I started therapy with the therapist, I think. *On Becoming a Person* had a profound effect on me. It was the first thing that gave me an inkling that the answer was inside of me, rather than outside. And that I could trust myself. I remember that—oh, that was just fantastic, the effect it had on me. That was the budding of my personhood, was reading that book and realizing that I could trust part of myself. And then, to feed that part and to bring it into full bloom, it was the ensuing years that did it, but. . . .

The marriage was valuable in that interim, too, of course, but I can't —I used to give Eric all kinds of credit for things. Well, in this case, I can give him some, but it's all mine. It's my doing. I went into therapy without his okay, a couple of times, and against his wishes—and that made a big difference. And then I knew I could stand on at least one foot at a time on my own and not have to rely on his okay to do something. But it was important enough for *me* to do it. Does that answer it for you?

ME: Well, if you think of other ideas, I'd love to have them, but that does give a partial answer. I'll just comment, as an aside, that I think the change from a really nonperson who is molded by others to a person in his own right is one of the most fascinating things that goes on anywhere.

ERIC: I'd like to comment on Denise's therapy. It seemed to me that the years in therapy with Dr. G. the first time—what they really did was enable you to kind of cope with the world, so that Denise was adjusted to the world, in a sense. You know, things didn't upset her too much, she could kind of cope with things. And that provided a kind of leisure for her to begin to enjoy life and find some happiness. We began to have fun together and do things together for fun. We learned how to play a little bit. Up to that time most of her energy had been absorbed in maintaining a sick character structure—that's somebody's term. You use all your energy to maintain that defense system, and so on.

But then the second phase of the therapy, when you got into the bioenergetics, and got into the yoga, was a totally different scene. That had nothing to do with adjusting or coping. That was a way of beginning to really start to grow some powers inside yourself. You know, to let emerge what wanted to unfold from you. The former part had been to keep her from being destroyed too much by the world, and this part then began to be an unfolding process. A real different turning point, when she got into bioenergetics.

THE MARGARET EPISODE

But then we haven't talked about the Margaret episode as being a crucial part in doing whatever has happened to us.

DENISE: That's when I said my first no. I had said a lot of yeses, but I'd never said *no*. This was three years ago. I hadn't gotten into the bioenergetics yet. I'd had one workshop in it and you'd had one workshop in it. We knew about it and had been exposed to it, but I hadn't. . . .

Eric fell in love with this student up at college, and this had been going on for several months without my knowledge. I got back from a trip to his parents. I had had the kids back there for a month. When I came back is when he told me about it, and I guess this was stronger than any love he'd had outside of ours—in all the other relationships he'd had with women. And it was really tearing him up, that he finally had to—well you ought to tell that part of it. But out of this came. . . .

ME: Tell your side of it, how it seemed to you.

DENISE: I was tremendously shocked. I hadn't anticipated this at all. For some reason I had hidden—you see this was his second or first year teaching away from home at college. He commuted and spent three days there and came home. And I was so proud of, you know, that my man had that kind of freedom—that I trusted him—and then for him to tell me this came as a tremendous shock.

Looking back, I think it was very dumb and stupid of me not to have expected this to happen, but part of me really put its head in the sand.

ME: I have one question here, because evidently it was not the fact that he was having intercourse with the girl—that wasn't what shocked you. That had happened before, if I understand you correctly. It was the fact that he really was very deeply involved with this girl.

DENISE: Yes. That's true. But another thing I wanted to add—one reason, too, it came as a surprise, because we had been out of this experimenting business for a couple of years, I thought, becoming more and more monogamous—I completely so. I hadn't realized that he had not, as much as I. So that was a surprise element. But it had been a couple years since anything like that had happened. We had considered it too painful to continue to explore, and not worth the emotional energy it drained—it was just demanding an awful lot, that kind of lifestyle, and we wanted to kind of take it easy from that.

Anyway, out of this crisis I tried to incorporate the idea of having a three-way relationship here. And I went as far as I could in saying yes to this. As I remember, it did not work, for reasons of yours at one point. You did not want it to be three-way at one point. But I could not tolerate his having two different lives, separating hers and mine. If it was together, that's one thing, but to have two different—him to be two different places and two different women—I just couldn't tolerate that. So I said *no. Period.* And that was the big no. And I have never felt stronger in my life.

ERIC: But that arrangement was precisely what I wanted. It was terribly attractive to me. To be able to have my family and Denise, and to be able to be off, you know, three days a week, several months a year. And have another woman whom I loved very much, who excited me in a completely different way, and who was willing to accept that kind of life. That was very, very attractive to me. And it was so powerfully attractive to me that I was insisting on it. I really was saying, "That's what I'm going to have, that's my nature, that's what I want and what I can have, and why shouldn't I?" And I was saying, "There's kind of an excitement there, a kind of power in that kind of life, that I really like —and it turns me on."

Denise's "no" seemed to tap into all the old social prohibitions and the jealousies; you know how you feel when you're in that kind of situation; I assume you do. And so I said, "I'm not going to give up this chance for a kind of excitement and beauty in life, you know, to live according to all those fucking rules that we had long ago abandoned, and give in to your feelings of being threatened," because—you know, I kept saying to Denise, which I think was true, that in some ways never had our relationship been any better than during that period. And I said, "What do you object to? It can be nothing more than simple jealousy and threat, and those are petty emotions."

And what happened was that Denise just got like a bitchy lion, possessive and powerful and demanding of what was her right and what she wanted and what she demanded, and out of those demands, and out of that strength in her, came a kind of a beauty and a power that had never been there before. You know, a personhood, which is what I had always—you know, it had been the curse of our marriage. What is Denise's person, you know, who is she? Other than an echo or something. And the relationship between us got so powerful and so intense that I just kind of forgot about the other woman. I mean, when I didn't see Margaret for three or four days, and Denise and I were into it—you know, there would be a chance to go see Margaret—I didn't want to, I wanted to stay with Denise, I wanted to stay with what we had going there. It was that kind of a power that emerged out of that crisis, because Denise was driven to the wall. And instead of falling apart, as she had done before, she emerged, you know—she put on all her "aspects and attributes" and came out covered with glory.

Now, you know, I mean, you could talk about all kinds of subconscious motivations and what-have-you. I know that for many years, after Denise's breakdown, and then when it was repeated, you know, a second and third time, I used to have nightmares that Denise was going to fall to pieces again, that she wasn't strong—that, you know, I had to be very careful, I shouldn't do anything that would threaten her, that I was *trapped* by her sickness. That was a lever, you know. I didn't dare fuck around with another woman—that would scare her too much and she'd flip out. I didn't dare be weak and irresponsible and say, "Screw it, I don't feel like working, I'm going to become a bum," because Denise couldn't handle that. It may have been that at some level I was trying to get out of that trap. And what happened was, when I tried to get out of that trap, Denise came through and it became very, very apparent to me that I didn't need to have that fear any more.

DENISE: The night that I was going to walk out—I did walk out—then he knew I was all right.

ERIC: It wasn't as simple as that.

DENISE *(interrupting)*: I'd done that before that.

ERIC: Yeah, this was different. I was ready to leave and go live with Margaret, and your strength and your beauty, you know, in insisting on what you wanted and what you were and what you wanted from me, just overwhelmed me. That's what happened. But, see, this is another example of what I mean when I say that all the growth in our marriage has come out of the most horrible kinds of crises.

"I CAN CHOOSE TO BE SICK!"

ME: Part of what I understand you to be saying is that—even before the Margaret situation—you were sort of controlled in your behavior by Denise's sickness. And I'd like to ask you, Denise, were you ever *sick?*

DENISE: Well, I've had my serious doubts about whether that's a good word to use about it, I really have. I don't know how to answer that, really. But I wanted to tell you one thing, Carl. The last time—it was during the end of the Margaret episode, and I was getting—we were drinking a lot at night, and we were bitterly trying to work it out. This was after he'd decided, "Okay, I'll do it your way. I'll stay, I'll give her up." But we were really still in the thick of it. And I started feeling as if I was getting fuzzy around the edges, unsure of my ego. All kinds of weird sensations. And I remember sitting in the hanging chair, with that drink in my hand and rocking back and forth, and I said to myself, "By golly, I have a choice here. I could really let go and encourage that 'sickness' and cause a lot of trouble. I have a *choice* in this matter." It was the first time I had looked back on the big break, and then the two afterward, realizing that a part of my organism *chose* to do that.

And then the sense of power that I could or could not do that, and then realizing I didn't *want* to do it. And within a day or so I was all right. The fuzziness went away. But it was a big discovery to know that it was a matter of *choice*. So then I had to own my past actions in a different way and realize that I had caused a lot of pain, but then I had been hurting myself too. But I think it's more a weakness of the organism —unable to have the power to withstand that sort of thing happening to it. I was a creature of my circumstances so utterly, I mean people could just impress me so easily, that I can feel sorry for myself or pity for that person back there, but I can understand why a little better.

ERIC AND DENISE'S "SICKNESS"

ME (*to* **ERIC**): I had planned not to say this until toward the end, but I really would like your comment on it. The first time I remember meeting the two of you was up at that beach house that Pete had. There was a party up there and you were both there. I talked with you alone, Eric, was much impressed by you as a person, and was very puzzled—and by the time I got away was really horrified—by the way you talked about Denise. Knowing that I was a psychologist, you wanted me to know that her diagnosis was such and such, I've forgotten what the hell it was, and she had to have her drugs every so often and all that. But it was not what you said, but the way that you said it—it was as though, here is an object that is very fragile and I have to really give a lot of thought to this and a lot of careful attention to it. It wasn't completely uncaring, but it was terribly objective and it was also very unlike any *marriage*. That was the impression I had. I'd just be interested in your comment on that.

ERIC: I look back on that period now. I was both very, very responsible and very bitter. I didn't love Denise in the way I know what love means now. I had loved her earlier when we were married because she excited me and turned me on and we had all these romantic ideas. And then after the breakdown I just didn't love her any more. I mean, she was a *problem,* and you don't love a problem. You know, you don't love someone who's constantly making—she was a *case.* She was someone who made my life full of threat and fear, difficulty, loneliness, all kinds of things. I was bitter, I was angry, yeah, no question about it. But I also had enough of a kind of basic integrity, I think, that I desperately wanted that to be different. You know, I wanted her to be well, I wanted to not have to fear any more. That's part of the commitment. I had some kind of integrity there, which kept us going part of that time, and then Denise has one that kept us going another—maybe I'll say a word about that. During about the first three or four years—actually the breakdown business went on for four years, really—and the other two breakdowns, later. I just had a goddamn monkey on my back, I mean I was just carrying everything on my back, including the fear that I was going to grow up with small children and a wife who was *nuts*. You know, if not in a mental hospital, at least just crazy. I knew enough crazy people to know what kind of hell that could be. And I stuck with it, you know. I didn't run away, and I really tried my damnedest to do what was right, and I did a lot of stupid things and a lot of very good things. You know, get the right kind of help and not get suckered into thinking that therapy was going to be magic and solve everything.

THE AFTERMATH

Then when it became very apparent that Denise was going to be all right—there came a time when it was very apparent that she *was* going to be all right—this was shortly after the Gilbert and Vera business, this was the couple that we formed a kind of quadruple alliance with for a period—I just went to pieces. And I started drinking heavily, heavily—every night I'd drink myself into a stupor and every day I'd go through in a hangover, and several times I went into absolute fits—the alcohol allowed me to do it; crawling under the bed and curling up on the floor and screaming and crying and clawing at the carpet and things, and refusing to do anything. I did no work, no responsibility—nothing. And Denise came through. I mean she took over and took responsibility then. So her integrity came through at that point.

DENISE: I'd like to add to that. These last two or three years, where I consider myself as a totally functioning person, and independently integral outside of Eric's relationship with me, for the first time me being the adult, it allows him to be the child. And for the past couple of years, he has been very childlike in a lot of ways, where he never had the freedom to be so before. So the tables have been turned. I've been playing the parent to his child a lot, then he gets fed up with that sometimes, and then we'll come back to the adult-adult. But it's the first time in our relationship—these last two, three years—where my being able to be the adult has allowed him to be the child or to be sick or to be nuts if he wants to just act nutty and irresponsible, and so he has the freedom from that monkey, I think *forever,* now.

ERIC: I'd never thought about that before, Denise. I mean I had thought about the fact that my career success has allowed me to be childish. That is, I've been successful enough financially that I have the freedom —I can play, I can be irresponsible, I can split for two weeks for a vacation, if I want to, I can play tennis instead of work. You know, I can act like a child in a lot of ways—playful. But I never thought about the fact that you have given me the permission, I mean the freedom to do that for the first time, and that's really true, you have.

DENISE *(laughing)*: You bet your sweet bippy!

ERIC: I mean, in some ways, you're mama, and you run the house and let me go play.

ME: Maybe that's a good point to take a break.

OTHERS: Okay.

LOVERS OUTSIDE OF MARRIAGE

ME: The only thought that has occurred to me during the break is the fact that a great many young people are experimenting with free interrelationships of the sort you evidently went through—I gather right now that's not the matter of greatest interest to you, and yet I think that it would be very informative to many young people if you would tell a little bit of what the problems were, why you finally quit the deal.

DENISE: The first thing that came to my mind to share was that what made it possible for me, and one of the most important aspects of the necessary ingredients, is that all three people love each other. In other words, when Eric was in love with Pris, she and I were like sisters. And that was the important ingredient for me—to be able to share Eric's love. If it was someone who threatened the hell out of me or I felt inferior to, I could never even try—it's just impossible for me to envision for us a triad relationship—and the same with Eric. He had to respect and really dig the person that I loved before he could even incorporate it into his day-to-day reality. So that's the first thing that came to my mind. The memory is very clear of that. I still think it could be done and I think it is an enlarging of one's life experience, or thoroughness of living life, but I think we *play* with it too much. You have to have a good strong bond in the marriage going—nothing can be wrong there, very seriously wrong, because that's one thing we found out. When we worked this thing with the other couple, that one link was a little weak and the whole thing went down the drain—the other man was not really ready to do this. But I think it can be a beautiful experience. But it's so hard to be able to be sure of the other people you're involved with, let alone yourself. So if you—there are so many daring risks involved that it's just—it's a fiery game to play. But I do believe—ultimately I believe we'll be able to do this. And more successfully than we have—I'm not just speaking of Eric and me—I'm not speaking of our life in the future, right now. I'm speaking, in general, about marriages.

ME: Part of what you're saying is that a person—well, that all four people have to be very grown up before it becomes even possible. Let me just get quite clear as to the facts. What you said had to do with your relationship with this other couple, where you had a relationship with the man and Eric with the woman, is that right? *(Nods)* Okay.

DENISE: I think too that quartets are easier than triads. *But,* it's harder to find two other people who are that solid in their marriage. It's in some ways simpler to find one unattached person. We never did quite make two triads. In other words, Eric had an outside other and I had an outside other, but they both would have melded into our marriage—not that the other two would have had anything to do with each other. We had overlapping things going at one time, but it never really worked out. The only thing with the triad that didn't work, it seemed to me, was that one person always felt left out. And that if both parties had an important other outside the marriage at the same time, then that facilitated things a little easier.

SEX IS JUST PLAY—OR IS IT?

ERIC: I don't know, you say that you think people have to be really mature to do that—maybe really immature. I know some people, around college, among the students—I was hearing in some detail about a situation yesterday. There's a girl there whose whole kick is in orgies. You know, two or three men and her, and she wants two or three women and a man, and she goes around almost proselytizing, you know, that this is the way to have sex. It's a way to get rid of our hangups, and so on. Well, I mean, if you want to consider sex to be *play* and nothing more, fine. But for me and for Denise sex is a lot more than playfulness—having a good time, you know, and getting your kicks. It's a profound kind of communication. And to the extent that it's a profound communication, it gets degraded by being diluted, I guess maybe that is the best way to say it. It gets degraded by being diluted.

ERIC'S JEALOUSY

Let me say something about our relationships outside the marriage. I have always had lovers. I've never had what I felt to be a great urgency to have a lover. I haven't gone around looking for women, looking for affairs, but for most of the fifteen years of our marriage I have had a lover. There has been someone that I met that I just really fell in love with and we got together. That does not seem to have been linked to whether things were going well or badly between Denise and me at all. It does not seem to be correlated. If anything, it's correlated with things going well between us. Because that seems to be the time in which I'm sort of the happiest, most liberated, full of energy, full of love and life and what-have-you. And my love affairs have been, pretty much without exception, a good experience for me. Only in a couple of cases have I felt that they damaged Denise's and my relationship. In a couple of cases I thought they were the best thing in the world, as we were talking a while ago about Margaret.

But damnit, I'm not willing for Denise to have lovers. I mean, I don't want to think about her making love to another man. I've always felt that way. I mean the jealousy of thinking about you and Gus or you and Ed together just tore my guts out. And we got into this a while back, you know, and finally we got into sort of a funny kind of bind where we said, in terms of all our values, everything we believe, all our rational kind of approach to the thing, we say my having a lover or Denise having a lover if she wants one may add to the marriage, it may enhance our growth, there is no reason it needs to be destructive, yet—I mean we're not free, you know, we're not free, independently choosing organisms. There are certain kinds of responses that seem to be programmed into our bodies, and jealousy is one of them—bitter, horrible jealousy. So the conclusion we came to a couple of years ago is that if something like this does happen—we fall in love with someone else and it gets to be a difficult thing—we'll keep that difficulty private, to ourselves. You know, we won't say, okay, let's have a triad now, let's incorporate someone else into the marriage or let's get together with another couple. If Denise meets somebody somewhere or I meet somebody somewhere and it turns into an electric kind of an affair thing, we'll keep it private, and if we can't keep it private, we just won't do it.

ME *(interrupting)*: You mean private from each other?

ERIC: Yeah. And I think that probably has meant that it's not apt to happen, because neither of us is very good at being private from the other one. And furthermore, you see, once you say that it's going to be private, then you automatically mean that there are certain cases in which you have to lie or mislead. And then that is destructive, and so that's a bind that you can't get out of. But I don't think the solution, as Denise says, is to make it open, because I don't think we can handle that either. It's funny, Carl, because the control which Denise and I put on each other—a very realistic control—about not having love affairs with other people, which is one we've wrestled with, deeply, is just about the only control we put on each other's behavior. Most couples I know really try to control each other a lot—social behavior, the way they dress, the kind of work they do, how hard they work—we don't do that. We do almost none of that. Denise can go for weeks, doing what she damn pleases, with hardly any suggestion or reaction from me that she ought to do something different. And she treats me the same way. I can be any way, from the maddest kind of naked prophet running on the beaches, to the most disciplined sort of social scientist teaching my students, and she accepts it. You know, whatever!

ME: I think that's one of the things that has kept our own marriage alive and really lively—though it's had its ups and downs, like every other marriage—is that we don't seem to feel any need to control each other. And that makes an awful lot of difference. If I want to goof off, I goof off. It wouldn't occur to me that Helen would ever object or anything.

DENISE'S HURT AND POSSESSIVENESS

ME (*turning to* **DENISE**): What I want to ask you is, he's spoken very freely of how he's felt, when you were having affairs with other men. How did you feel, before this present arrangement, when you knew that he was having some kind of affair with somebody else?

DENISE: I'm trying to remember the first time I found out. And I cannot remember.

ME (*interrupting*): Did you find out through his telling you?

DENISE: He's been the one that I found it out from. But you didn't tell me about some until years and years and years afterward. I found out about the whole rigmarole through the Margaret thing, but up until that point I had not known about a lot of them. I knew about the most important ones, because that involved our whole lifestyle. And those were the ones that threatened the marriage or threatened the style of our living. The first impression was—I was very hurt—I felt as if something had been taken from me that was rightfully my own. But that became diminished. The gut-level hurt is there if you want to go back and experience it, and taste it and bring it out and feel it, and things like that—but what I tried to do, particularly when it was someone whom I cherished also—you see, I kind of started the whole thing, by an experience at a group with another man, and I experienced what it was like to love two people simultaneously, totally differently, but simultaneously. So I knew it was possible. So when I found this out, I knew that it did not diminish Eric's love for me. I was equating the way I was with him. It didn't diminish my love for him at all, for my loving this Ed. So

I tried just to impute that to Eric's relationship, particularly when it was someone I cared for. And that helped me disregard the hurt and try to work toward really putting into action what I believed, which is that you can live together and love people, more than one at a time. The sexual aspect of it is the trickiest thing to work out. Because privacy is important. We never all three went to bed together. It was always a one-to-one relationship. That's why it was hard for Eric to be able to work it with two of his women at the same time. I'm sure that's one of the reasons why, because you're such a sexual creature. I always wanted it domesticated though. My idea to work it out was to bring the other woman into the home. It would have been fine if she had had children by Eric, anything like that. In two cases I was like that—Vera and Pris. I was willing and able to do that. Eventually with Margaret, maybe, but you were not at a place where you could tolerate that.

ME: One thing I'd like to ask—you're very clear on a lot of that, but can you give me any more of the taste and the flavor of what that kind of hurt is, when you do bring it out and look at it?

DENISE: I'm ashamed of it, because I think it comes from possessiveness and I'm trying to grow away from that. However, it's posed a real dichotomy within me because, as he says, one of my greatest glories was when I was most possessive, over the Margaret thing, when I came on so strong. So part of me is still trying to work that out. It's not working out yet to my satisfaction. But I think the hurt is there because you take it as a blow to your ego. As if something was being taken away from you that was rightfully yours. If you can get past that point, it seems to me. . . .

ME: What's being taken away?

DENISE: Well, it's like a hangup from the previous codes, that the sexual act between a married couple is sacred and unto itself, and when that's shared with another person, then that diminishes the original sanctity. And I still can't shake that.

ERIC: I don't think it's just a religious code or something. When Denise and I make love—and sometimes we just screw and go to sleep—but when we really make love, there is a kind of an intimacy and total openness and tenderness, and we just melt into one being. You can't do that with more than one person somehow. It's different with more than one person. It's no longer as genuine. It's like the profundity of sexual union carries with it a message that this is an exclusive thing you and I have—I don't know why, but it does. It does for me. And if it's not an exclusive thing, then it's different, its character has changed.

DENISE: Well, that's exactly what I'm saying, so then if you—it *is* changed. The actual act, the accoutrements of the whole thing. When you're in love with two different people and you have sex with both people, and you really make love with both people, then that's changed, you're saying.

THE PARADOX

ERIC: It's a paradox. On the one hand, the way we made love last night and my whole feeling for that is I am totally committed and unified with you, I want nothing but you, we flow together, we are each other, in a way. I mean, that's what that sexual act carries with it in meaning. Now suppose tonight I go off somewhere and make love with another woman and have that same kind of feeling with her? That's very strange. I mean, it seems like that cannot be the case. In fact, it *is* the case, it can happen. That's why I say it's a paradox. I've known that experience, to have that kind of feeling with two women at once. You know, very close together, two women, loving them both very much. And yet it seems to me that it's got to be wrong. I mean, there's got to be something that's not working right about that. But I'll be damned if I know what it is.

DENISE: I want to say that I haven't had that experience of what he's talking about—the sexual union feeling—simultaneously. I haven't, ever.

ERIC: Yeah, that's an interesting thing that maybe ought to be said, Carl, in this discussion about our extramarital relationships, is that—you've had what, four or five intimate relationships—they for the most part have not been good. They have not been happy things. Mine have been good, for the most part. The relationships that I've had with other women have been really good ones. Now, I don't know whether that's an accident, you know, or what it is. So that, in a sense, makes us have kind of different attitudes about that whole thing. I think I could quite happily—I know I could quite happily—accept the idea of having lovers now and then, if that happens. And the reason I don't is because Denise can't accept it. On the other hand, I couldn't accept her doing it.

WHAT IS POSSESSIVENESS?

ME: One term you've used—I'd like to see what it means to you. What do you mean by "possessiveness"?

DENISE: When you possess something, you have it unto yourself. It's yours. It's yours. Well, possessiveness means it's yours.

ME: Sort of like a jewel, perhaps, which you can't control, but nonetheless it's yours—this piece of jewelry that is yours. Or do you mean possessiveness in the sense that this is mine, so I manage it?

DENISE: Well, much of the time I've wanted to manage it. Yeah, I mean, that's my whole inclination. Trying to grow away from that is one of my goals. I don't want to manage Eric. Because I realize that the greatest happiness I can give him is his freedom, and that's the uniqueness of me, too. And I've gotten the same impression and reaction when other people have heard what's happened to us. It's that I seem to have the unique capacity to be able to share. I mean, to be able to love that other woman. Many times the other women—they were too possessive—they couldn't share Eric with me. They could not put themselves in my position, so they could not make it a threesome.

ERIC *(interrupting)*: Who?

DENISE: Pris. She wasn't able to, she said that.

ERIC: Yes, but that's because she wanted to have a baby very badly, and thought there would be all kinds of social problems involved.

DENISE: But I've also had it said to me, "If I were in your shoes, I couldn't do what you're doing."

THE PLACE OF DRUGS

ME: This is extremely insightful and very thought-provoking. There's one other question that I want to ask, though I don't want to shut you off. *(Pause)* As you say, you've smoked pot and used LSD. Do you feel that has had any particular influence one way or the other on your marriage?

ERIC: I suppose I might just as well be iconoclastic, Carl. I think grass and LSD have probably had a more profound effect on our marriage than anything else we've talked about. Part of it because part of the problem with our marriage in the early years, aside from the ones we've already talked about that came out of Denise, was a problem that I had, to which grass is an effective antidote. And that is the problem of being uptight. I wanted things to be done my way. I had, you know, a hyperanalytical, hyperrational, contentious, debater's mentality—in love with the processes of the intellect and pretty much dead sensuously. I didn't enjoy my body, I didn't listen to music, I didn't really learn how to touch things and look at things, and I got really pissed off at Denise all the time, because she was not analytical and critical and evaluative, because she could spend a whole day doing nothing but playing the piano and playing with the kids and walking around on the beach—and what kind of a life was that to lead!

Well, when I started smoking grass, I began to say, "Hey. Denise knows some things I never knew!" Until grass broke down that sort of hyperanalytical facility and allowed me to become more of a sensory person like Denise is, then I began to respect her way of being, in a way I'd never respected it before. The LSD, now that's a different story. That just changed my self-identity in a way that's really complicated and allowed some new structures to be built. But grass has been terribly important in our marriage—it's been a very important aspect and part of our marriage. Now, see, Denise never smokes grass any more. And I smoke a lot of grass, almost every day. And that's very comfortable. In some ways when I smoke grass, we relate better—it does a lot of different things to me. It makes me much more focused in on whatever is happening at that time—it frees up my rapping apparatus in a way that alcohol does for some people. I feel a lot more like talking about all kinds of things, sharing ideas and stuff. I tend to be much quieter otherwise. More private, more withdrawn. With grass I tend to be a lot more communicative.

DENISE: Since that time seven years ago, when you took LSD and started smoking pot, even when he's not smoking pot, it has changed his behavior modes and patterns. So that you don't have to smoke it every day to have this groovy thing going with me.

ERIC: Many of my tastes, which now are with me all the time, are tastes which were developed on grass. For instance, like rock music—I learned to like with grass. I never—it wasn't that I didn't like it before, I just wasn't even aware of it, I never heard it. It was alien to me. Now I really like rock. And a lot of other things like that too. I think grass has been the important thing, on the one hand, sort of for the sensory period, that I was talking about earlier, and the bioenergetics has been the other important thing.

ME: Let me ask one question just to make sure I'm partially understanding you. I understand that the LSD is a complicated story and you didn't care to get into it, but it sounds as if that had more to do with you than with your marriage, where pot really has changed you from a head-tripper to someone who's aware of his whole self and of relationships.

ERIC: Maybe I can draw a parallel. Visualize the prophet who goes off on a mountaintop by himself—goes off and contemplates the world and comes to understand the structure of the cosmos, on the one hand. And visualize on the other hand the sort of Dionysian mode of someone who learns how to sing and dance and eat and make love. The LSD has been more the mountaintop, where you say, "Oh, now I have a different picture of the cosmos and myself, and what I mean and what this means." And the grass has been more of a convivial thing—the singing and dancing bit. It's been a way of dropping a lot of your structures, your patterns, which program your behavior, and opening up to new kinds of interpersonal, intersensory kinds of experiences.

DENISE: Unlike alcohol, which lets down the barriers, and lets you be uninhibited. Alcohol deadens and the pot livens. *(Pause)*

YOUTH AND "OVER THIRTY"

ME: This certainly changes the direction, but I want to get this information at some point. How old is each of you?

DENISE: I am thirty-four.

ERIC: I am thirty-six.

DENISE: We were nineteen and a half and twenty-one and a half when we were married.

ERIC: Another comment perhaps worth making is if I were to meet Denise as she was when she was nineteen today, or if she were to meet me when I was twenty-one today, we would probably find each other the most unattractive people we could imagine! That's an interesting idea, Carl, which we've talked about a lot. When people think about marriages, they usually say if people get married very young, they grow away from each other. If people get married when they're older, they've gone through their major changes, so they have a better foundation for the marriage. What's happened to us is that both of us have changed in dramatic, profound ways, but we've changed in parallel directions. You know, so that it's a whole new ballgame.

ME: I really dig that, because we've often talked of exactly that same thing. If either of us as we are now met the other as he or she was at twenty-two, when we were married, my God, we wouldn't have anything to do with the other person. We just wouldn't be in the least interested. But we have been very fortunate in growing together. And some of the things that Helen says these days, I tell her, "What would people back in your hometown think about *that!*"

ERIC: We've thought about this same kind of thing, in connection with what I will now put in quotes as "Denise's breakdown." Which is that every day either of us does twenty things which ten years ago we would have locked each other up for. You know, that we would have defined as insane. Now we accept them as a normal part of our lives, because we've changed our definition of what life is.

MARRIAGE AS PROCESS

I think that people normally talk about marriage as an institution, or they think of marriage as a structure, and it's not, it's a *process.* It's a *set of processes* which people engage in and you never know where they're going to go. But I think you can define what those processes are. And if you thought about marriage in terms of a set of processes which people decide to set in motion, you know—physical, sexual intimacy, probably procreation, sharing economic responsibility for one another, and so on, somehow paralleling commitments in terms of where you're going to live and things like that—these are very definite processes. And so you say, "Okay, marriage consists of those processes, and that's *all.* You set them in motion. And that's what marriage is." Then you have quite a different attitude toward it than if you say, "It's an institution" or "It's a structure of some kind."

ME: I've about run out of questions, but I'd be glad to have you talk a lot more.

ERIC: When we talk about the success of our marriage—we're kind of flippant about it, and it *is* successful, we're really happy—but we're really lucky. I'm thirty-six, right? I just turned thirty-six, you just turned thirty-four. We're both very healthy, we're bright, we're both very attractive, we're far better-looking and more attractive sexually than we were when we were nineteen and twenty-one. I mean, you know, we've got a lot of stuff going for us, and we shouldn't sit around talking about what wonderful things we've done to make this work and that work and things like that. We've really lived in blessed circumstances in a lot of ways. Okay, we've made a lot of good choices. . . .

DENISE *(interrupting):* Okay, but the reason we are, at thirty-six and thirty-four, looking and being what we are is because we *did* that *work.* A lot of things happened because we chose to do with our own bodies what we did. And chose the therapy or the forms of growth experience that we did. And so we can take credit for it. I'm for taking credit for it. We could have copped out so many times.

ME: I agree with you, Denise, because you could be someone with a drawn face and a tight mouth, and Eric could be the head-tripper he was when I first knew him, but no, you've both changed enormously. Be willing to take a little credit for it. On the matter of appearance, I think you build your own appearance in part. On the matter of health, you are very fortunate. And so luck does enter into it, I'm not denying that, but on the other hand you do *build* a changing marriage, it doesn't just happen, because of luck or because you're good-looking or something. You make yourself good-looking.

ERIC'S CONCLUSION

ERIC: I've got something I wanted to say, Carl—about our marriage. This is an evaluation or an analysis of some kind. Both of us are pretty unconventional in sort of social and intellectual terms, given the kind of milieu in which we operate. We don't act in very standard ways. And the reason we have the freedom to be that way is because we have so much strength in our home. The power, the strength, the refuge of our marriage, has given us a kind of core to operate from which has allowed both of us to be very much mavericks in most social terms. And my hunch is that that's far more important than most people generally think. My hunch would be, for instance, that if you see a man who is very conventional, very frightened, you know, very unsure of what directions to move and always looking at how his peers evaluate him—my bet is you can predict he doesn't have a very good marriage. Because if he did, he wouldn't have to do that. He'd find his core, his identity and his being somewhere else. And these things would be secondary, as they ought to be.

ME: I really think that's an idea that has rarely, if ever, been voiced, and I think there's a great deal of truth in it—that if you have a solid base camp, to use military terms, you can go out on all kinds of wild patrols and wild adventures. And if you don't have, you're going to be very, very cautious.

ERIC: I don't care if I lose my job. My identity is not wrapped up in my rank or my publications. It's wrapped up in my wife and my children. I mean, that's so much more powerful than that other stuff.

ME: And that's terribly rare. *(Pause)* Well, this has been a lot of fun, as far as I'm concerned.

MY COMMENTS AND LEARNINGS

Some of Eric's final comments are masterful statements, deserving careful rereading. This unique marriage has gone through various stressful stages, and in going through them the partners seem to have acquired a wisdom from which each of us may learn.

I would like to state some of the elements in their marriage which particularly struck me, though your own reactions and insights may be quite different. For each of my statements I will give either the section heading or the page references or both, so that you may check back if you wish to make a judgment about my thoughts.

To an unusual degree, Eric and Denise have built their own

world around their marriage, rather than asking the social environment how they should be and behave. They are not building their marriage into the expectations of a community, nor even into a network of long-term friendships. They are listening to the internal rhythms of their own organisms to determine what their behavior and their relationship will be. This is a daring way to live (which they fully recognize), and many would be too frightened to take such a stance or would disagree with it. They, however, see that either the community or friendships can be used as an escape from marriage, and they do not intend to utilize these escapes (The Pioneering Move, pp. 162–165 Living by Internal Rhythms, pp. 166–167).

They have discovered in their own lives the disastrous consequences of endeavoring to live by parental and cultural expectations. Even though Denise was "content" with a marriage and a home and baby for five years, living very conventionally, it did not keep her from having a "mental breakdown" (The Period of Social "Oughts," pp. 166–169).

Their marriage illustrates very well the fact that almost all young couples start marriage with an overestimate of their psychological maturity and an underestimate of their childish and juvenile qualities. This is natural enough. It is *how* they deal with this natural unreadiness for a major and continuing relationship which is important (p. 168).

The severe conflict which can be brought about by differing values, especially religious values, is certainly made clear in Denise's life. Added to this is the genuine impossibility of real and free communication, if religious views are held rigidly, as was the case with her parents (pp. 168–169).

Their realization that crises had often saved their marriage was for me a particularly striking statement. Note that it was never the crisis itself that saved the marriage but the fact that they used a crisis as an opportunity for growth. Whether consciously or unconsciously, in these critical periods they became more open with each other, more differentiated from each other, acquiring more separateness as distinct human beings, and thus were able to move to new levels of relating and being with each other. The description of the two kinds of fights in which they engage shows the clear differences between a fight as an expression only of bitterness and a fight as an opening for moving forward (p. 164; Marriage Saved by Its Crises, pp. 170–171).

As in so many of the other marriages we have considered, the crucial, almost desperate importance of becoming a self with an internal locus of evaluation, in which the "rightness" or "wrongness" of a course of action is determined by listening to one's own experience, not to the judgment of others, is well illustrated. It means, as Denise puts it so well, acquiring enough trust in one's real self to nurture it lovingly into bloom. Amazingly enough she attained the point where she was well enough acquainted with her self to recognize when she was letting her self fuzzily fade away, and where she could *choose* whether or not she would be "mentally ill" again (p. 169; How Did You Achieve Personhood? pp. 172–174; I Can Choose To Be Sick, pp. 177–178).

One point on which I am sure readers will stoutly disagree among themselves is, where did they acquire the *desire* to work through each crisis without giving up or running away? Religious upbringing? Cultural conditioning? Natural strength? Or?

To me their explanations of their deep commitment to each other seem somewhat weak and often contradictory. To Denise, it is a mystical karma which binds them together, perhaps from a previous incarnation. To Eric, it is the product of a narrow but deeply ingrained determination (from childhood) to make marriage last. But he also thinks their desire to work things out grows out of a fantastic sexual relationship. At another point he attributes it to a somewhat mystical biological linkage which comes with the bearing of children and the responsibility for those children. Again he offers as an elucidation the fact that Denise is the only person he has met who never bores him—though at times he may be furious with her. Taken separately or together these do not for me constitute a fully satisfying explanation of the fact—which is very clear—that they have *wanted* the marriage to work and have been willing to endure conflict and pain and discord in order to make that come true. (The Underlying Link—Differing Views, pp. 171–172).

The process of change in their sexual and love relationships outside of marriage is fascinating. Denise first discovered for herself that it is possible to love two men simultaneously. However, her willingness to accept Eric's frequent "affairs" is unusual, as is her desire to be warm and friendly toward the other woman, with whom she is (temporarily) sharing her man. But then, as her own independence grew, she found that she could not let Eric live two separate lives, be as much in love with, as much involved with Margaret as with herself. Here, in Eric's words, she became "a bitchy lion," and somehow he found in this strength, in her ability to say "NO!" and in her willingness to leave him if necessary the kind of free independent person he had always wished her to be —no longer potentially "sick" but a person capable of being a full partner in living and loving, and he opted for this in place of the double life which had had such romantic drawing power for him ("The Margaret Episode," pp. 174–177; Lovers Outside of Marriage, pp. 180–181).

It is noteworthy that they found the attempt to live a sexually free life with another couple simply too draining of psychological energy to continue. They still feel, intellectually at least, that to achieve such a relationship—similar to the group marriages of some communes—would be a splendid goal to achieve, but a very difficult one (Lovers Outside of Marriage, pp. 180–181).

Although each has been "fully willing" for the spouse to have an "outside other," it gradually emerges that this willingness is only in the mind. Eric experiences a full measure of primitive jealousy when he knows she is having sexual relationships with another man. And Denise, though ashamed of her feeling, is hurt when he is sexually involved with another woman, a hurt she feels even though she has been similarly involved with other men. She feels that the hurt not only takes away something which is her own, but diminishes—and here she uses a very strange word for such a modern woman—the sanctity of the sexual love they share. Eric confirms this, with an almost lyrical description of their deep sexual union. Yet he sees this as a paradox, because he knows he can feel the same experience with another woman (Eric's Jealousy, pp. 182–184; Denise's Hurt and Possessiveness, pp. 184–186; The Paradox, pp. 186–187).

So they have come to a somewhat peculiar accommodation. If either feels such attraction to another person that he/she wants it to come to a climax in a sexual relationship, so be it. But they will keep these matters private from each other, simply because openness brings too much pain and hurt. But since they are accustomed to an astonishing degree of complete openness with each other, such deceit does not come easily and the result is to make them more monogamous! (p. 183).

They have now reached the point where, after much experience, very open mutual consideration, and much responsible thought, they have decided that there is only one control they put on each other: "We will not have love affairs with other people." From their statements even this is a very loose control, but it is their aim. I suspect they would be the first to say that this is their solution for *them*. They are not trying to tell others what to do. In every other respect they grant each other an almost absolute freedom to be a separate person, to act in any way which each might choose, without attempting to impose any kind of restraint. It is clearly a marriage without nagging—fights yes, but nagging no. Whatever possessiveness exists in the marriage is something they are striving to eliminate, not perpetuate (pp. 183–186; What is Possessiveness? p. 187).

No doubt in part because they have been so involved in making sexual relationships truly meaningful, whether in or out of marriage, Eric has nothing but scorn for the pseudosophisticated who see sex as simply a way of getting "kicks" out of life. He regards this as highly childish and degrading of an experience which he knows can be much more (p. 182).

Let me turn to another important sequence in their remarks. Eric describes graphically the trap in which a person finds himself when he tries to be directly *responsible* for the psychological life of a person with whom he is directly involved. He cannot control or stop Denise's "mental illness," but he feels directly responsible and is also controlled by it. It is a "monkey on his back." He cannot do this or that because it might worsen Denise's condition. Was she unconsciously controlling him by her behavior? At this point we certainly cannot know. Many parents go through the same kind of anguish which Eric suffered with their adolescent children. To feel absolutely responsible, but without the power or control which is the natural accompaniment of responsibility, is indeed a situation peculiarly devised to induce suffering (p. 176; Eric and Denise's "Sickness," pp. 178–179).

The extent to which Eric felt the strain of being so trapped is measured—when he was reassured of Denise's independent strength—by the extent to which he went to pieces. He really went slightly "crazy" himself and let Denise carry the responsibility for him (pp. 179–180).

The full measure of Denise's fulfillment as a person is that she can now be not only Eric's mate in the fullest possible sense, but can also be his "mother" when he feels childish or irresponsible or "crazy," and can also let him return to his grown-up status when he wishes. This is a far cry from the early Denise (The Aftermath, pp. 179–180).

It may be somewhat of an aside—but one on which I feel very strongly—to point out that "mental breakdown," "mental illness," "schizophrenia," and the like are, except in very special cases, *not diseases.* Circumstances may be so overwhelming, or conflicts so great, or the self so unknown and so weak, that bizarre behavior may be the only way to cope with or manage the interpersonal world. But this is vastly different from a physical illness. Denise's attempt to live as the person manufactured by her parents, the conflict between that person and the one acceptable to Eric, her "mental breakdown," her gradual discovery of and nurturing of her own self into a strong, vigorous, exciting woman is a classic example of this ("I Can Choose To Be Sick!," pp. 177–178).

Let me turn now to a very different topic, one on which I am far from expert. It is absolutely clear to Eric and Denise that the smoking of marijuana enabled Eric to become much more of a whole person, to appreciate the emotional aspects of Denise's way of life, and to enrich their marriage in many, many ways. I have known of others with similar stories. The use of LSD by Eric seems to have been a potent experience, but, according to him, it had no great effect on their marriage. The coldly rational, highly intellectual Eric whom I first knew certainly has changed into a warm, feelingful, whole person. If marijuana was to any degree responsible, then it certainly helped both their marriage and Eric as a person (The Place of Drugs, pp. 187–189).

As one sign of the enormous change and growth in their marriage it is amusing to think that each feels that if they now were to meet each other as they were at nineteen and twenty-one, each would find the other totally unattractive. I think this should be true of every developing marriage (Youth and "Over Thirty," pp. 189–190).

Eric, toward the end, describes marriage as a *process*, not an institutional structure. I can in no way improve on his statement and would simply, with all my heart, underscore it, say "Amen!" and suggest that it be reread.

I feel the same way about his final statement. A marriage which is continually being transformed by the development of each spouse is without doubt one of the greatest sources of security a man can know. From it he can venture into daring, innovating, challenging behavior, can work freely to change his world, can take risks, because he knows he can return to his secure relationship. Even this is security in change and process, not in something static. But a core of this continually blossoming security is, to me, marriage at its best (Marriage as Process, pp. 190–191; Eric's Conclusion, pp. 191–192).

9 ℐ Threads of Permanence, of Enrichment

IT IS CLEAR TO ME as I have worked intimately with the materials given so freely by Eric and Denise, by Dick and Gail, Roy and Sylvia, Irene, Hal, and all the rest, that some partnerships "work"—seem satisfying, enriching, growthful, even permanent. Others, sometimes involving some of the same people, do not work and end in unhappiness as well as separation or divorce. And so I have asked myself, are there any threads which appear to distinguish the one from the other? Could I observe elements in a given partnership which would give me some confidence that it would be meaningful to both parties and likely to continue, or other elements which would point to an opposite outcome? I would like to share with you my thinking about this, in a way which I hope will allow you to draw your own conclusions, whether they resemble mine or not.

I. DEDICATION? COMMITMENT?

The first thread I discern has something to do with the two terms in the headings, though the question marks indicate that I am satisfied with neither. Let me trace for you the pathway of my thinking on this topic.

"I love you"; "We love each other." We have seen plenty of examples in this book to indicate how fundamentally meaningless these statements are as any guarantee of a satisfying or lasting partnership—though they may well describe the attitudes existing in some transient relationships. It is not that the statements are meaningless—they may be the absolute truth of the moment; but we have seen them—in Irene's life for example, in Chapter 5— change so easily into "I *thought* I loved you."

"I commit myself wholly to you and your welfare"; "I am more concerned for you than I am for myself." Noble sentiments. But we have seen them lead to disaster in Jennifer's marriage to Jay (Chapter 1), and Hal's hard-working attempts to do the things that would please his first wife (Chapter 6). Beautiful as this attitude may seem at the moment, it can lead to a submergence of self which is fatal to the partnership.

"We will work hard on our marriage." This too is a fine purpose, but it is too vague and implies something too static. We glimpse something of this in the final portion of the account by Dick and Gail (Chapter 2), but it is not very convincing. What they were saying, and what it too often means, is, "We will do our best to make this box we are in a beautiful box." That is *not* enough.

"We hold the institution of marriage sacred, and it will be sacred for us"; "We pledge ourselves to each other until death do us part." It takes only a glance at the separation, divorce, and dissolution statistics to see that no matter how intensely a couple mean such vows, they cannot hold to them unless the marriage is satisfying. If it is not, they either demean or destroy themselves or each other, or they break the bonds—and sometimes they do all these things. The value of such outward commitment appears to me to be just about nil.

"We are destined for each other; we are bound by deep biological bonds through our children; we are determined (through our childhood conditioning) to make our marriage last." Such a multiple dedication is voiced very eloquently by Eric and Denise (Chapter 8) and yet, quite honestly, I question whether those statements account for their lasting marriage. So many individuals have voiced, with equal intensity, each of these views, only to see the partnership dissolve into dust or, even worse, to leave a legacy of bitterness and spoken or unspoken blame.

"I commit myself to working on the process of our relationship, which means a great deal to me." Now, in my opinion, we are getting a bit closer to the nub of whatever dedication means. It views a partnership as a continuing process, not a contract. The work which is done is for *personal* as well as mutual satisfaction. I think we see this most clearly in Irene's third marriage (Chapter 5) in which Joe—quietly, insistently, without fanfare—devotes himself to the *process* of their relationship, even though Irene resolutely refuses to accept this, at first. He will not listen to her "horror stories"—accounts of her tragic past. He focuses on the process of their present relationship and gradually she comes to join him, through her marvelous conversation with herself in the window. From that point onward it is a process relationship, a growing relationship, and exists well before there are any vows exchanged or any marriage legalized.

We see something of the same thing in Becky, I believe (Chapter 6), though unfortunately we do not have her direct personal perceptions. She works on the process of their relationship because she loves and has chosen Hal, and gradually this gets through to him in spite of all the obstacles he must have seen to a black-white marriage. But she is committed to building that relationship.

So, little by little, and largely through a process of elimination, I have arrived at a statement which satisfies me—for the present. It is an attempt to put into words—too many words, I fear—the real meaning of a term like "dedication" as it applies to a partnership. It is a statement which I believe describes one of the threads of permanence and enrichment in any lasting relationship. Here it is. Every word in it has been carefully considered and has weight for me:

"We each commit ourselves to working together on the changing process of our present relationship, because that relationship is currently enriching our love and our life and we wish it to grow."

That says it, so far as I am concerned. Perhaps any explication is unnecessary, but I cannot resist it. The commitment is individual, but the constant, difficult, risky work—which I will try to describe later—is of necessity work that is done together. It recognizes that a relationship is lasting only if that lasting quality exists in the present moment. It makes no major attempt to clear up past or future difficulties, except as they make mutual life unhappy right now. It sees the relationship as a flowing stream, not a static structure which can be taken for granted. It focuses not so much on the other individual, nor on oneself—though of that I will also have more to say later—but on the immediate relationship of loving and living which exists between the two. And so, occasionally, it achieves the transcendent quality which Buber describes so well, and which perhaps suffers when it is abbreviated, but a few of his sentences have great meaning for me. "The primary word *I-Thou* can only be spoken with the whole being. . . . When *Thou* is spoken, the speaker has no thing for his object. . . . He takes his stand in relation. . . . *Thou* has no bounds. . . . (In an *I-Thou* relationship) No deception penetrates here; here is the cradle of the Real Life" (Buber, pp. 3, 4, 7).

When dedication and commitment are defined in the manner I finally formulated, then I believe they constitute the cradle in which a real, related partnership can begin to grow.

II. COMMUNICATION

What a morass of diverse and contradictory elements are contained in this word. It covers everything imaginable. "Pass the butter." That is communication, and is about as far as the term goes in many marriages. "My mother always said you were a louse, and you are!" This too qualifies as communication, and such accusations, judgments, evaluations possibly do more to harm partnerships than any other one factor I know. Or Sylvia, trailing her long hair lovingly over Roy's back, without saying a word—that too is communication; just as much as are the silent glare, or the look of disgust, or Hal's first wife's pulling away when he wanted to kiss her. Nonverbal communication can be very powerful indeed.

So the statement that a partnership should be communicative says nothing at all really. All marriages are communicative, verbally or nonverbally, for better or for worse. Yet somewhere in this welter of meanings I find a thread of enrichment, one which greatly increases the chances of permanence, of happiness. Let me see if I can tease it out and clarify it—perhaps by negative as well as positive examples.

In one sense commitment to the process, which I have just endeavored to describe, is basic to the best of communication. But communication has many elements.

The Persisting Feeling. Let me take a very commonplace example. The husband finds himself bothered by his wife's appearance at the breakfast table, bedraggled, in a rumpled robe, and in curlers. If he lets this build up and build up in himself, it will come out *sometime,* usually in an explosive accusation: "Why do you look like a *slut* in the morning?" But if he is sufficiently aware of his own inner feelings, then after a few recurrences of this attitude he can voice it as something in *himself:* "You know, I find I'm annoyed at the way you appear each morning." This is sure to draw a response and the ensuing communication will probably not be pleasant, but each will learn a great deal about the other, *if* each can continue voicing only his own feelings and not accusations about the other. This is not a trick or a technique, and will fail completely if used as such. But if it is firmly based in the attitude "I want to share myself and my feelings with you, even when they are not all positive," then a constructive process can almost be guaranteed.

Risk. Such communication always involves risk. You are exposing a hitherto unknown—and hence vulnerable—facet of yourself. When a woman takes a deep breath and decides to risk herself, and says to her partner, "I don't know the reasons, whether it's in me or you, but I find very little real satisfaction in our sex relationship," she is doing two things. She is risking the whole relationship for the sake of the process of growing it. She is also sharing a hidden, frightening part of herself, which may be rejected or misunderstood or seen as an accusation—she is laying the relationship on the line. Yet such a statement cannot be denied. She is the only one who knows whether it is true. And it can become a datum, staring each in the face, which encourages a deep sharing.

We have seen example after example of this in the chapters. Dick and Gail, who could accuse each other so easily, voiced their *own feelings* in regard to sex and found the partner understanding and compassionate (Chapter 2). Irene (Chapter 5), who tried so desperately and in so many ways to communicate a false image of herself, including a false picture of achieving orgasm, gradually relaxed into communicating all the horrible ways in which she saw herself, and was loved in return.

There is one effect of such deeply vulnerable communication which most people cannot believe until they have tried it. That is that the sharing of the deepest feelings one can discover in oneself almost inevitably draws similar sharing from the other. When Peg (Chapter 1) reveals all she can of her "awful self" to her husband, he responds with his feelings about himself, and she discovers he "has been down in hell too." Such sharing provides an enormous body of sensitive, quivering data with which they can deal to improve the quality of the process of their relationship.

One of the most fortunate things about the kind of communication I have been describing is that it can be started by *one* member of the partnership. This surely takes courage, but it is possible.

Here is my attempt to put as concisely as I can the various aspects of this second elusive thread of a developing partnership. Again, this is more than a casual statement.

"I will risk myself by endeavoring to communicate any persisting feeling, positive or negative, to my partner—to the full depth that I understand it in myself—as a living, present part of *me*. Then I will risk further by trying to understand, with all the empathy I can bring to bear, his or her response, whether it is accusatory and critical or sharing and self-revealing."

I wish that statement too could be condensed, but my organizing mind insists on trying to take into account all conceivable situations. At any rate, I believe that you will find, in this book and in the lives about you, that when this complex quality of sharing, risking, receptive communication exists even partially, you have a great likelihood of a developing, releasing relationship. It is especially evident in Irene's third marriage, and in Eric and Denise, but it is to be observed in all the partnerships which are moving toward a process, rather than a static mode of relating. The less that there is hidden in the present relationship (not digging into the past), the more change and development are nurtured. And *one* member can start that ball rolling, though if the communication remains continuously one-sided, the prospects for growth become dismal.

III. THE DISSOLUTION OF ROLES

One element which we have seen playing both a positive and a negative part, depending on the stance taken toward it, is that of expectations arising from the culture or subculture. To live by role expectations seems consistently in opposition to a marriage which is going somewhere, which is in process. Whether we are talking of the Tepoztlán woman who is submissive to her husband because she is supposed to be that way, or Joan marrying because all her friends and parents expect her to marry Max, or of Dick and Gail (Chapter 2) finding themselves after marriage suddenly thrust into new boxes not of their own making, we are speaking of a relationship which is *static* or going downhill.

So in the only marriages which seem enriching and satisfying roles play a lesser and lesser part until, as in the case of Eric and Denise, the expectations practically disappear. To follow—more or less blindly—the expectations of one's parents, of one's religion, of one's culture is to bring to disaster the ongoing, differentiating process of a developing partnership.

This is not to say that all these expectations are in themselves "bad." Indeed, a person might choose, after mature consideration, to follow a course of action which his parents too think is wise. But this is because he *chooses* to do so, not because they expect it. And here, as one easily recognizes, it becomes tricky. Is it because your own feelings, your own "natural rhythms" move you toward this course of action, or are you deceiving yourself by saying that you choose it? To know one's feelings is not easy or simple. It is in fact a lifetime effort. But to the extent that you can listen to your own organism and move in the directions that "feel right" to it and to you, to that extent you are moving away from behavior guided by role expectations. And to that extent you are moving toward a complexity of partnership, a richness of living together which is far less simple than living by a role, and far more satisfying. So, for me, here is another thread which unites those partnerships which are becoming. They do not permit themselves to be molded by expectations, no matter how compelling these may seem to be. "We will live by our own choices, the deepest organismic sensings of which we are capable, but we will not be shaped by the wishes, the rules, the roles which others are all too eager to thrust upon us."

IV. BECOMING A SEPARATE SELF

In a process partnership one of the most important factors making for a truly growing relationship may seem a rather paradoxical one. It is simply that when each partner is making progress toward becoming increasingly his or her own self, the partnership becomes more enriching. It is almost like saying that the more separate you become, the greater is the chance for a strong union. This is not to be taken quite literally, for obviously it can lead to breakup as well. Yet almost every instance in this book supplies evidence. A *living* partnership is composed of two people, each of whom owns, respects, and develops his or her own selfhood. Nowhere is this better illustrated than in the case of Denise and Eric. As Denise takes faltering steps away from being a nonentity, molded by her parents or her husband, the marriage grows. As she becomes more and more a strong and independent self, each step in that progress aids their partnership. But what is meant by becoming your own self? Let me try to tell what it means to me.

DISCOVERY OF ONESELF. It means first that he/she (damn these pronouns!) is continually trying to get closer to his inner feelings. He moves toward a greater closeness to, and awareness of, whatever he is experiencing in his own organism. Joan (Chapter 1) is a brief and pathetic example of how—too late for her first marriage—she learns that she has feelings and that they are trustworthy. Every individual finds that what he is experiencing inwardly is complex and varied, ranging from wild, "crazy" reactions to solid, socially approved ones.

ACCEPTANCE OF SELF. He moves toward accepting all this changing complexity as a real part of himself—a crazyquilt of variety of which he does not need to feel ashamed. He begins to *own* himself—a very precious possession. The more he owns himself, the more he can *be* himself. I have most often seen this process come about in therapy or in encounter groups, but it could equally well come about in our education, if we ever came to recognize that helping persons to be *persons* is far more basic than helping them to become mathematicians or French conversationalists or what-have-you.

So if the person in a partnership looks acceptingly on all the awful and crazy and hideous and tender and beautiful and competent aspects of him/her self, he is becoming more of a person to live with. Irene and Joe (Chapter 5) are classic examples—worth rereading. But to study the slow progress of Denise (Chapter 8) or of Roy and Sylvia (Chapter 3) is to learn what a tough, difficult, lifelong process this is—one of the elements which gives a partnership its exciting unpredictable loveliness as well as pain. When two unique persons live together intimately and sharingly—Wow!

DROPPING MASKS. It almost goes without saying that in this process he/she is moving away from façades, armor-plated defenses and pretenses. She is not a frightened immature child, hiding behind the mask of a sophisticated glamour girl. He may seem to be a living example of *machismo*, of supermasculinity, of strength, but he can drop that façade. Inside he is often childish, dependent, in need of mothering, just as at times she needs the fatherly care which can mean so much to a frightened little girl.

Each can be what he changingly is, without the fear that he will remain cast in that mold forever. I have often suggested to individuals that they be good and kind and careful of the child they always carry within. And if my mate can also love this boy that is part of me, that becomes doubly enriching and enables me also to be the man that I know I am.

EXPERIENCING VALUES. All of this means that each partner is developing what I like to call an "internal locus of evaluation." By this I am saying that the value, the meaning that an experience has for you is not determined by what your partner says or your parents decide or your church rules or your school evaluates, but by the way it "feels" to you in your very deepest level of experiencing. For instance, all the outside influences I mentioned may say that a given experience of sexual intercourse in your marriage is right, and legal, and proper, and shows love. You know all this. And yet you may also know, in the deepest recesses of your being, that it was one person being used by another, that it was a pretense, a fraud, and contained no real love. When you have an *internal* center of evaluation, it is this second type of judgment on which you rely and which guides your next behaviors. It also implies that you are not governed by the "shoulds" and "oughts" which all the aspects of our culture are so ready to substitute for the values you are discovering in and by yourself.

When a person is making progress, in all the ways I have described, toward becoming his own separate self, then he/she is a worthy partner—not a slave or slaveowner, not a shadow or an echo, not always a leader nor always a follower, not a person to-be-taken-for-granted, and certainly, as Eric points out, not a boring person.

GROWTH FOR BOTH. Finally, it is so rewarding to be in process of becoming one's real self, that it is almost inevitable that you will permit and encourage your partner in the same direction, and rejoice in every step that he or she takes. It is *fun* to grow together, two unique and intertwined lives.

I should add that if this kind of growth toward selfhood occurs only in one partner and fails to be encouraged or fostered in the other, then the increasing distance can become awesome, and the partnership, without some sort of near miracle, is headed straight for the rocks.

"PERHAPS." I should like to try to put this final intricate strengthening thread into personal terms, as I have the others. Again the words are not lightly chosen.

"Perhaps I can discover and come closer to more of what I really am deep inside—feeling sometimes angry or terrified, sometimes loving and caring, occasionally beautiful and strong or wild and awful—without hiding these feelings from myself. Perhaps I can come to prize myself as the richly varied person I am. Perhaps I can openly *be* more of this person. If so, I can live by my own experienced values, even though I am aware of all of society's codes. Then I can let myself be all this complexity of feelings and meanings and values with my partner—be free enough to give of love and anger and tenderness as they exist in me. Possibly then I can be a *real* member of a partnership, because I am on the road to being a real person. And I am hopeful that I can encourage my partner to follow his or her own road to a unique personhood, which I would love to share."

ONLY FOUR?

I honestly supposed that I could discover many of these "threads" which bind partnerships together in an enriching, not a confining way. But the four I have described are all I have come up with. More things are notable by their absence than by their presence. Take, for example, "mutual satisfaction in the sexual relationship," often listed as a sine qua non of a permanent relationship. But I do not find it to be basic of itself—it can almost surely be developed, if the four gossamer threads are present in a partnership. So I have omitted a great many of the superficial descriptive statements which can often be made about "successful" marriages, because they do not explain how they came about. To me it has seemed that I have drawn out four of the more basic, the more causal, the more processmaking elements—commitment to the relationship process, risking the communication of one's own feelings, ceasing to live by roles, and discovering and sharing more of one's separate real self.

But I have no illusions that my analysis is correct or that it is the only correct one. I hope you will build your own.

10 ✍ So?? What Do We Do?

LET ME DEPART A BIT from marriage and its various alternatives and creep up on the problem, as it were, from a fresh angle.

The experimental laboratory is one of the core elements of American society. Hardworking physicians and their technical colleagues spend vast sums investigating the causes and cure or amelioration of various failures of the human organism to function normally. The government increases its investment in the exploration of cancer. Pharmaceutical companies spend millions, and the government adds many millions more, to explore new ways of controlling disease through medication and to investigate failures and disastrous results of some prescribed drugs. This has come about because we no longer regard a plague or a rampant disease as an evidence of God's wrath, simply to be borne in silence.

We have space laboratories which devote themselves to the problems of reaching outer space and living in it, and getting to the bottom of every mechanical or human failure. Billions of dollars are not enough to support these pioneering exploratory ventures, whose outcome no man can predict. They fly in the face of the tradition that man is bound to this planet.

Automotive companies have elaborate laboratories to study every portion of the functioning of the modern car, trying to improve it, to reduce breakdowns, to make them safer. With a bit of government prodding they even recall thousands upon thousands of automobiles which *might* fail, even though that breakdown might only occur in one out of a hundred thousand cars. We have come a long way from the derisive shouts at the automobile, "Get a horse!" And we have come that distance through freely conducted laboratory experiments.

Any modern industry is judged in part by the size of its investment in R and D—research and development. It is recognized that a company cannot succeed unless it is eliminating past failures, exploring new possibilities, studying new materials for its products.

In agriculture it is a truism that modern agriculture, with its tremendous rate of improvement in the production of crops, meats, poultry, and the like, could not have come about without countless laboratories—governmental, commercial, private—exploring past failures and future possibilities, and supported by endless funds.

I won't belabor this point. Experimentation is central to all our technological advances, no matter how many traditions it overthrows. It is not only accepted, but financed and admired by the public. Change is the name of the game, and this is known to and accepted by almost everyone. The industrial revolutions— more than one: the revolution in health care, in agriculture, industry, war technology, space technology—are all recognized. We know that these nonviolent revolutions have brought incredible alterations in our ways of life.

Now let us turn to the subject of this book. Marriage and the nuclear family constitute a failing institution, a failing way of life. No one would argue that these have been highly successful. We need laboratories, experiments, attempts to avoid repeating past failures, exploration into new approaches.

I believe that in this book we see what a vast laboratory in just these problems is being conducted by our young people. Unheralded and unsung, explorations, experiments, new ways of relating, new kinds of partnerships are being tried out, people are learning from mistakes and profiting from successes. They are inventing alternatives, new futures, for our most sharply failing institutions, marriage and the nuclear family. So then, the government supports these laboratories with its billions, and young people are highly respected for experimenting with new values and new patterns? This quiet nonviolent revolution is being strongly supported by a concerned public? What nonsense! Everyone knows that just the reverse is true. In this area we are so frightened of change that we see an enemy under every bed—no, *in* every bed would be more accurate. We pass laws and ordinances to kill this budding, promising laboratory. We can only point to its failures and are too frightened to look at its successes. We do our best to cut off financial support to anyone so bold as to experiment with change in the institution of marriage. We are—in this area—back in the Middle Ages, when the scientist—Galileo, for example—was tried and found guilty of having made discoveries, and forced to recant. We still hold that tradition and religious sanctions, and codes of morality taken from the past must never be broken, and woe to the person whose values, discoveries, and ways of living violate these sanctions.

To me it seems high time that here too we begin to move into the twentieth century. It is high time that we recognize and respect the fact that quiet revolutionary as well as evolutionary experiments are a fortunate, not an unfortunate, aspect of our cultural life. Can we accept the fact that here too the name of the game is change, and that we are desperately in need of just such a revolution in the area of living partnerships and family life as has taken place in industry, agriculture, flight, space, and all the other aspects of life? Can we respect our explorers? This is the great question which we face. And if we did, what would we do?

FREEDOM TO BE EXPERIMENTAL IN PARTNERSHIPS

It fascinates me that as I look over the list of names of the people who have so honestly filled this book with themselves, the great majority of them have, in their struggles for a better partnership, engaged—either in the past or present—in practices which federal, state, or local laws would class as illegal. To give them their old-fashioned names, "living in sin," "committing adultery," "lewd and lascivious conduct," "fornication," "homosexuality," "ingesting illegal drugs," even "soliciting"—these have all been present in these pages, though when they are actions engaged in by individuals struggling to find a better pattern of partnerships, the old-fashioned names are, frankly, ridiculous.

So perhaps one thing we as a culture might do which would preserve this enormously valuable laboratory, these pioneering ventures into new relationship space, would be to relieve them of the ever-present shadow of moral reproach and criminal action.

If we only dared to say, "We will not interfere," this would be an enormous step forward in facing reality. Suppose we passed a law which declared that any partnership pattern entered into by mutually consenting adults is now legal, providing it does no clear injury to other persons. This would make for honest, rather than clandestine explorations, and would let these laboratories in partnerships operate openly and honestly. I wonder if we are, as a culture, capable of such action? Change and freedom, especially when they are meant "for real," are terms which make the American public shiver in its boots. We seem to hate to remember that this was a nation molded by revolutionaries, both nonviolent and violent. So perhaps we will be too frightened to say to members of partnerships of various kinds: "You *are* free; we accept the inevitability, and the conceivably great advantages, of *change.*" But I believe that if, collectively, we had the courage to say even this, we would have set the stage for a partnership revolution, a relationship revolution.

EDUCATION FOR HUMAN INTERACTION, HUMAN COMMUNICATION

One of the elements which stands out for me, in so many of the marriages described in this book and in other marriages that I have known, is that young people start out without the foggiest notion of how to live in human, personal interaction—literally without any experience in real interpersonal sharing communication with persons. Sometimes I feel our education has as one of its major goals the bringing up of individuals to live in isolation cages.

So, in moments of bemused thinking, I wonder if it would truly be too much to ask of our educational system that it include one new goal, in addition to those they have defined so intellectually, so precisely. I wonder if they would be willing not only to believe, but to prove by their actions that *one* goal of education is to assist the young person to live as a person with other persons.

It seems to me a modest hope, in some ways. It would not require vast new expenditures, new buildings, added teaching staff. It would simply mean that we would need a changed attitude in teachers, a changed climate in classrooms, a changed attitude—perhaps the most difficult to achieve—in school administrators.

If all elementary, high school, and college personnel could simply recognize and accept the fact that they are fallible persons dealing with fallible persons, our educational system would be revolutionized overnight. If they could recognize that human interaction is something that will go on all through their lives and all through their students' lives, then they might be willing to include a real and open and sharing communication as a part of the educational experience. This would be an enormous start, a beginning preparation for living in the world of people.

Yet even such a suggestion often arouses, as I know, profound fear in teachers and administrators. For the teacher to become a person to his students reveals him as vulnerable, with moods, with feelings, making mistakes, occasionally inspired. Gone would be the steady, unchanging, infallible mask which is the most prized possession of nearly every teacher (see Dillon, *Personal Teaching*, 1971, for a personal account of his fumbling attempts to drop such a mask).

But I and others have, especially in recent years, written about such human possibilities in the schools and I do not wish to repeat myself. So, if you are interested, read Rogers, 1969, Lyon, 1970, Leonard, 1968, Herndon, 1968, and many, many others whom you will find mentioned in these books.

Instead let me turn to a new suggestion, which I have not seen made before. If a group of serious parents wish to start a "learning laboratory" for their children, why not give them a certificate to go ahead and experiment? The time could be limited to five years, if that would make the bureaucrats more satisfied, but otherwise, except for reasonable health and sanitation precautions, we could free these parents from all the restrictive state laws about curriculum, requirements, grades—the whole crippling and imprisoning bit. How could one be opposed to this? There are only two reasons: if we do not trust parents to want the best for their children, we would not do it; if, as bureaucrats, we are afraid that in the long run it might endanger our jobs and all the elaborate structure of teacher certification, required textbooks, and the framework of entrenched educators and their system, we would not approve it. But we would be losing a priceless opportunity for diversity, and humanizing influences, and exploration of new avenues. And children learn in spite of us, as many studies show, and parents would most assuredly learn, in such an experiment. I hope we are not fearful of the emotional development, and honest expression of feelings, and purposeful learning which might go on in such laboratories.

EDUCATION FOR PARTNERSHIP

There is enormous furor today about sex education in the schools, and surely if it is done it should be carried on in free and honest discussions by persons who are real.

But even more basic, to my mind, is the need for learning to be partners. An individual can get a college degree today without ever having learned anything about how to communicate, how to resolve conflict, what to do with anger and other negative feelings. He/she can be completely ignorant of the fact that in part every man is feminine, dependent, childish; every woman in part strong, independent, mature—and vice versa for each.

One cannot read this book without realizing that though modern marriage is a tremendous laboratory, its members are often utterly without preparation for the partnership function. How much agony and remorse and failure could have been avoided if there had been at least some rudimentary learning before they entered the partnership.

Again you may ask, "How can this be done?" and again I feel that a culture that is even, perhaps, making progress in dealing with smog, most certainly could do *something* to lift the fog which surrounds the beginning partnership. If, for example, encounter groups for teachers and students, led by the kind of people who do not cause psychological damage (and we now know something about that) could be a part of the learning process, many things would be achieved. The communication of real feelings, positive and negative; the resolution of conflicts and antagonisms; the pathway to a self-accepting personhood—all of these might be at least partially achieved (Rogers, 1970). And if the means for adequate and intelligent follow-up were developed, these gains could be maintained.

But I mention this only as one way—there must be many more. Creative dance could contribute; cooperation in artistic and literary creativity encouraged. It is fundamental, I believe, that the learning be experiential—education "from the neck up" will *not* be sufficient for a living, changing, growing partnership.

COUPLES AND FAMILIES AS A RESOURCE

But it is not only in our educational system that we could educate for partnership. There are various resources involving the family itself.

The most exciting one, because most directly related to the problem, is the group conducted for young people who are "going together," considering marriage or living together, or are engaged. Here, as I have seen in my experience, the opportunity is very great. Given a nonjudgmental and facilitative person as organizer of such a group, young people can openly explore their differing expectations of each other and of the partnership, their conflicting aims and desires, their independent strengths, and their mutually interdependent support—each for the other. This can involve communication on a deep level, and can be preventative of future difficulties. (See Rogers, 1970, for a general picture of groups and their outcomes.)

I think of one young couple in a group I conducted, and the results of their more open interaction. He thought that she was considerably inferior to him—which came as a shock to her—and each found that they had very different expectations for marriage. They had cared for each other for a long time, had been living together for some time, and yet neither had ever communicated much of his inner self to the other. At the time, I felt that this sharing of their highly divergent feelings could not help but have a positive outcome. Either they would decide they were not for each other, and "split" before serious damage had been done, or they would continue to work through these problems openly with each other. The letters, a wedding invitation, and Christmas messages for the past several years, indicate that it was the second alternative which occurred.

So to deal directly with young people who are considering partnership, in groups which permit them to be open, is one important way of building for more lasting relationships.

Then the increasing spread of couples' groups, in which the approach and the facilitation would be similar to that which I have described, has been of great help to many couples. Again, in a deeply disturbed and incompatible relationship, experience in such a group may lead toward separation or divorce, but for the great majority it helps toward more interpersonal sharing, more willingness to express differences and resolve them, more recognition of their mutual caring and strength.

Another approach through the family is the inauguration of family group meetings, held regularly, where everyone has the right fully to express his complaints, his hurts, and his good feelings concerning every other member of the family. Obviously at least one parent must be capable of receiving, understanding, and accepting such feelings if the attempt is to have any success. But where a climate of acceptance can be fostered, not only do parents learn—often for the first time—some of their children's deeper feelings about them and about each other, but the children learn of the parents' feelings too. Again, it is often for the first time that children recognize that their parents are human—with failings and moods, loving feelings and critical ones—that they are not simply "grownups," meaning beings whom the young cannot possibly understand.

In one of the cassette series listed in the bibliography, a mother tells of the very moving events which occurred when they first inaugurated family sessions, starting with embarrassed silences, and giggles, but leading gradually to some totally unknown feelings on the part of the oldest boy. She also tells some of the amusing and unpredictable ways in which the family, working as a problem-solving unit in these meetings, has resolved some issues which were major sources of irritation to one or more of the members of the family. (See Rogers, Cassettes on Personal Adjustment, #7.)

All such efforts in the family circle give, I believe, to parents and children alike, learnings in what it means to be human with another person.

Let me turn to quite a different area in which I am convinced we could take more positive steps. This is the dilemma of children whose parents are divorced. Our present treatment of them is legalistic and medieval. So often it consists of dividing the child down the middle and giving one miserable portion to one parent, the other to the other. Yet at no time in their lives are these children in greater need of love, of a caring environment. They need to be nurtured as persons and respected as persons.

How could this be done? Are we saying that a culture which, through its laboratories, got us off the ground into space quails before this problem? There should be dozens of differing attempts, from improved versions of the kibbutzim to solutions as yet undreamed of. Surely it is not our imagination which is lacking. It is a lack of will, and a failure to believe that the development of a truly separate, expressive, creative, secure child is worthy of enormous effort in imagination, in financing, in humans being human with one another.

ONE FINAL REMARK

This chapter has but one purpose: to get people thinking about how to change—yes, even revolutionize—a failing portion of its culture—marriage and all its ramifications and alternatives.

I want to add that the concept of partnerships—married or not—as a vast and promising laboratory has been forced on me by my learnings from these couples. I did not start with this idea at all. I tried to choose reasonably representative people. They did not—and do not—seem to me to be unusual couples or unusual persons, except for their surprising willingness to tell of their life as it is. Only gradually did I see that here is an enormous, exploring experiment, going on all about us. What will be our stance toward it?

For myself I can only say that my experience with these persons has led me to an even deeper feeling of trust in their capacity to find growthful, healing solutions to the problems of living together—if we will give them half a chance. They represent a rich resource for our country and especially for its future, if we can bring ourselves to accept and trust the seriously meaningful revolution which is taking place in partnerships.

To Carry On ✐
An Annotated Bibliography
For Further Search

THIS BOOK HAS MERELY opened up topics of a very broad range: varieties of marriage and divorce; sexual difficulties; differing kinds of marital relationships; the problems of communications; the future of marriage; a few of the problems of child rearing. Many readers will want to push further into specific fields. For this reason I have asked my extremely well-read friend Dr. Alice Elliott to prepare the following annotated bibliography, to which I have added some titles. I believe that from this list (and the carefully written brief descriptions) you can choose both the topics you would like to pursue further and the level of "lightness" or "heaviness" in your reading. It is doubtful that you will find many answers, but your thinking will most certainly be enriched.

Dr. Elliott says: ". . . Marriage is so multi-faceted that I have chosen to recommend a few books in each of several categories including: historical perspectives, sex, sex education, love, communication, 'games,' divorce, communal living, humor, poetry, satire, studies on marriage and sex, child rearing, infertility, self-awareness, future possibilities, and other topics. Then, in addition to books, I have added films and taped cassettes which bear on these topics."

BOOKS

Abbott, Elisabeth, *The Fifteen Joys of Marriage* (New York: The Orion Press, 1959).
A medieval satire (illustrated in color) warning a young man of the "pains and torment" of married life and the joys of bachelorhood.

Allard, William A., "The Hutterites—Plain People of the West," *National Geographic*, July, 1970, *138*, 98–125.
A good summary of the longest-lived group of communes in existence, best known for their pacifism. Some of their characteristics will strongly appeal to young people, and some may repel them, but the fact that they have lasted is thought-provoking.

Armour, Richard, *A Short History of Sex* (New York: McGraw-Hill, 1970).
Armour is a master at satire. Read this and laugh through the history of sex from Adam and Eve through the Kinsey Report to today's home movies, television, and the Pill.

Augsburger, David W., *Cherishable: Love and Marriage* (New York: Pyramid Books, 1971).
An excellent book for the young especially. A book that will challenge anyone to examine what it means to be married, to be a man, to be a woman, to communicate, to be a parent, to be sexual, to make conflict creative, and to be faithful.

Bach, George R., & Deutsch, Ronald M., *Pairing* (New York: Avon Books, 1970).
This is a book about the art of communicating and making contact with others. A new look at the word "intimacy." The authors see it as an essential for emotional survival. Provocative and practical new insights for making warm human relationships.

Bartell, Gilbert D., *Group Sex* (New York: Peter H. Wyden, 1971).

The author, an anthropologist at Northern Illinois University, spent three years in this pioneering study of "swingers." The number of people in the United States involved in this "group sex" has been estimated as high as 5 million. Assisted by his wife, this author studied over 280 "middle-class swingers" without participating in such activities. The basic motivations of the swingers are very complex but there seems to be an underlying hope that they can improve their marriages. A sad tale about people who do not know how to make warm human relationships and perhaps the sad result of the importance the media has put upon sex.

Beauvoir, Simone de, *The Second Sex*, H. M. Parshley ed. and trans. (New York: The Modern Library, 1968).

The Patriarchial Times states that this famous French woman believes that life in our Western culture forces women to take a secondary place in society. This is done by social tradition and education controlled by men. Until these conditions change, woman cannot take her rightful place in society with a sense of human dignity and is relegated to dependency and subservience. Easily read and understood. This book is a classic in its field.

Bernard, Jessie, *The Sex Game* (Englewood Cliffs, N.J.: Prentice Hall, 1968).

An outstanding book on communication between the sexes. Aware of the biological and emotional differences between the sexes, Jessie Bernard has written a well documented, penetrating study. It is easy reading and highly interesting. Excellent bibliography.

Berne, Eric, *Games People Play* (New York: Grove Press, 1964).

As the title implies, people consistently play games in their interpersonal relationships. Thirty-six games are analyzed in seven categories including marital games and sexual games. At times superficial, but often provocative

Bertocci, Peter A., *Sex, Love and the Person* (New York: Sheed & Ward, 1967).

Bertocci stresses the interrelatedness of sex, love, and the person. An excellent book on the pros and cons of premarital sex, and the implications for a happy marriage.

Bird, Joseph, & Bird, Lois, *Marriage Is for Grownups* (Garden City, N.Y.: Image Books, 1971).

An analysis of common marriage problems and guidelines which will help you toward a more meaningful relationship in marriage. Both authors are marriage counselors who raise questions, but do not necessarily provide answers. The first chapter, "So You Have a Problem," will give you their assumptions. In the following chapters they discuss "major problem spots." Emphasis is on communication.

Blake, Robert R. & Mouton, Jane S., *The Marriage Grid* (New York: McGraw-Hill, 1971).

Both authors are psychologists for a behavioral science firm called Scientific Methods Incorporated. A book about personal explorations. If you're interested in improving your marriage, try using this grid to help you understand your feelings and behavior toward the end of actualizing your own potential and your marriage relationship. A most interesting and easily readable book. Excellent bibliography.

Bossard, James H. S., & Boll, Eleanor S., *Why Marriages Go Wrong* (New York: The Ronald Press, 1958).

The authors believe that many of our current social values and beliefs make the achievement of happiness in marriage difficult. Navigators find charts of reefs and shoals essential to safe voyaging. This book provides a similar chart for the unmarried.

Breasted, Mary, *Oh! Sex Education!* (New York: Praeger Publishers, 1970).

The author made a detailed investigation into the pros and cons of the teaching of sex education in the schools today. She is not happy with the conclusion she reached: neither side is being honest with the young. However, she learned to understand both the pros and the cons. You will too if you read this interesting up-to-date book on the sex education dilemma in our society.

Buber, Martin, *I and Thou*, R. G. Smith, trans. (Edinburgh: T. & T. Clark, 1937; New York: Charles Scribner's Sons, 1958).
This book will appeal to some and repel others. It is essentially a great philosophical prose poem, written with something of the sweeping grandeur of the King James Version. It is also finally addressed to the eternal *Thou*, the "wholly other . . . the wholly Same, the wholly Present," whom men have often termed God. It is a book which will make you think, written by a man of great wisdom.

Capon, Robert F., *Bed and Board: Plain Talk About Marriage* (New York: Simon & Schuster, 1965).
An Episcopal priest, husband, father of six, writes with wit and gusto about marriage. What is it, really? If bed and board—love and nourishment—are its foundations, its sacraments, what else is involved? Reinhold Niebuhr, the theologian, said that the author had snatched the subject away not only from the adjustment engineers but from the sexologists concerned with technique and from the sentimental moralists.

Carden, Maren L., *Oneida: Utopian Community to Modern Corporation* (Baltimore, Md.: The Johns Hopkins Press, 1969).
The history of one of the most successful of the communal societies founded in America about 1800. This book is the result of much research of original source materials.

Chapman, A. H., *Sexual Maneuvers and Strategems* (New York: G. P. Putnam's Sons, 1969).
As the title implies, sexual gamesmanship is discussed in depth, primarily through case studies. Interesting, enlightening, and humorous.

Chesser, Eustace, *Is Chastity Outmoded?* (London: The Windmill Press, 1960).

Dr. Chesser is a well-known psychiatrist and a prolific writer in the fields of love, sex, and marriage. The material appeared first as a chapter in a booklet entitled *Getting Married*, published by the British Medical Association. It caused such a furor that after two hundred thousand copies had been sold the decision to suspend sales was taken and both editors (Dr. Chesser and Dr. Winifred de Kok) resigned from the BMA. This book, an extension of that chapter, is an excellent work by a qualified writer which will give you an understanding of the process of changing attitudes from generation to generation.

————, *Love and the Married Woman* (New York: G. P. Putnam's Sons, 1969).

Another valuable book by the same author. Aware of the importance of sex in marriage, he tells us that knowledge is not enough and why love cannot be made by the book. This book covers the relationships from the honeymoon to the menopause, and Dr. Chesser states that if the book is read in the right spirit, it will help you toward a deeper understanding of your sexual nature.

————, *Unmarried Love* (New York: David McKay Company, 1965).

The title aptly describes what the book is about. A compassionate book whose author stresses the moral responsibility of one human being to another.

Ciardi, John, *I Marry You* (New Brunswick, N.J.: Rutgers University Press, 1958).

A beautiful book of poetry about love between a man and a woman, beginning with the initial love through all the years of married life with their realities and vicissitudes and inevitable death.

Constantine, L., & Constantine, Joan. This couple is making an ongoing study of group marriages and what they term "multilateral relations." Some of their earlier work is published, but the richcᴉ findings are still to appear—some of them in the *Journal of Sex Research*. They can be reached at 23 Mohegan Road, Acton, Mass. 01720.

Cuber, John F., and Harroff, Peggy, *The Significant Americans* (New York: Appleton-Century-Crofts, 1965).
An intimate study of intelligent American couples and the marital and extramarital lives that they lead. It was precedent-setting for its date. One of its major findings is that almost every conceivable marital arrangement works—for some.

Daniels, Anna K., *It's Never Too Late to Love* (New York: Pyramid Books, 1956).
A famous gynecologist gives wise counsel in layman's language. Illustrated by her factual case studies, this book is primarily concerned with women and their special problems. For those who wish to achieve a more satisfying sexual and emotional life.

De Vinck, Jose, & Catoir, John T., *The Challenge of Love: Practical Advice on Freedom of Conscience and Happiness in Marriage* (New York: Hawthorn Books, 1969).
This book aims to help "the thinking Catholic" achieve happiness and success in marriage. (Practical advice for married couples.)

Dillon, J. T., *Personal Teaching* (Columbus, Ohio: Charles E. Merrill, 1971).
A completely human and personal account by a high school teacher telling of his attempts, often fumbling and groping, to combine a genuine personal affection for students with professional skill. He describes it as "putting the person you are into your teaching and encouraging the students to put the persons they are into their learning." His style is easy and humorous, yet the struggles are real. Teachers at any level could almost certainly profit, and students and high school students might take heart at learning that *some* teachers give

no tests, insist that students give their own grades, take no attendance, and talk about the topics students want to talk about.

Donelson, Kenneth, & Donelson, Irene, *Married Today, Single Tomorrow* (Garden City, N.Y.: Doubleday & Co., 1969).
This helpful book discusses various aspects of the emotional and legal breakup of a marriage, and has useful suggestions for rebuilding a new life.

Duvall, Evelyn M., *Love and the Facts of Life* (New York: Association Press, 1968).
For young teen-agers, this book tries to answer every basic question while taking into account their concern for the deeper meaning involved in boy-girl relationships, and in marriage.

Ellis, Albert E., *Sex Without Guilt* (New York: Hillman Periodicals, 1959).
Based on research and case material from his private practice of psychotherapy and marriage counseling. Dr. Ellis is a prolific writer in the field of sex. No one except the *Independent* would publish this material when originally written because of its controversial nature.

Ellis, Havelock, *Psychology of Sex* (New York: The New American Library, 1960).
Copyright 1933 and in its seventh printing in 1960, this book is a classic in the field of sex and marriage. Not as easily read as some. However, if you're interested in an historical perspective of beliefs and attitudes, you'll want to read this.

Emrich, Duncan, ed., *The Folklore of Weddings and Marriages* (New York: American Heritage Press, 1970).
Marriage customs and traditions compiled by a specialist in folklore, make interesting, amusing reading.

Fast, Julius, *The Incompatibility of Men and Women, and How to Overcome It* (New York: M. Evans & Co., 1971).
What are the causes of strife between the sexes? The author,

after interviewing both laymen and professionals, has come up with some very readable insights into what it means to be a man or a woman in this culture.

Francoeur, Robert T., *Utopian Motherhood: New Trends in Human Reproduction* (Garden City, N.Y.: Doubleday & Co., 1970). We are on the threshold of being able to control human reproductive processes, and thus man will be able to shape his own evolution. If you expect to be alive in 1984, read this book and avoid "future shock." Scientific but not too technical, this makes interesting reading. Excellent bibliography.

Friedan, Betty, *The Feminine Mystique* (New York: Dell Publishing Company, 1964). At the time of publication called "The year's most controversial best-seller." Betty Friedan points out the discrepancies between reality and the levels of expectancy to conform suffered by American women. In her search she discovered that many women suffer a schizophrenic reaction to the mystique our culture has about women. You may like this book or regard it as superficial.

Fromm, Erich, *The Art of Loving* (New York: Harper & Row, 1956). Though written long ago, this is a basic book in understanding exactly what the title suggests—the *art* of loving.

Fromme, Allan, *The Ability To Love* (New York: Pocket Books, 1971). What is love? Man has been involved in answering this question for thousands of years. In this book the author examines the many aspects of love from "What is it?" to "Mature love." Not a book to be read at one sitting but one you'll return to for thought-provoking answers. Well worth the effort.

Futurist, April, 1970, *iv*, 2. Contains a special eighteen-page section with first-class condensed articles on the future of marriage and the family, the outlook for group marriage, and living together without marriage, all done by competent writers. Stimulating and controversial. (World Future Society, P. O. Box 19285, 20th Street Station, Washington, D.C. 20036, is the publisher of the *Futurist*.)

Geddes, Donald P., ed., *An Analysis of the Kinsey Reports on Sexual Behavior in the Human Male and Female* (New York: New American Library, 1959).
The title of this book adequately covers the contents. Sixteen experts in sociology, education, medicine, journalism, etc., analyze the meaning of these reports for you and future generations.

Gordon, Thomas, *Parent Effectiveness Training*. (The "no-lose" program for raising children.) (New York: Peter H. Wyden, 1970).
Marriage often involves the rearing of children. Not nearly enough books are written about communication and effective means of living with and loving children. This one, however, you'll find to be full of excellent ideas for your future children. It may even help you now to communicate with your parents.

Gustaitis, Rasa, *Turning On* (New York: The Macmillan Company, 1969).
A personal account of visits to many "growth centers," encounter groups, marathons (including one nude), and accounts of a few communes. Chapter 8 describes the deteriorating stage of Morningstar Ranch, a commune completely opposed to all values of our present society including health and sanitation rules.

Hall, Elizabeth, & Poteete, Robert, "A Conversation With Robert H. Rimmer," *Psychology Today*, January 1972, 5, 8.
Rimmer is, of course, famous for *The Harrad Experiment, Proposition 31*, and *The Rebellion of Yale Marratt*. The first book describes a fictional college with assigned roommates— a boy and a girl in each room—and their subsequent histories. *Proposition 31* advocates group marriage. *Yale Marratt* deals with, among other things, a triad which "works." This interview brings Rimmer up to date, covering lasting triads, group

marriage, church approval of various alternatives, and some of the problems and potentialities of the various arrangements. For those unfamiliar with his work, this might give an introduction to the man and his thinking.

Halloway, M., *Heavens on Earth: Utopian Communities in America, 1680–1880*, 2nd ed. (New York: Dover Books, 1966).
Good bibliography. For those who wish to study the early communal attempts, especially Oneida, this is a valuable book.

Hathorn, Raban, Genne, William H., & Brill, Mordecai, eds., *Marriage: An Interfaith Guide for All Couples* (New York: The Association Press, 1970).
Marriage is a contract, but it also is viewed variously as a vocation, a covenant, a sacrament by religious groups. This unique book, edited by a Benedictine monk, a Protestant minister, and a Rabbi, has much of value for couples of any faith.

Hedgepeth, William, & Stock, Dennis, *The Alternative* (London: Collier Books, 1970).
Subtitled *Communal Life in New America*, this is an interestingly written and beautifully illustrated book about the "now generation" and its involvement in communes, mostly rural.

Herndon, James, *The Way It Spozed to Be* (New York: Simon & Schuster, 1968).
Ghetto life in San Francisco Bay Area schools. The problems and frustrations of both students and teachers as they try to change the ways they think "it spozed to be."

Houriet, Robert, *Getting Back Together* (New York: Coward-McCann & Geoghehan, 1971).
This is a fascinating book by a man who has *lived* in many different communes for longer or shorter periods and visited others, and is now endeavoring to start one of his own. For the first time the problems and the joys of communal living are

given in first-person terms. Here too is represented the range of types of group living which pass for "communes."

Howard, Jane, *Please Touch* (New York: McGraw-Hill, 1970).
Subtitled *A Guided Tour of the Human Potential Movement.* Miss Howard's experiences will help the reader to understand the growing number of people who are aware that not expressing themselves and coming to know what they really feel can affect them, their marriages, their interpersonal relationships, and society as a whole.

Hunt Morton M., *The Affair* (New York: New American Library-Signet, 1971).
"Affairs" are one way of dealing with marital difficulties. This book is an interesting study of these extramarital "voyages." A nonjudgmental compilation of a large variety of attempts at meeting personal needs. The most significant factor the author found in his research was the "degree of involvement." He invites the reader to lay aside judgment and examine this phenomenon of our society. A well-researched and interestingly written book. Excellent bibliography.

————, *The World of the Formerly Married* (New York: McGraw-Hill, 1966).
This unique book reports on "the mores, problems, and experiences of people who inhabit a half-secret subculture. . . ." The separated and divorced are virtually forced out of conventional social and family life. How do they adapt to their new state, make new friends, find new partners? The answers are interesting and varied.

Huxley, Aldous, *Island* (New York: Harper and Row, 1962).
Island is the story of ideal life on the fictitious island of Pala as seen through the eyes of an English journalist. The islanders practice hypnosis, eugenics and employ interesting child rearing methods in addition to utilizing the art of awareness. This book is as powerful as *Brave New World* with many possibilities for solutions to the problems of today's world. The value system of *Island* is well worth exploring.

Ibsen, Henrik, *A Doll's House*, Peter Watts, trans. (Baltimore, Md:, Penguin Books, 1965).

> A hundred years ago at the conclusion of Ibsen's play *A Doll's House*, Nora slammed a door. The concept of a woman having a duty to herself as well as to her husband and children was as startling to the audience as the slam of the door. This is the story of Nora's shattered illusions and the immense role that lack of communication played in her marriage.

Kantor, Rosabeth M., "Communes," *Psychology Today*, July, 1970, 4, 53.

> A good analysis of the many different reasons and motives for communal living. The author is particularly interested in what makes for permanence and brings in facts from her earlier study of the Utopian communities of the last century.

Kaufman, Sherwin A., *New Hope for the Childless Couple* (New York: Simon & Schuster, 1970).

> Every aspect of infertility is discussed by this medical specialist.

Klock, Frank, *Apes and Husbands* (Alhambra, Cal.: Borden Publishing Company, 1970).

> An exciting well-documented look at man from earliest records of domestic relationships to now. The author plans another book on his "favorite subject—women." After reading this, you'll look forward to the next. An historical perspective which will enlighten you but will also make you wonder how far man has advanced.

Landis, Judson T., & Landis, Mary G., *Building a Successful Marriage* (Englewood Cliffs, N.J.: Prentice-Hall, 1968).

> This is the fifth edition of this book. It is often used as a text in "family living" classes because of its complete coverage of the aspects of relationships in each stage of the life cycle— dating, marriage, parenthood, and later years of life. It also covers handling money, legal problems, adoption, insurance, etc.

Larsson, Clotye M., ed., *Marriage Across the Color Lines* (Chicago, Ill.: Johnson Publishing Company, 1965).

Based upon surveys and case histories, this is an appraisal of interracial marriages, especially between blacks and whites, and of the difficulties, stresses, and strengths of such unions.

Lash, Joseph P., *Eleanor and Franklin* (New York: W. W. Norton, 1971).

This revealing story recounts the process by which Eleanor Roosevelt grew from a truly "ugly duckling" into one of the world's most renowned women. Drawing heavily on her personal papers, it tells of her relationship and her difficulties with her famous husband, and her attempts to influence him —sometimes successfully, sometimes not. It manages to focus on both, and the political and wartime world is only a backdrop. As a record of growth, it is hard to match. Very readable.

Lederer, William J., & Jackson, Don D., *Mirages of Marriage* (New York: W. W. Norton, 1968).

Is marriage in America today anchored in anachronisms? The authors think so, but it's nice to find a book with prescriptions and suggestions for how to make a marriage work. It discusses false assumptions, techniques for appraising a marriage, communication techniques for improving marriage, and the pros and cons of marriage counseling. Excellent, easy reading. Excellent bibliography.

Leonard, George B., *Education and Ecstasy* (New York: Delacorte Press, 1968).

If you're interested in a look at what might be done in education, you'll want to read this book of revolutionary ideas for students and curriculum.

Lewis, C. S., *The Four Loves* (London: Collins, Fontana Books, 1960).

A philosophical treatise on affection, friendship, Eros, and charity and how each merges into the other. For many years an atheist, this distinguished Oxford scholar became one of the most influential of Christian scholars. This small book is well worth the effort of reading.

Lewis, Oscar, *Tepoztlán: Village in Mexico* (New York: Holt, Rinehart & Winston, 1960).
This small book (only 104 pages) is a condensation of the two studies done by the author in 1943–48 and 1956–57. It gives a good overall picture of the village life but the chapters on the family and the life cycle, from pregnancy to marriage to old age and death, will probably be of most interest to readers of this book.

Liswood, Rebecca, *First Aid for the Happy Marriage* (New York: Pocket Books, 1971).
This book is described as "a book for the very people who think they need it least." It covers all aspects of marriage and makes an excellent reference.

Loomis, Mildred J., *Go Ahead and Live* (New York: Philosophical Library, 1965).
How and why does a young couple get out of the rat race and join the Green Revolution? Ron and Laura Baker joined not a commune but a community where they could have their own homestead, maintain their marriage without any group-sex experimentation, raise much of their food, and rear their children.

Lyon, Harold C., Jr., *Learning to Feel: Feeling to Learn* (Columbus, Ohio: Charles E. Merrill, 1971).
A whole series of vital methods by which the classroom teacher can make learning an exciting voyage of discovery. He has a philosophy developed out of an extremely varied career and his account minces no words, spells out details, and names names. It is useful to anyone interested in education for the whole man—who feels as well as thinks, and learns in both areas.

Mindley, Carol, *The Divorced Mother* (New York: McGraw-Hill, 1969).

> This "guide to readjustment" was written by the mother of two sons to furnish the information, suggestions, and help every potential divorcee with children needs.

O'Neill, Nena, & O'Neill, George, *Open Marriage* (Philadelphia, Pa.: Lippincott, 1971).

> Marriage, the O'Neills believe, should and can enrich life and open it. The outcome should be growth and renewal, but this must be based on an honest and communicating relationship, realistic expectations, and the awareness of the importance of selfhood.

Packard, Vance, *The Sexual Wilderness. The Contemporary Upheaval in Male-Female Relationships.* (New York: David McKay Company, 1968).

> The author, well known for his social analyses, spent four years in research throughout much of the Western world, consulted with over three hundred specialists—doctors, sociologists, psychologists, etc.—and had a questionnaire answered by over two thousand respondents analyzed by a university team of social scientists. The book reveals "how chaotic and conflicting" are the generally held beliefs and the general behavior as regards male-female relationships. The latter part of the book proposes new sexual and marital codes. Whether one agrees or not, they make provocative reading.

Perls, Frederick S., *Gestalt Therapy Verbatim* (Lafayette, Cal.: The Real People Press, 1969).

> Dr. Perls states that "To suffer one's death and to be reborn is not easy." Christ said, "Ye must be born again." The task of becoming truly human is illustrated in this book, which is a report of the interpersonal relationships of Dr. Perls and those whose sufferings you can read in the Dream Seminars included in the book.

————, *In and Out of the Garbage Pail* (Lafayette, Cal.: The Real People Press, 1969).

The autobiography of the late Dr. Perls. An authentic report of an individual's struggle toward self-actualization. Delightful, honest, and profound. To become truly aware of one's self in interpersonal relationships is a vital step in answering the question "Who am I?" This book will help you in that process.

Rogers, Carl R., *Carl Rogers On Encounter Groups* (New York: Harper & Row, 1970).

One can learn a great deal about communication as well as about encounter groups from this book, which discusses the process, the training and functions of the facilitator, and the many personal and relationship changes which emerge from the experience. According to Philip Slater, the noted sociologist: "Finally . . . a real book has been written on encounter groups. Clear, lucid, simple, evocative. . . ."

————, *Freedom to Learn* (Columbus, Ohio: Charles E. Merrill, 1969).

The theme of this book is freedom and trust. While the book is directed to the necessary changes that need to be brought about in education, the book's approach to learning, valuing, and trusting in all interpersonal relationships will help the reader in the search for lasting relationships and a heightened self-awareness.

————, "Interpersonal Relationships: USA 2000," *Journal of Applied Behavioral Science*, 1968, *4*, 3: 265–280.

This article raises first the question of how rapidly man can adapt to the ever-increasing rate of change. Then it projects the positive and negative possibilities in urban crowding, interpersonal communication, man-woman and parent-child relationships, education, industry, religion, minority groups, at the beginning of the next century.

————, *On Becoming a Person* (Boston: Houghton Mifflin, 1961; Sentry Edition paperback, also published by Houghton Mifflin, 1970).

Although only one chapter refers directly to marriage and family life, the book abounds in material related to discovering and being oneself, and in the ways by which we can learn to communicate.

Saxton, Lloyd, *The Individual, Marriage, and the Family* (Belmont, Cal.: Wadsworth Publishing Co., 2d ed., 1972).
An excellent book in every way. Crammed with facts, interestingly written. Covers everything from dating to specific means of contraception; from physiological aspects of sex and orgasm to marital conflict and divorce. By an experienced marriage counselor who also teaches marriage and the family courses to undergraduates.

Shedd, Charlie W., *Letter to Philip* (on how to treat a woman) (Garden City, N.Y.: Doubleday & Co., 1968).
Written at his son's request, this is a marvelous book of advice by a minister who believes that the family holds the key to the future of our society. Another charming book is *Letters to Karen*, which his daughter requested him to write before she married. Young people love these books. Parents will find that the Reverend Shedd has said many things they would like to say to their own children.

Shostrom, Everett, & Kavanaugh, James, *Between Man and Woman. The Dynamics of Intersexual Relationships.* (Los Angeles, Cal.: Nash Publishing Co., 1971).
The authors analyze the "role playing" that takes place in what they call the "Marriage-go-Round." They emphasize that personal growth is painful, but that it can take place in a man-woman marriage relationship if they can become aware of how a "rhythmic relationship" can be established. This is a book about how to stop games and role playing and find the real meaning of intimacy in marriage. At times academic, and at times very personal, this is an irregular but useful book.

238

SIECUS (Sex Information and Education Council of the United States), Eds., *Sexuality and Man*, introduction by Mary S. Calderone, M.D. (New York: Charles Scribner's Sons, 1970).

In nontechnical and nonjudgmental language this book explains a wide range of topics, and would be very useful for parents as well as for those working with children and young people. The last three chapters discuss sex education, science, and how moral values may be examined, determined, or taught. The appendix offers many resources for sex education programs, including a list of films available.

Smith, Gerald W., *Me and You and Us* (New York: Peter H. Wyden, 1971).

This book will appeal especially to those who like how-to manuals. It contains forty-seven exercises the author has used with married couples at Esalen and elsewhere. A sample which he regards as very revealing is for a couple to plan something together—what to do Sunday afternoon, for example. He believes this reveals how they deal with power, who is in charge, and is even revealing of the nature of their sexual relationship, as well as the quality of their communication. This last is a central concern of the book.

Tenenbaum, Samuel A., *A Psychologist Looks at Marriage* (New York: A. S. Barnes & Co., 1968).

Dr. Tenenbaum believes that in a good marriage the individuals give each other the courage to live and be. Maturity and the capacity for loving and for sacrifice are essential, and this easily read book will help you attain these goals. A good chapter on communication.

Thorp, Roderick, & Blake, Robert, *Wives: An Investigation* (Philadelphia, Pa.: Lippincott, 1971.

A unique study of wives, rich and poor, educated and uneducated, from age twenty-four to fifty-two, who reveal their struggles to make their marriages work. Men who want to hear the way these wives see it will profit as will women who secretly harbor the fears, frustration, and loneliness existent in many marriages, as described by these wives.

Toffler, Alvin, *Future Shock* (New York: Random House, 1970).
Change is inevitable. How does it affect you? Will you be overwhelmed by it as the changes come faster and faster? How will it affect your patterns of love, friendship, marriage, etc.? And finally, how will it affect rational decision and health? The author explodes a lot of clichés as he probes the future to help us today.

Van De Velde, Theodor H., *Ideal marriage. Its Physiology and Technique* (New York: Random House, 1965).
Written by an internationally famous Dutch gynecologist, translated into many languages, enthusiastically received by both the medical profession and the lay public, this book, the first of a trilogy, aims at increasing the forces of mutual attraction in marriage. Much more than a how-to manual, it includes delightful literary quotations and references, and the author's own philosophy. It has gone through innumerable printings since its first publication some forty years ago and has become a classic in the field. The 1965 edition was revised to include information on contraception, fertility, etc.

Viorst, Judith, *It's Hard to Be Hip Over Thirty and Other Tragedies of Married Life* (New York: New American Library, 1968).
Delightful humorous poetry. Domestic problems turned to laughter with great insight.

Williams, Mary McGee, *Marriage for Beginners* (New York: The Macmillan Company, 1967).
Written for young engaged couples, this book in three sections—Your Love, Your Life, Your Home—is a complete and common-sense manual. Whether discussing how to prepare for marriage, how to handle the inevitable and varied problems, or the most efficient way to clean house, the author is warm and helpful.

Wyse, Lois, *I Love You Better Now* (Cleveland, Ohio: Garrett Press, 1970).
The author of *Love Poems for the Very Married* and *Are You Sure You Love Me?* among others, has written another charming book of poems about love and marriage.

Yablonsky, Lewis, *The Tunnel Back: Synanon* (New York: The Macmillan Company, 1965; also in Pelican paperback).
Possibly the best account of the whole Synanon movement for dealing with serious drug addiction. It was started in a storefront by Check Diedrich, its leader, has developed into a very large enterprise with many houses, and developed the "Synanon" for dealing with interpersonal problems of drug addicts. Has a high rate of success, *if* the person stays.

CASSETTES

Each of these constitutes a series of cassettes, available from Instructional Dynamics, Inc. 166 East Superior Street, Chicago, Illinois 60611. Prices vary according to the number of cassettes in the series:

Bach, George R., *How to Fight Fair: Understanding Aggression*.
Dr. George Bach describes how all of us can deal creatively with the perplexing problems of human anger and violence. He advocates a release for the aggression that many of us are afraid to express.

Rogers, Carl R., *How to Use Encounter Group Concepts*.
Dr. Rogers talks about process, practice, and procedures in encounter groups, sometimes in dialogue with others. He discusses what actually happens in an encounter group, the social significance of such groups, danger signals, and the training of facilitators. Very informative.

———, *Personal adjustment*.
Dr. Rogers speaks directly and intimately, just as he might in

a person-to-person conference. He discusses the importance of being the person you are. The series is aimed at increasing self-understanding and the ability to be.

Whitaker, Carl, *What's New in Husband-Wife Counseling?*
Dr. Whitaker discusses the psychology and mechanics of marriage from the days of courtship to the days when grown children are ready to leave home. He explains what is involved in order to ensure a lasting physical and emotional bond in marriage.

FILMS

A Doll's House.
This film of Ibsen's great play, written nearly a century ago, shows what role a lack of communication can play in a marriage. Distributed through Encyclopaedia Britannica Educational Corporation.

Because That's My Way.
A group containing a narcotics agent, young drug users and non-users—blacks and whites—and a convicted drug pusher. Facilitated by Drs. Carl Rogers and Anthony Rose. Color film, sixty minutes, produced by W. H. McGaw and Station WQED, Pittsburgh, Pa. Available through Great Plains Instructional Television Library, University of Nebraska, Lincoln, Nebraska. The film indicates how hostile individuals can build relationships.

Games people play: The practice; Games people play: The theory.
A series of interviews with Eric Berne, author of the book *Games People Play.* In two parts, each thirty minutes. Available through NET Film Service A.V. Center, Indiana University, Bloomington, Indiana 47401.

Journey into Self.
An encounter group experience with Carl Rogers and Richard Farson as facilitators. An Academy Award-winning film,

produced by W. H. McGaw. Available through Western Behavioral Sciences Institute, 1150 Silverado, La Jolla, California 92037.

Mother Love.
A twenty-six-minute film about Dr. Harry Harlow's studies on monkeys and the importance of tactile communication. (CBS, New York.)

Self-Actualization.
Dr. Abraham H. Maslow emphasizes and illustrates the aspects of self-actualization he has stressed in his writings. Sixty minutes. In color. Available through Psychological Films, Inc., 205 West 20th Street, Santa Ana, California.

Sessions in Gestalt Therapy.
Dr. Frederick Perls illustrates and discusses his methods of communication and awareness. Media-Psych. Corp., Box 7707, San Diego, California 92107.

Some Personal Learnings About Interpersonal Relationships.
A filmed lecture by Dr. Carl Rogers. 16 mm. black-and-white film, 33 minutes. The title of the film indicates the subject matter of the lecture. Developed by Dr. Charles K. Ferguson, UCLA, distributed through the University of California Extension Media Center, Berkeley, California, 94720.

Three Approaches to Psychotherapy.
Drs. Carl R. Rogers, Fritz Perls, and Albert Ellis consecutively interview the same woman, Gloria, during the day, using very different approaches to a helping relationship. Gloria's problems center around man-woman and parent-child relationships, as well as gaining an understanding of herself. Each interview 45 minutes. Available through Psychological Films, Inc., 205 West 20th Street, Santa Ana, California.